SCOTT, FORESMAN AND COMPANY

CHICAGO

ATLANTA

DALLAS

NEW YORK

SAN FRANCISCO

SCOTT, FORESMAN AND COMPANY

CHICAGO
ATLANTA
DALLAS
NEW YORK
SAN FRANCISCO

AMERICAN

POETRY

EDGAR ALLAN POE

RALPH WALDO EMERSON

WALT WHITMAN

EMILY DICKINSON

ROBERT FROST

T. S. ELIOT

EDITED BY

RANDALL STEWART, BROWN UNIVERSITY

DOROTHY BETHURUM, CONNECTICUT COLLEGE

American Poetry *is one of four books constituting* Living Masterpieces of American Literature: *Book One,* Concord Idealism, *Emerson and Thoreau; Book Two,* Classic American Fiction, *Poe, Hawthorne, Melville, and James; Book Three,* Modern American Narration, *Mark Twain, Hemingway, and Faulkner; Book Four,* American Poetry, *Poe, Emerson, Whitman, Dickinson, Frost, and Eliot.*

FOREWORD

Few readers are likely to quarrel seriously with our choice of the six American poets here brought together. Certain important figures of course will inevitably be missed: Bryant, Longfellow, Lowell, and Lanier, for example, in the nineteenth century, and Robinson, Lindsay, and a score of others in more recent times. But few readers are likely to insist upon the replacement of our six by any of these. In short, if we are to have six poets and no more in a convenient volume, most readers, the editors believe, will be happy with those here presented.

The advantages of the present arrangement seem clear enough. The number of poets is neither too large for intensive study nor too few for a comprehensive coverage. And the present assemblage makes conveniently possible a study that is comparative as well as analytical.

The opportunities for comparison and contrast are many and fascinating. They can be suggested here only in part by a few examples of the kind of questions to which the student might profitably give his attention. In what respects were Poe and Emerson antipodal figures, and why did each find the other's work uncongenial? Are there underlying resemblances between the two? Are the elements of a New England tradition discoverable in the poetry of Emerson,

Dickinson, and Frost? Why is Dickinson regarded today as a greater poet than Emerson? Does Frost belong at all in their succession? What is the nature of Whitman's affinity to Emerson ("I was simmering, simmering," he said, "and Emerson brought me to boil.")? Does the affinity seem difficult to account for in the light of certain radical dissimilarities between the two? Does Eliot derive at all from the others? What is his case against nineteenth-century poetry (is it applicable to Frost in part?), and how valid does the case seem today in the light of the poetry here presented? These and many other inquiries involving comparison will occur to the student as he peruses the contents of this volume.

Matthew Arnold once urged the importance of our knowing the best that has been thought and said. The present volume contains a considerable part of America's best in poetry. Not the least valuable result of the student's labors will be the growing realization that America has produced poetry important both as knowledge and as a criticism of life, and which therefore repays an attentive, sympathetic study.

Randall Stewart
Dorothy Bethurum

CONTENTS ∎∎∎∎∎∎∎∎∎∎∎∎∎∎∎∎∎∎∎∎∎∎∎

NINETEENTH-CENTURY ROMANTICS

■ ■

WALT WHITMAN

EMILY DICKINSON

ROBERT FROST

T.S. ELIOT

AMERICAN POETRY

EDGAR ALLAN POE

RALPH WALDO EMERSON

WALT WHITMAN

EMILY DICKINSON

ROBERT FROST

T. S. ELIOT

NINETEENTH-CENTURY ROMANTICS ∎∎∎∎∎∎

EDGAR ALLAN POE

RALPH WALDO EMERSON

WALT WHITMAN

EMILY DICKINSON

The poets of the nineteenth century, both in England and America, wrote for the most part "romantic" poetry. "Romanticism," however, has many facets, and the term "romantic," many connotations. To call a poet or a poem "romantic" without specifying in what particular way or ways he or it is so is to be guilty of inexactness. It is necessary, therefore, to explore some of the meanings of the word as it is ordinarily used. Various attempts at definition have been made, but it is doubtful if a generalization can be devised that will comprehend all romantic phenomena. One must be content with a descriptive account of certain salient aspects.

THE NATURE OF MAN

One of the more important aspects of romanticism is the belief that man is innately good and infinitely perfectible, and that his shortcomings are owing to his surroundings. T. E. Hulme defined "romantics" as those who reject the doctrine of original sin, and there is a good deal to be said for this definition. If not "the root of all romanticism," as Hulme maintained, it is at least one of its principal branches. One class of romantics, among whom Emerson was chief in America, discounted evil as an active force in human life.

Emerson maintained that good is the only reality:

> Good [he said] is positive. Evil is merely privative, not absolute: it is like cold, which is the privation of heat. All evil is so much death or nonentity. Benevolence is absolute and real. . . . Absolute badness is absolute death.

All men, Emerson thought, have the positive principle of goodness at work within them, however obscured it may be for a time. Emerson was by temperament an optimist. He believed that the Calvinist

dogma of human depravity was a libel on mankind. His own humble-
bee (in the poem of that title) is a beautiful emblem of himself:

> Wiser far than human seer,
> Yellow-breeched philosopher!
> Seeing only what is fair,
> Sipping only what is sweet. . . .

Whitman—disciple of Emerson that he was—strongly endorsed
the view that man is innately good and infinitely perfectible. He re-
acted even more emphatically than Emerson—if that was possible—
against the Puritan emphasis upon man's sinfulness. In "Song of
Myself," he admires the animals because they are untouched by
the blight of Puritanism: "They do not lie awake in the dark and
weep for their sins."

To Whitman, life is immensely good in all its manifestations, and
human beings are incarnations of divinity. While leaning on the
rail of the ferryboat (in "Crossing Brooklyn Ferry"), he saw, he
said, "fine centrifugal spokes of light round the shape of my head in
the sunlit water." Later in the poem, he notes that these spokes of
light diverge not only from his head, but from "anyone's head." The
inference, of course, is that, in Whitman's vision, all men wear
halos, all men are saints.

Whitman believed not only in man's saintliness but in his great
powers of growth. The concept of evolution gave to him (as it did to
Emerson) added confidence in man's future. No one has ever advocated more eloquently than Whitman the doctrine of progress. "My
feet strike an apex of the apices of the stairs," he says in "Song
of Myself," "all below duly travel'd, and still I mount and mount!"

Dickinson's view of the nature of man is not nearly so unequivocal
as that of Emerson or Whitman. There are passages in her poetry
that suggest Emerson's influence. Her "liquor never brewed" matches
Emerson's "wine which never grew in the belly of the grape." The
ability of "our statures," under certain conditions, to "touch the
skies" suggests Emerson's confidence in what he called "the infinitude
of the private man." But the Puritan tradition persists in Dickinson.
Her poetry presupposes the Christian doctrine of the Fall. Evil is a
reality in her world; man's sinfulness is a reality, and the wages of
sin are an inescapable part of human experience. "I like a look of
agony," she says, "because I know it's true." The "agony" is a type
of retributive suffering; it is, by extension, the agony of Christ on
the cross. In the sense in which romanticism is being considered in
the present context, Miss Dickinson's awareness of sin and suffering
is an "unromantic" trait.

Poe is so little the moralist that he seems almost irrelevant in this
discussion of the romantic view of the nature of man. And yet his
work is not without certain moral implications. Poe represents man
as unhappy, as yearning toward a perfect state (as in "Israfel") ; he

suggests the existence of diabolical powers (as in "The City in the Sea"); he embodies evil in grotesque forms. He is obviously not an Emersonian optimist: he takes a dark view of human fate.

THE RETURN TO NATURE

A second major aspect of nineteenth-century romanticism is that which has often been called the "return to nature." It is perhaps related to the first aspect in that man's goodness, it was widely believed, is best called forth and nurtured when he lives in close contact with the natural world.

To the romantics, nature was a thing of beauty worthy of aesthetic response. Following the example of Wordsworth, Emerson wished to awaken in the reader an appreciation, especially, of the commonplace aspects of nature. He expressed delight in the fact that (as he put it in "The American Scholar") "the near, the low, the common," were being "explored and poetized." Carrying this attitude even further than Emerson (or Wordsworth), Whitman found in "leaves of grass" the symbol of all poetry.

There are several characteristic notes in the romantic description of nature. One is a new particularity, based upon close, imaginative observation. Emily Dickinson is one of the best poets to show this characteristic: consider, for example, her account of the snake moving rapidly through the grass—"a whip-lash / Unbraiding in the sun." Another note in romantic nature description is a rich sensuousness, best illustrated perhaps by Whitman. Consider, for example, this impression of the sea: "Cushion me soft, rock me in billowy drowse, / Dash me with amorous wet. . . ." One finds a special emphasis of the tactile sense in Whitman, as here, and of the visual in Emerson and Dickinson—in, for example, "The Rhodora" and "The Humming Bird." And another note (among still others) is religious sentiment. To Emerson, nature is a symbol of the divine. To Dickinson and to Whitman, it is rich in religious suggestion: Emily would rather worship in an orchard than in a church edifice; Whitman regards the grass as a veronica, "the handkerchief of the Lord."

To most of the romantics, nature is beneficent. Man's struggle against a hostile nature received comparatively little attention in nineteenth-century poetry. Nor did the struggle within nature itself, and the corresponding scientific notion of survival, make much of an impression upon the romantic poets. Nature is ordinarily peaceful and happy; the flower enjoys the air it breathes. Nature comforts, restores, and fortifies the troubled spirits of men. Nature repays human trust: Wordsworth's famous declaration of faith, in "Tintern Abbey"—"Nature never did betray / The heart that loved her"— was reaffirmed nearly a half-century later in Emerson's assertion in

"Wood-Notes" that "Nature ever faithful is / To such as trust her faithfulness."

Poe again stands apart from his American contemporaries. His nature "resembles nothing that is ours." One has only to compare the "perfumed sea" of "To Helen," or the "lurid sea" of "The City in the Sea," with the sea of Whitman; or the "leaves crispèd and sere" and the "alley Titanic of cypress" with the garden world of Dickinson to see how much of an outcast Poe was from the standard nature of nineteenth-century poetry. Poe's nature is grotesque and unrealistic. It is also significantly symbolical, a reflection and projection of the mental states that he describes.

THE WONDERFUL AND STRANGE

Allied with the two large aspects of romanticism already discussed is a third, which Theodore Watts-Dunton called "the renascence of wonder." The eighteenth-century mind seemed prosaic and unimaginative to the nineteenth century. The romantics, like Shakespeare's Miranda, discovered a brave new world. The poet strove to see and feel; his habitual attitude was one of wonder at the mystery and beauty of all created things. Emerson described the poet as "Lover of all things alive, / Wonderer at all he meets." Whitman carried the attitude of wonder perhaps further than anyone else: he regarded all phenomena as miraculous—"As to me," he declared, "I know of nothing else but miracles."

If some poets found the wonderful in the commonplace, others sought for it in the exotic, the strange, the grotesque. Medieval poems like Coleridge's "Christabel" and Keats' "Eve of St. Agnes" (as well as Gothic fiction like Walpole's *Castle of Otranto* and Mrs. Radcliffe's *Mysteries of Udolpho*) were in a sense a quest for the wonderful in the strange and faraway. Poe, who was greatly influenced by these English writers, was the chief American representative of the Gothic school. He is romantic, therefore, in a very different sense from that which is applicable to Emerson or Whitman or Dickinson. For if they are romantic in a Wordsworthian sense, then Poe's romanticism may be said to correspond to that of Coleridge, who dealt with the "supernatural," and who endeavored (as he himself said with reference to his own poetry) to "procure for these shadows of imagination that willing suspension of disbelief for the moment which constitutes poetic faith."

Some critics have thought that Poe was a trickster, and that his horror is artificial. Poe himself declared that the "horror was of the soul." A growing number of readers today are disposed to agree with him, being impressed by his emotional sincerity and the integrity of his art.

LANGUAGE, VERSIFICATION, STYLE

The romantic poets enlarged the scope of poetry. At the end of the nineteenth century, a greater range of subjects was open to the poet than had been considered proper or legitimate a hundred years earlier. The romantics also enlarged the vocabulary of poetry, and the freedom and variety of verse forms.

Emerson in some ways harked back to the English metaphysical poets of the seventeenth century, and it is interesting to note that Andrew Marvell was one of his favorites. His pregnant, functional use of metaphor recalls the author of "To His Coy Mistress." A poem like Emerson's "Grace" might have been written by George Herbert. His fondness for the octosyllabic couplet may reflect a debt to Milton's "L'Allegro" and "Il Penseroso." These affinities with the seventeenth century distinguish Emerson from his English contemporaries, and ally him with the future: with Emily Dickinson, and with the twentieth-century revival of the seventeenth-century metaphysicals. But Emerson looks forward in ways other than those that pertain to the seventeenth century. He sometimes has a Yankee earthiness that anticipates Robert Frost, as in these lines from "Hamatreya":

> Bulkeley, Hunt, Willard, Hosmer, Meriam, Flint,
> Possessed the land which rendered to their toil
> Hay, corn, roots, hemp, flax, apples, wool, and wood.

And in the freedom and flexibility of the versification of a poem like "Bacchus" or "Merlin," he anticipates the moderns.

Poe defined poetry in "The Poetic Principle" as "the rhythmical creation of beauty." His concept of beauty was "Gothic": he liked to quote Francis Bacon's dictum, "There is no excellent beauty that hath not some strangeness in the proportion." Poe gave meticulous attention to melody and to regularity of meter. Double rhyme and verbal repetition are favorite devices. Emerson was unappreciative when he called Poe the "jingle-man," for his melodies and rhythms, as well as his images, are artfully contrived and have had for many readers (especially for the French symbolists, with whom Poe was a great favorite) a psychic and a spiritual significance.

Whitman wanted to write democratic poetry, to compose what he called "the great psalms of the republic." In the Preface to *Leaves of Grass* he laid down the following propositions, among others of like import: "The United States themselves are essentially the greatest poem. . . . The genius of the United States is always most in the common people. . . . A bard is to be commensurate with a people. . . . His spirit responds to his country's spirit. . . . The proof of a poet is that his country absorbs him as affectionately as he has absorbed it." Whitman's aim was to give the new American democracy a new poetic embodiment.

He went further than any predecessor in using the language of men, and in breaking down the distinction between the language of verse and the language of prose. Whitman's poems contain Americanisms, colloquialisms, and slang expressions. "I had great trouble," he said, "in leaving out the stock 'poetical' touches, but succeeded at last." Many of his lines are indistinguishable from prose; indeed, he transferred lines from the prose Preface to the poems without change. Whatever license poets since Whitman may have used, probably no poet before him ever put into a poem lines so "unpoetic" as (to take an example almost at random) "Say, old top-knot, what do you want?"

Whitman's verse is unrhymed and unmetrical, though often having a fine rhythm. The unit of composition is the line, which is regularly end-stopped. Lines are combined to form verse paragraphs—they can hardly be called "stanzas" because as a rule they lack stanzaic organization. Lines can be added and subtracted at will (as they were, in fact, in Whitman's many revisions) without destroying the fabric of the whole. The lines of a sequence are often held together by parallelism and initial repetition, and are usually grammatically coordinate. Whitman undoubtedly regarded such a "form" as peculiarly appropriate for democratic poetry, and as a kind of symbol of a democratic society, where each member (like the individual verse line) is self-contained, approximately equal to each of the other members and coordinate with them, important but not indispensable to the ensemble, and joined with the others in a loose confederation. Whitman's verse was a harbinger of the modern freedoms. It is indeed "free," though perhaps it should not be called "free verse" (*vers libre*), the later poetry so named having a more calculated technique than Whitman's.

Few poets have employed language so precisely, so pregnantly, so cryptically, as Emily Dickinson, or with such a disregard for conventional meaning and construction. More than any other nineteenth-century poet in America, she extended the semantic and syntactical boundaries. Close analysis is necessary to the understanding of the poet's multiple suggestions. She is also the most metaphorical (Whitman being the least so, and Emerson being her closest rival in this respect) of the four poets who are being considered in this introduction; her poems are often expanded metaphors. She has, moreover, a "metaphysical" quality (Emerson again being comparable, though in a lesser degree) that recalls the age of Donne and Marvell. Allen Tate has described Dickinson's metaphysical quality by saying (in his essay "Emily Dickinson," included in the volume *Reactionary Essays*, 1936): "She sees the ideas, and thinks the perceptions. . . . Miss Dickinson is probably the only Anglo-American poet of her century whose work exhibits the perfect literary situation—in which is possible the fusion of sensibility and thought."

Dickinson's basic verse form is the hymn stanza (the 4–3–4–3 quatrain, rhyming *abcb*). Most of her poems either conform to, or are recognizable variations of, this pattern. The hymns are almost certainly (though no actual demonstration has as yet been made) an important source for Dickinson beyond the supplying of her favorite stanza. Near rhymes, or slant rhymes, like hers are not uncommon in the hymns; much of her imagery, too, can be found there. The influence is not surprising in view of her early indoctrination in Protestant hymnology.

THE APOTHEOSIS OF THE POET

The poet achieved a new apotheosis in the nineteenth century. Never before, in England or America, had poets held such an exalted opinion of their importance in the scheme of things, or expressed such an opinion so insistently. Most nineteenth-century poets believed that they were divinely inspired, and that their poetry would contribute mightily to man's improvement. Many of their works, both in verse and prose, describe the poet, the poet's function, and the nature of poetry.

Poe's concept of poetic inspiration seems to be based primarily upon the poet's delicate sensibility, his sensitiveness to aesthetic influences. He defines "the poetic principle" as "the human aspiration for supernal beauty." "The manifestation of the principle," he says, "is always found in *an elevating* excitement of the soul—quite independent of that passion which is the intoxication of the heart, or of that truth which is the satisfaction of the reason." In the work of a true poet, he says, "we are often made to feel, with a shivering delight, that from an earthly harp are stricken notes which *cannot* have been unfamiliar to the angels." Poe, it would seem, exalts the poet to angelic status.

It would be interesting and instructive to compare the "idealisms" of Poe and Emerson. Though both owed something to Coleridge, Emerson's idealism is essentially different from Poe's. "Beauty," Emerson said with Puritan accent, "is the mark God sets upon virtue." Poe's "supernal beauty" has no moral ingredient; it is as dissociated from ethical considerations as mathematics or music, a union of which, indeed, seems to have constituted his concept of the "Ideal."

Emerson in his essay "The Poet" emphasizes the poet's comprehensiveness, his inspired condition, his importance: "He stands among partial men for the complete man. . . . The poet . . . traverses the whole scale of experience. . . . He is a sovereign, and stands on the centre . . . he announces that which no man foretold . . . the birth of a poet is the principal event in chronology." These pronouncements, and many others of similar import, stress the poet's bardic character. Poe's poet would be a "partial man" by Emerson's standard.

Certain passages in Emerson's essay read like a prophecy of Whitman. "We have yet had," he declared, "no genius in America, with tyrannous eye, which knew the value of our incomparable materials." Whitman felt a messianic mission to supply this lack. Pointing out the symbolic nature of all language, Emerson went on to say that "bare lists of words are found suggestive to an imaginative and excited mind"—a statement that must have seemed to Whitman an endorsement of his catalogues. Whitman would have agreed with Emerson's main argument in "The Poet." His Preface to the 1855 *Leaves of Grass* is a restatement and detailed application of Emersonian principles: it goes beyond Emerson—if at all—in giving a special emphasis to the United States, and to the value of the poet in a democracy like our own. The poet, he declares, "is the equalizer of his age and land . . . he supplies what wants supplying and checks what wants checking. If peace is the routine, out of him speaks the spirit of peace. . . . In war he is the most deadly force of the war. . . . He is no arguer . . . he is judgment. . . . He is a seer. . . . The attitude of great poets is to cheer up slaves and horrify despots." The poet's *apologia* could go no further.

Unlike Poe, Emerson, and Whitman, Emily Dickinson wrote no essay on the subject of poetry and the poet. But here and there in her poetry can be found views of the subject, which are summed up well enough in the following lines:

> This was a Poet—it is that
> Distills amazing sense
> From ordinary meanings,
> And attars so immense
> From the familiar species
> That perished by the door
> We wonder it was not ourselves
> Arrested it before.

Dickinson's concept is less bardic than Emerson's or Whitman's; her claim is, in comparison, unpretentious and Wordsworthian, yet large enough to guarantee to the poet a place of prime importance among his fellow men.

The romantic poets—of whom the four considered here are excellent representatives—contributed much to the enrichment of the human spirit. Despite the twentieth-century deprecation of certain aspects of their work, the modern sensibility would be seriously impoverished if deprived of their contribution. They awakened a human sympathy and stimulated the humanitarian impulse. They made us aware of the beauty and wonder of the world of nature and of the world of men, women, and children. They made our perceptions finer, attuning them to supersensual vibrations, so that we could hear the music of the spheres and see the miracles that lie about us always.

EDGAR ALLAN POE ■■■■■■■■■■■■■■■■■■■

Edgar Allan Poe was born in Boston in 1809 of actor parents, both of whom were dead within three years after his birth. He was admitted to the family of John Allan, a Richmond merchant, but never legally adopted. Between 1815 and 1820 he was in England with his foster parents. He spent brief periods at the University of Virginia (1826) and West Point (1830). In 1835 he became editor of the *Southern Literary Messenger*, and in 1836 he married his cousin, Virginia Clemm. From 1838 to 1843 he was in Philadelphia, and during part of that time was editor of *Graham's Magazine*. From 1844 till his death he lived at Fordham. His *Tales of the Grotesque and Arabesque* appeared in 1840; *The Raven and Other Poems*, in 1845. His prolific contributions to the magazines included prose tales, poetry, book reviews, and critical essays. His philosophical treatise, "Eureka," was written and published in 1848. He died in Baltimore under mysterious circumstances on October 7, 1849. His reputation, though considerable in America and in England, has been greatest in France, thanks especially to the enthusiasms of Baudelaire and Mallarmé.

The standard edition of the *Works* is that edited by James A. Harrison in seventeen volumes (1902). The best lives are by G. E. Woodberry (1909) and A. H. Quinn (1941). The most authoritative scholarship is found in Killis Campbell's *The Mind of Poe and Other Studies* (1933) and Margaret Alterton's *Origins of Poe's Critical Theory* (1925). For perceptive criticisms see W. C. Brownell's *American Prose Masters* (1909) and Allen Tate's *The Forlorn Demon* (1953).

SONNET—TO SCIENCE

Science! true daughter of Old Time thou art!
Who alterest all things with thy peering eyes.
Why preyest thou thus upon the poet's heart,
Vulture, whose wings are dull realities?
How should he love thee? or how deem thee wise,

Who wouldst not leave him in his wandering
To seek for treasure in the jewelled skies,
Albeit he soared with an undaunted wing?
Hast thou not dragged Diana from her car?
10   And driven the Hamadryad from the wood
To seek a shelter in some happier star?
Hast thou not torn the Naiad from her flood,
The Elfin from the green grass, and from me
The summer dream beneath the tamarind tree?
1829

TO HELEN

Helen, thy beauty is to me
    Like those Nicéan barks of yore,
That gently, o'er a perfumed sea,
    The weary, way-worn wanderer bore
    To his own native shore.

On desperate seas long wont to roam,
    Thy hyacinth hair, thy classic face,
Thy Naiad airs have brought me home
    To the glory that was Greece,
10   And the grandeur that was Rome.

Lo! in yon brilliant window-niche
    How statue-like I see thee stand,
The agate lamp within thy hand!
    Ah, Psyche, from the regions which
    Are Holy-Land!
1831

LENORE

Ah, broken is the golden bowl! the spirit flown forever!
Let the bell toll!—a saintly soul floats on the Stygian river;
And, Guy De Vere, hast *thou* no tear?—weep now or never more!
See! on yon drear and rigid bier low lies thy love, Lenore!
Come! let the burial rite be read—the funeral song be sung!—
An anthem for the queenliest dead that ever died so young—
A dirge for her the doubly dead in that she died so young.

"Wretches! ye loved her for her wealth and hated her for her pride,
And when she fell in feeble health, ye blessed her—that she died!
How *shall* the ritual, then, be read—the requiem how be sung   10
By you—by yours, the evil eye,—by yours, the slanderous tongue
That did to death the innocence that died, and died so young?"

Peccavimus; but rave not thus! and let a Sabbath song
Go up to God so solemnly the dead may feel no wrong!
The sweet Lenore hath "gone before," with Hope, that flew beside,
Leaving thee wild for the dear child that should have been thy bride—
For her, the fair and *debonair,* that now so lowly lies,
The life upon her yellow hair but not within her eyes—
The life still there, upon her hair—the death upon her eyes.

"Avaunt! to-night my heart is light. No dirge will I upraise,   20
But waft the angel on her flight with a Paean of old days!
Let *no* bell toll, then,—lest her soul, amid its hallowed mirth,
Should catch the note, as it doth float—up from the damnèd Earth!
To friends above, from fiends below, the indignant ghost is riven—
From Hell unto a high estate far up within the Heaven—
From grief and groan, to a golden throne, beside the King of Heaven."
1831

THE SLEEPER

At midnight, in the month of June,
I stand beneath the mystic moon.
An opiate vapour, dewy, dim,
Exhales from out her golden rim,
And, softly dripping, drop by drop,
Upon the quiet mountain-top,
Steals drowsily and musically
Into the universal valley.
The rosemary nods upon the grave;
The lily lolls upon the wave;   10
Wrapping the fog about its breast,
The ruin moulders into rest;
Looking like Lethe, see! the lake
A conscious slumber seems to take,
And would not, for the world, awake.
All Beauty sleeps!—and lo! where lies
(Her casement open to the skies)
Irene, with her Destinies!

13. **Peccavimus:** We have sinned.

O lady bright! can it be right—
20   This window open to the night?
The wanton airs, from the tree-top,
Laughingly through the lattice drop—
The bodiless airs, a wizard rout,
Flit through thy chamber in and out,
And wave the curtain canopy
So fitfully—so fearfully—
Above the closed and fringèd lid
'Neath which thy slumb'ring soul lies hid,
That, o'er the floor and down the wall,
30   Like ghosts the shadows rise and fall!
O lady dear, hast thou no fear?
Why and what art thou dreaming here?
Sure thou art come o'er far-off seas,
A wonder to these garden trees!
Strange is thy pallor! strange thy dress!
Strange, above all, thy length of tress,
And this all solemn silentness!

The lady sleeps! Oh, may her sleep,
Which is enduring, so be deep!
40   Heaven have her in its sacred keep!
This chamber changed for one more holy,
This bed for one more melancholy,
I pray to God that she may lie
Forever with unopened eye,
While the dim sheeted ghosts go by!

My love, she sleeps! Oh, may her sleep,
As it is lasting, so be deep!
Soft may the worms about her creep!
Far in the forest, dim and old,
For her may some tall vault unfold—
50   Some vault that oft hath flung its black
And wingèd panels fluttering back,
Triumphant, o'er the crested palls,
Of her grand family funerals—

Some sepulchre, remote, alone,
Against whose portal she hath thrown,
In childhood, many an idle stone—
Some tomb from out whose sounding door
She ne'er shall force an echo more,
Thrilling to think, poor child of sin!
60   It was the dead who groaned within!
1831

TO HELEN[1]

I saw thee once—once only—years ago:
I must not say *how* many—but *not* many.
It was a July midnight; and from out
A full-orbed moon, that, like thine own soul, soaring,
Sought a precipitate pathway up through heaven,
There fell a silvery-silken veil of light,
With quietude, and sultriness, and slumber,
Upon the upturn'd faces of a thousand
Roses that grew in an enchanted garden,
Where no wind dared to stir, unless on tiptoe—   10
Fell on the upturn'd faces of these roses
That gave out, in return for the love-light,
Their odorous souls in an ecstatic death—
Fell on the upturn'd faces of these roses
That smiled and died in this parterre, enchanted
By thee, and by the poetry of thy presence.

Clad all in white, upon a violet bank
I saw thee half reclining; while the moon
Fell on the upturn'd faces of the roses,
And on thine own, upturn'd—alas, in sorrow!   20

Was it not Fate that, on this July midnight—
Was it not Fate (whose name is also Sorrow)
That bade me pause before that garden-gate,
To breathe the incense of those slumbering roses?
No footsteps stirred: the hated world all slept,
Save only thee and me. (Oh, Heaven!—oh, God!
How my heart beats in coupling those two words!
Save only thee and me). I paused—I looked—
And in an instant all things disappeared.
(Ah, bear in mind this garden was enchanted!)   30
The pearly lustre of the moon went out:
The mossy banks and the meandering paths,
The happy flowers and the repining trees,
Were seen no more: the very roses' odors
Died in the arms of the adoring airs.
All—all expired save thee—save less than thou:
Save only the divine light in thine eyes—
Save but the soul in thine uplifted eyes.
I saw but them—they were the world to me.
I saw but them—saw only them for hours—   40
Saw only them until the moon went down.

1. This poem refers definitely to Sarah Helen Whitman of Providence, Rhode Island.

What wild heart-histories seemed to lie enwritten
Upon those crystalline, celestial spheres!
How dark a wo! yet how sublime a hope!
How silently serene a sea of pride!
How daring an ambition! yet how deep—
How fathomless a capacity for love!

But now, at length, dear Dian sank from sight,
Into a western couch of thunder-cloud;
50 And thou, a ghost, amid the entombing trees
Didst glide away. *Only thine eyes remained.*
They *would not* go—they never yet have gone.
Lighting my lonely pathway home that night,
They have not left me (as my hopes have) since.
They follow me—they lead me through the years.
They are my ministers—yet I their slave.
Their office is to illumine and enkindle—
My duty, *to be saved* by their bright light,
And purified in their electric fire,
60 And sanctified in their Elysian fire.
They fill my soul with Beauty (which is Hope),
And are far up in Heaven—the stars I kneel to
In the sad, silent watches of my night;
While even in the meridian glare of day
I see them still—two sweetly scintillant
Venuses, unextinguished by the sun!
1848

TO ONE IN PARADISE

Thou wast that all to me, love,
    For which my soul did pine—
A green isle in the sea, love,
    A fountain and a shrine,
All wreathed with fairy fruits and flowers,
    And all the flowers were mine.

Ah, dream too bright to last!
    Ah, starry Hope! that didst arise
But to be overcast!
10   A voice from out the Future cries,
"On! on!"—but o'er the Past
    (Dim gulf!) my spirit hovering lies
Mute, motionless, aghast!

For, alas! alas! with me
   The light of Life is o'er!
No more—no more—no more—
   (Such language holds the solemn sea
To the sands upon the shore)
   Shall bloom the thunder-blasted tree,
Or the stricken eagle soar!   20

And all my days are trances,
   And all my nightly dreams
Are where thy grey eye glances,
   And where thy footstep gleams—
In what ethereal dances,
   By what eternal streams.
1835

ISRAFEL

In Heaven a spirit doth dwell
   "Whose heart-strings are a lute";
None sing so wildly well
As the angel Israfel,
And the giddy stars (so legends tell),
Ceasing their hymns, attend the spell
   Of his voice, all mute.

Tottering above
   In her highest noon,
   The enamoured moon   10
Blushes with love,
   While, to listen, the red levin
   (With the rapid Pleiads, even,
   Which were seven,)
   Pauses in Heaven.

And they say (the starry choir
   And the other listening things)
That Israfeli's fire
Is owing to that lyre
   By which he sits and sings—   20
The trembling living wire
   Of those unusual strings.

But the skies that angel trod,
   Where deep thoughts are a duty,

Where Love's a grown-up God,
    Where the Houri glances are
Imbued with all the beauty
    Which we worship in a star.

Therefore, thou art not wrong,
    Israfeli, who despisest
An unimpassioned song;
To thee the laurels belong,
    Best bard, because the wisest!
Merrily live, and long!

The ecstasies above
    With thy burning measures suit—
Thy grief, thy joy, thy hate, thy love,
    With the fervour of thy lute—
    Well may the stars be mute!

Yes, Heaven is thine; but this
    Is a world of sweets and sours;
    Our flowers are merely—flowers,
And the shadow of thy perfect bliss
    Is the sunshine of ours.

If I could dwell
Where Israfel
    Hath dwelt, and he where I,
He might not sing so wildly well
    A mortal melody,
While a bolder note than this might swell
    From my lyre within the sky.
1831

DREAM-LAND

By a route obscure and lonely,
Haunted by ill angels only,
Where an Eidolon, named NIGHT,
On a black throne reigns upright,
I have reached these lands but newly
From an ultimate dim Thule—
From a wild weird clime that lieth, sublime,
    Out of SPACE—out of TIME.

Bottomless vales and boundless floods,
And chasms, and caves, and Titan woods,
With forms that no man can discover
For the tears that drip all over;

Mountains toppling evermore
Into seas without a shore;
Seas that restlessly aspire,
Surging, unto skies of fire;
Lakes that endlessly outspread
Their lone waters, lone and dead,—
Their still waters, still and chilly
With the snows of the lolling lily.   20

By the lakes that thus outspread
Their lone waters, lone and dead,—
Their sad waters, sad and chilly
With the snows of the lolling lily,—
By the mountains—near the river
Murmuring lowly, murmuring ever,—
By the grey woods,—by the swamp
Where the toad and the newt encamp,—
By the dismal tarns and pools
   Where dwell the Ghouls,—   30
By each spot the most unholy—
In each nook most melancholy,—
There the traveller meets, aghast,
Sheeted Memories of the Past—
Shrouded forms that start and sigh
As they pass the wanderer by—
White-robed forms of friends long given,
In agony, to the Earth—and Heaven.

For the heart whose woes are legion
'Tis a peaceful, soothing region—   40
For the spirit that walks in shadow
'Tis—oh, 'tis an Eldorado!
But the traveller, travelling through it,
May not—dare not openly view it;
Never its mysteries are exposed
To the weak human eye unclosed;
So wills its King, who hath forbid
The uplifting of the fringéd lid;
And thus the sad Soul that here passes
Beholds it but through darkened glasses.   50

By a route obscure and lonely,
Haunted by ill angels only,
Where an Eidolon, named NIGHT,
On a black throne reigns upright,
I have wandered home but newly
From this ultimate dim Thule.
1844

THE BELLS

1

Hear the sledges with the bells—
 Silver bells!
What a world of merriment their melody foretells!
 How they tinkle, tinkle, tinkle,
  In the icy air of night!
 While the stars that oversprinkle
 All the heavens, seem to twinkle
  With a crystalline delight;
  Keeping time, time, time,
   In a sort of Runic rhyme,
To the tintinnabulation that so musically wells
 From the bells, bells, bells, bells,
  Bells, bells, bells—
From the jingling and the tinkling of the bells.

2

Hear the mellow wedding bells—
 Golden bells!
What a world of happiness their harmony foretells!
 Through the balmy air of night
 How they ring out their delight!—
  From the molten-golden notes,
   And all in tune,
  What a liquid ditty floats
To the turtle-dove that listens, while she gloats
  On the moon!
 Oh, from out the sounding cells,
What a gush of euphony voluminously wells!
  How it swells!
  How it dwells
  On the Future!—how it tells
  Of the rapture that impels
 To the swinging and the ringing
  Of the bells, bells, bells—
  Of the bells, bells, bells, bells,
   Bells, bells, bells—
To the rhyming and the chiming of the bells!

3

Hear the loud alarum bells—
 Brazen bells!
What a tale of terror, now, their turbulency tells!
 In the startled ear of night

How they scream out their affright!   40
Too much horrified to speak,
They can only shriek, shriek,
Out of tune,
In a clamorous appealing to the mercy of the fire,
In a mad expostulation with the deaf and frantic fire,
Leaping higher, higher, higher,
With a desperate desire,
And a resolute endeavor
Now—now to sit, or never,
By the side of the pale-faced moon.   50
Oh, the bells, bells, bells!
What a tale their terror tells
Of Despair!
How they clang, and clash, and roar!
What a horror they outpour
On the bosom of the palpitating air!
Yet the ear, it fully knows,
By the twanging
And the clanging,
How the danger ebbs and flows;   60
Yet the ear distinctly tells,
In the jangling
And the wrangling,
How the danger sinks and swells,
By the sinking or the swelling in the anger of the bells—
Of the bells,—
Of the bells, bells, bells, bells,
Bells, bells, bells—
In the clamor and the clangor of the bells!

4
Hear the tolling of the bells—   70
Iron bells!
What a world of solemn thought their monody compels!
In the silence of the night,
How we shiver with affright
At the melancholy menace of their tone!
For every sound that floats
From the rust within their throats
Is a groan.
And the people—ah, the people—
They that dwell up in the steeple,   80
All alone,
And who tolling, tolling, tolling,
In that muffled monotone,
Feel a glory in so rolling
On the human heart a stone—

They are neither man nor woman—
They are neither brute nor human—
They are Ghouls:—
And their king it is who tolls:—
90 And he rolls, rolls, rolls,
Rolls
A pæan from the bells!
And his merry bosom swells
With the pæan of the bells!
And he dances, and he yells;
Keeping time, time, time,
In a sort of Runic rhyme,
To the pæan of the bells—
Of the bells:—
100 Keeping time, time, time,
In a sort of Runic rhyme,
To the throbbing of the bells—
Of the bells, bells, bells—
To the sobbing of the bells;
Keeping time, time, time,
As he knells, knells, knells,
In a happy Runic rhyme,
To the rolling of the bells—
Of the bells, bells, bells:—
110 To the tolling of the bells—
Of the bells, bells, bells, bells,
Bells, bells, bells—
To the moaning and the groaning of the bells.
1849

THE RAVEN

Once upon a midnight dreary, while I pondered, weak and weary,
Over many a quaint and curious volume of forgotten lore—
While I nodded, nearly napping, suddenly there came a tapping,
As of some one gently rapping, rapping at my chamber door.
" 'Tis some visitor," I muttered, "tapping at my chamber door—
Only this and nothing more."

Ah, distinctly I remember it was in the bleak December;
And each separate dying ember wrought its ghost upon the floor.
Eagerly I wished the morrow;—vainly I had sought to borrow
10 From my books surcease of sorrow—sorrow for the lost Lenore—
For the rare and radiant maiden whom the angels name Lenore—
Nameless *here* for evermore.

And the silken, sad, uncertain rustling of each purple curtain
Thrilled me—filled me with fantastic terrors never felt before;
So that now, to still the beating of my heart, I stood repeating,
" 'Tis some visitor entreating entrance at my chamber door—
Some late visitor entreating entrance at my chamber door;—
     This it is and nothing more."

Presently my soul grew stronger; hesitating then no longer,
"Sir," said I, "or Madam, truly your forgiveness I implore;   20
But the fact is I was napping, and so gently you came rapping,
And so faintly you came tapping, tapping at my chamber door,
That I scarce was sure I heard you"—here I opened wide the door;—
     Darkness there and nothing more.

Deep into that darkness peering, long I stood there wondering, fearing,
Doubting, dreaming dreams no mortal ever dared to dream before;
But the silence was unbroken, and the stillness gave no token,
And the only word there spoken was the whispered word, "Lenore?"
This I whispered, and an echo murmured back the word, "Lenore!"
     Merely this and nothing more.   30

Back into the chamber turning, all my soul within me burning,
Soon again I heard a tapping somewhat louder than before.
"Surely," said I, "surely that is something at my window lattice;
Let me see, then, what thereat is, and this mystery explore—
Let my heart be still a moment, and this mystery explore;—
     'Tis the wind and nothing more!"

Open here I flung the shutter, when, with many a flirt and flutter,
In there stepped a stately Raven of the saintly days of yore.
Not the least obeisance made he; not a minute stopped or stayed he;
But, with mien of lord or lady, perched above my chamber door—   40
Perched upon a bust of Pallas just above my chamber door—
     Perched, and sat, and nothing more.

Then this ebony bird beguiling my sad fancy into smiling,
By the grave and stern decorum of the countenance it wore,
"Though thy crest be shorn and shaven, thou," I said, "art sure no craven,
Ghastly grim and ancient Raven wandering from the Nightly shore—
Tell me what thy lordly name is on the Night's Plutonian shore!"
     Quoth the Raven, "Nevermore."

Much I marvelled this ungainly fowl to hear discourse so plainly,
Though its answer little meaning—little relevancy bore;   50
For we cannot help agreeing that no living human being
Ever yet was blessed with seeing bird above his chamber door—
Bird or beast upon the sculptured bust above his chamber door,
     With such name as "Nevermore."

But the Raven, sitting lonely on that placid bust, spoke only
That one word, as if his soul in that one word he did outpour.
Nothing farther then he uttered—not a feather then he fluttered—
Till I scarcely more than muttered, "Other friends have flown before—
On the morrow *he* will leave me, as my Hopes have flown before."
        Then the bird said, "Nevermore."

60

Startled at the stillness broken by reply so aptly spoken,
"Doubtless," said I, "what it utters is its only stock and store
Caught from some unhappy master whom unmerciful Disaster
Followed fast and followed faster till his songs one burden bore—
Till the dirges of his Hope that melancholy burden bore
        Of 'Never—nevermore.'"

But the Raven still beguiling my sad fancy into smiling,
Straight I wheeled a cushioned seat in front of bird and bust and door;
Then, upon the velvet sinking, I betook myself to linking
Fancy unto fancy, thinking what this ominous bird of yore—
What this grim, ungainly, ghastly, gaunt, and ominous bird of yore
        Meant in croaking "Nevermore."

70

This I sat engaged in guessing, but no syllable expressing
To the fowl whose fiery eyes now burned into my bosom's core;
This and more I sat divining, with my head at ease reclining
On the cushion's velvet lining that the lamp-light gloated o'er,
But whose velvet-violet lining with the lamp-light gloating o'er,
        She shall press, ah, nevermore!

Then, methought, the air grew denser, perfumed from an unseen censer
Swung by seraphim whose foot-falls tinkled on the tufted floor.
"Wretch," I cried, "thy God hath lent thee—by these angels he hath sent
    thee
Respite—respite and nepenthe from thy memories of Lenore;
Quaff, oh, quaff this kind nepenthe and forget this lost Lenore!"
        Quoth the Raven, "Nevermore."

80

"Prophet!" said I, "thing of evil!—prophet still, if bird or devil!—
Whether Tempter sent, or whether tempest tossed thee here ashore,
Desolate, yet all undaunted, on this desert land enchanted—
On this home by Horror haunted—tell me truly, I implore—
Is there—*is* there balm in Gilead?—tell me—tell me, I implore!"
        Quoth the Raven, "Nevermore."

90

"Prophet!" said I, "thing of evil!—prophet still, if bird or devil!
By that Heaven that bends above us—by that God we both adore—
Tell this soul with sorrow laden if, within the distant Aidenn,
It shall clasp a sainted maiden whom the angels name Lenore—
Clasp a rare and radiant maiden whom the angels name Lenore."
        Quoth the Raven, "Nevermore."

"Be that word our sign of parting, bird or fiend!" I shrieked, upstarting—
"Get thee back into the tempest and the Night's Plutonian shore!
Leave no black plume as a token of that lie thy soul hath spoken!
Leave my loneliness unbroken!—quit the bust above my door!   100
Take thy beak from out my heart, and take thy form from off my door!"
       Quoth the Raven, "Nevermore."

And the Raven, never flitting, still is sitting, *still* is sitting
On the pallid bust of Pallas just above my chamber door;
And his eyes have all the seeming of a demon's that is dreaming,
And the lamp-light o'er him streaming throws his shadow on the floor;
And my soul from out that shadow that lies floating on the floor
       Shall be lifted—nevermore!
1845

THE VALLEY OF UNREST

Once it smiled a silent dell
Where the people did not dwell;
They had gone unto the wars,
Trusting to the mild-eyed stars,
Nightly, from their azure towers,
To keep watch above the flowers,
In the midst of which all day
The red sun-light lazily lay.
Now each visitor shall confess
The sad valley's restlessness.   10
Nothing there is motionless—
Nothing save the airs that brood
Over the magic solitude.
Ah, by no wind are stirred those trees
That palpitate like the chill seas
Around the misty Hebrides!
Ah, by no wind those clouds are driven
That rustle through the unquiet Heaven
Uneasily, from morn till even,
Over the violets there that lie   20
In myriad types of the human eye—
Over the lilies there that wave
And weep above a nameless grave!
They wave:—from out their fragrant tops
Eternal dews come down in drops.
They weep:—from off their delicate stems
Perennial tears descend in gems.
1831

THE CITY IN THE SEA

Lo! Death has reared himself a throne
In a strange city lying alone
Far down within the dim West,
Where the good and the bad and the worst and the best
Have gone to their eternal rest.
There shrines and palaces and towers
(Time-eaten towers that tremble not!)
Resemble nothing that is ours.
Around, by lifting winds forgot,
Resignedly beneath the sky
The melancholy waters lie.

No rays from the holy heaven come down
On the long night-time of that town;
But light from out the lurid sea
Streams up the turrets silently—
Gleams up the pinnacles far and free—
Up domes—up spires—up kingly halls—
Up fanes—up Babylon-like walls—
Up shadowy long-forgotten bowers
Of sculptured ivy and stone flowers—
Up many and many a marvellous shrine
Whose wreathéd friezes intertwine
The viol, the violet, and the vine.

Resignedly beneath the sky
The melancholy waters lie.
So blend the turrets and shadows there
That all seem pendulous in air,
While from a proud tower in the town
Death looks gigantically down.

There open fanes and gaping graves
Yawn level with the luminous waves;
But not the riches there that lie
In each idol's diamond eye—
Not the gaily-jewelled dead
Tempt the waters from their bed;
For no ripples curl, alas!
Along that wilderness of glass—
No swellings tell that winds may be
Upon some far-off happier sea—
No heavings hint that winds have been
On seas less hideously serene.

But lo, a stir is in the air!
The wave—there is a movement there!
As if the towers had thrust aside,
In slightly sinking, the dull tide—
As if their tops had feebly given
A void within the filmy Heaven.
The waves have now a redder glow—
The hours are breathing faint and low—
And when, amid no earthly moans,   50
Down, down that town shall settle hence,
Hell, rising from a thousand thrones,
Shall do it reverence.
1831

ULALUME—A BALLAD

The skies they were ashen and sober;
  The leaves they were crispéd and sere—
  The leaves they were withering and sere;
It was night, in the lonesome October
  Of my most immemorial year:
It was hard by the dim lake of Auber,
  In the misty mid region of Weir—
It was down by the dank tarn of Auber,
  In the ghoul-haunted woodland of Weir.

Here once, through an alley Titanic,   10
  Of cypress, I roamed with my Soul—
  Of cypress, with Psyche, my Soul.
These were days when my heart was volcanic
  As the scoriac rivers that roll—
  As the lavas that restlessly roll
Their sulphurous currents down Yaanek
  In the ultimate climes of the Pole—
That groan as they roll down Mount Yaanek
  In the realms of the Boreal Pole.

Our talk had been serious and sober,   20
  But our thoughts they were palsied and sere—
  Our memories were treacherous and sere;
For we knew not the month was October,
  And we marked not the night of the year
  (Ah, night of all nights in the year!)—
We noted not the dim lake of Auber
  (Though once we had journeyed down here)—

Remembered not the dank tarn of Auber,
   Nor the ghoul-haunted woodland of Weir.

30

And now, as the night was senescent
   And star-dials pointed to morn—
   As the star-dials hinted of morn—
At the end of our path a liquescent
   And nebulous lustre was born,
Out of which a miraculous crescent
   Arose with a duplicate horn—
Astarte's bediamonded crescent
   Distinct with its duplicate horn.

And I said: "She is warmer than Dian;
   She rolls through an ether of sighs—
   She revels in a region of sighs.
She has seen that the tears are not dry on
   These cheeks, where the worm never dies,
And has come past the stars of the Lion,
   To point us the path to the skies—
   To the Lethean peace of the skies—
Come up, in despite of the Lion,
   To shine on us with her bright eyes—
Come up through the lair of the Lion,
   With love in her luminous eyes."

40

50

But Psyche, uplifting her finger
   Said: "Sadly this star I mistrust—
   Her pallor I strangely mistrust:
Ah, hasten!—ah, let us not linger!
   Ah, fly!—let us fly!—for we must."
In terror she spoke, letting sink her
   Wings till they trailed in the dust—
In agony sobbed, letting sink her
   Plumes till they trailed in the dust—
   Till they sorrowfully trailed in the dust.

60

I replied: "This is nothing but dreaming:
   Let us on by this tremulous light!
   Let us bathe in this crystalline light!
Its Sibyllic splendor is beaming
   With Hope and in Beauty to-night!
   See!—it flickers up the sky through the night!
Ah, we safely may trust to its gleaming,
   And be sure it will lead us aright—
We safely may trust to a gleaming,
   That cannot but guide us aright,
   Since it flickers up to Heaven through the night."

70

Thus I pacified Psyche and kissed her,
   And tempted her out of her gloom—
   And conquered her scruples and gloom;
And we passed to the end of the vista,
   But were stopped by the door of a tomb—
   By the door of a legended tomb;
And I said: "What is written, sweet sister,
   On the door of this legended tomb?"
   She replied: "Ulalume—Ulalume!—   80
   'Tis the vault of thy lost Ulalume!"

Then my heart it grew ashen and sober
   As the leaves that were crispéd and sere—
   As the leaves that were withering and sere;
And I cried: "It was surely October
   On *this* very night of last year
   That I journeyed—I journeyed down here!—
   That I brought a dread burden down here—
   On this night of all nights in the year,
   Ah, what demon has tempted me here?   90
Well I know, now, this dim lake of Auber—
   This misty mid region of Weir—
Well I know, now, this dank tarn of Auber,
   This ghoul-haunted woodland of Weir."

Said we, then—the two, then: "Ah can it
   Have been that woodlandish ghouls—
   The pitiful, the merciful ghouls—
To bar up our way and to ban it
   From the secret that lies in these wolds—
   From the thing that lies hidden in these wolds—   100
Have drawn up the spectre of a planet
   From the limbo of lunary souls—
This sinfully scintillant planet
   From the Hell of the planetary souls?"
1847

ANNABEL LEE

It was many and many a year ago,
   In a kingdom by the sea,
That a maiden there lived whom you may know
   By the name of Annabel Lee;—
And this maiden she lived with no other thought
   Than to love and be loved by me.

She was a child and *I* was a child,
　　In this kingdom by the sea,
But we loved with a love that was more than love—
　　I and my Annabel Lee—
With a love that the wingéd seraphs of Heaven
　　Coveted her and me.

And this was the reason that, long ago,
　　In this kingdom by the sea,
A wind blew out of a cloud, chilling
　　My beautiful Annabel Lee;
So that her highborn kinsman came
　　And bore her away from me,
To shut her up in a sepulchre
　　In this kingdom by the sea.

The angels, not half so happy in Heaven,
　　Went envying her and me:—
Yes! that was the reason (as all men know,
　　In this kingdom by the sea)
That the wind came out of the cloud, chilling
　　And killing my Annabel Lee.

But our love it was stronger by far than the love
　　Of those who were older than we—
　　Of many far wiser than we—
And neither the angels in Heaven above
　　Nor the demons down under the sea,
Can ever dissever my soul from the soul
　　Of the beautiful Annabel Lee:—

For the moon never beams without bringing me dreams
　　Of the beautiful Annabel Lee;
And the stars never rise but I see the bright eyes
　　Of the beautiful Annabel Lee;
And so, all the night-tide, I lie down by the side
Of my darling, my darling, my life and my bride,
　　In her sepulchre there by the sea—
　　In her tomb by the side of the sea.
　　1849

THE POETIC PRINCIPLE

In speaking of the Poetic Principle, I have no design to be either thorough or profound. While discussing very much at random the essentiality of what we call Poetry, my principal purpose will be to cite for consideration some few of those minor English or American poems which best suit my own taste, or which, upon my own fancy, have left the most definite impression. By "minor poems" I mean, of course, poems of little length. And here, in the beginning, permit me to say a few words in regard to a somewhat peculiar principle, which, whether rightfully or wrongfully, has always had its influence in my own critical estimate of the poem. I hold that a long poem does not exist. I maintain that the phrase, "a long poem," is simply a flat contradiction in terms.

I need scarcely observe that a poem deserves its title only inasmuch as it excites, by elevating the soul. The value of the poem is in the ratio of this elevating excitement. But all excitements are, through a psychal necessity, transient. That degree of excitement which would entitle a poem to be so called at all, cannot be sustained throughout a composition of any great length. After the lapse of half an hour, at the very utmost, it flags—fails—a revulsion ensues—and then the poem is, in effect, and in fact, no longer such.

There are, no doubt, many who have found difficulty in reconciling the critical dictum that the "Paradise Lost" is to be devoutly admired throughout, with the absolute impossibility of maintaining for it, during perusal, the amount of enthusiasm which that critical dictum would demand. This great work, in fact, is to be regarded as poetical only when, losing sight of that vital requisite in all works of Art, Unity, we view it merely as a series of minor poems. If, to preserve its Unity—its totality of effect or impression—we read it (as would be necessary) at a single sitting, the result is but a constant alternation of excitement and depression. After a passage of what we feel to be true poetry, there follows, inevitably, a passage of platitude which no critical pre-judgment can force us to admire; but if, upon completing the work, we read it again, omitting the first book—that is to say, commencing with the second—we shall be surprised at now finding that admirable which we before condemned—that damnable which we had previously so much admired. It follows from all this that the ultimate, aggregate, or absolute effect of even the best epic under the sun, is a nullity—and this is precisely the fact.

In regard to the *Iliad*, we have, if not positive proof, at least very good reason, for believing it intended as a series of lyrics; but, granting the epic intention, I can say only that the work is based in an imperfect sense of Art. The modern epic is, of the suppositious ancient model, but an inconsiderate and blindfold imitation. But the day of these artistic anomalies is over. If, at any time, any very long poem *were* popular in reality, which I doubt, it is at least clear that no very long poem will ever be popular again.

That the extent of a poetical work is, *ceteris paribus*,[1] the measure of its merit, seems undoubtedly, when we thus state it, a proposition sufficiently absurd —yet we are indebted for it to the Quarterly Reviews. Surely there can be nothing in mere *size*, abstractly considered—there can be nothing in mere *bulk*, so

---

1. ceteris paribus: other things being equal.

far as a volume is concerned, which has so continuously elicited admiration from these saturnine pamphlets! A mountain, to be sure, by the mere sentiment of physical magnitude which it conveys, *does* impress us with a sense of the sublime—but no man is impressed after *this* fashion by the material grandeur of even "The Columbiad." Even the Quarterlies have not instructed us to be so impressed by it. *As yet,* they have not *insisted* on our estimating Lamartine by the cubic foot, or Pollok by the pound—but what else are we to *infer* from their continued prating about "sustained effort"? If, by "sustained effort," any little gentleman has accomplished an epic, let us frankly commend him for the effort —if this indeed be a thing commendable—but let us forbear praising the epic on the effort's account. It is to be hoped that common sense, in the time to come, will prefer deciding upon a work of art rather by the impression it makes, by the effect it produces, than by the time it took to impress the effect, or by the amount of "sustained effort" which had been found necessary in effecting the impression. The fact is, that perseverance is one thing and genius quite another—nor can all the Quarterlies in Christendom confound them. By and by, this proposition, with many which I have just been urging, will be received as self-evident. In the meantime, by being generally condemned as falsities, they will not be essentially damaged as truths.

On the other hand, it is clear that a poem may be improperly brief. Undue brevity degenerates into mere epigrammatism. A *very* short poem, while now and then producing a brilliant or vivid, never produces a profound or enduring effect. There must be the steady pressing down of the stamp upon the wax. De Béranger has wrought innumerable things, pungent and spirit-stirring; but in general they have been too imponderous to stamp themselves deeply into the public attention, and thus, as so many feathers of fancy, have been blown aloft only to be whistled down the wind.

A remarkable instance of the effect of undue brevity in depressing a poem—in keeping it out of the popular view—is afforded by the following exquisite little Serenade:

> I arise from dreams of thee
> In the first sweet sleep of night,
> When the winds are breathing low,
> And the stars are shining bright;
> I arise from dreams of thee,
> And a spirit in my feet
> Has led me—who knows how?—
> To thy chamber-window, sweet!
>
> The wandering airs, they faint
> On the dark, the silent stream—
> The champak odors fail
> Like sweet thoughts in a dream;
> The nightingale's complaint,
> It dies upon her heart,
> As I must die on thine,
> O, beloved as thou art!

> O, lift me from the grass!
> I die, I faint, I fail!
> Let thy love in kisses rain
> On my lips and eyelids pale.
> My cheek is cold and white, alas!
> My heart beats loud and fast:
> Oh! press it close to thine again,
> Where it will break at last!

Very few perhaps are familiar with these lines—yet no less a poet than Shelley is their author. Their warm, yet delicate and ethereal imagination will be appreciated by all—but by none so thoroughly as by him who has himself arisen from sweet dreams of one beloved to bathe in the aromatic air of a southern midsummer night.

One of the finest poems by Willis, the very best in my opinion which he has ever written, has no doubt, through this same defect of undue brevity, been kept back from its proper position, not less in the critical than in the popular view.

> The shadows lay along Broadway,
> 'Twas near the twilight-tide—
> And slowly there a lady fair
> Was walking in her pride.
> Alone walk'd she; but, viewlessly,
> Walk'd spirits at her side.
>
> Peace charm'd the street beneath her feet,
> And Honour charm'd the air;
> And all astir looked kind on her,
> And call'd her good and fair—
> For all God ever gave to her
> She kept with chary care.
>
> She kept with care her beauties rare
> From lovers warm and true—
> For her heart was cold to all but gold,
> And the rich came not to woo—
> But honour'd well are charms to sell,
> If priests the selling do.
>
> Now walking there was one more fair—
> A slight girl, lily-pale;
> And she had unseen company
> To make the spirit quail—
> 'Twixt Want and Scorn she walk'd forlorn,
> And nothing could avail.
>
> No mercy now can clear her brow
> For this world's peace to pray;

> For, as love's wild prayer dissolved in air,
> Her woman's heart gave way!—
> But the sin forgiven by Christ in Heaven
> By man is cursed alway!

In this composition we find it difficult to recognize the Willis who has written so many mere "verses of society." The lines are not only richly ideal, but full of energy; while they breathe an earnestness, an evident sincerity of sentiment, for which we look in vain throughout all the other works of this author.

While the epic mania—while the idea that, to merit in poetry, prolixity is indispensable—has for some years past been gradually dying out of the public mind by mere dint of its own absurdity, we find it succeeded by a heresy too palpably false to be long tolerated, but one which, in the brief period it has already endured, may be said to have accomplished more in the corruption of our Poetical Literature than all its other enemies combined. I allude to the heresy of *The Didactic*. It has been assumed, tacitly and avowedly, directly and indirectly, that the ultimate object of all Poetry is Truth. Every poem, it is said, should inculcate a moral, and by this moral is the poetical merit of the work to be adjudged. We Americans especially have patronized this happy idea, and we Bostonians very especially have developed it in full. We have taken it into our heads that to write a poem simply for the poem's sake, and to acknowledge such to have been our design, would be to confess ourselves radically wanting in the true Poetic dignity and force:—but the simple fact is, that would we but permit ourselves to look into our own souls, we should immediately there discover that under the sun there neither exists nor *can* exist any work more thoroughly dignified, more supremely noble than this very poem, this poem *per se*, this poem which is a poem and nothing more, this poem written solely for the poem's sake.

With as deep a reverence for the True as ever inspired the bosom of man, I would nevertheless limit, in some measure, its modes of inculcation. I would limit to enforce them. I would not enfeeble them by dissipation. The demands of Truth are severe. She has no sympathy with the myrtles. All *that* which is so indispensable in Song is precisely all *that* with which *she* has nothing whatever to do. It is but making her a flaunting paradox to wreathe her in gems and flowers. In enforcing a truth, we need severity rather than efflorescence of language. We must be simple, precise, terse. We must be cool, calm, unimpassioned. In a word, we must be in that mood which, as nearly as possible, is the exact converse of the poetical. *He* must be blind indeed who does not perceive the radical and chasmal differences between the truthful and the poetical modes of inculcation. He must be theory-mad beyond redemption who, in spite of these differences, shall still persist in attempting to reconcile the obstinate oils and waters of Poetry and Truth.

Dividing the world of mind into its three most immediately obvious distinctions, we have the Pure Intellect, Taste, and the Moral Sense. I place Taste in the middle because it is just this position which it occupies in the mind. It holds intimate relations with either extreme, but from the Moral Sense is separated by so faint a difference that Aristotle has not hesitated to place some of its operations among the virtues themselves. Nevertheless, we find the *offices* of the trio marked with a sufficient distinction. Just as the Intellect concerns itself with Truth, so Taste informs us of the Beautiful, while the Moral Sense is regardful of Duty. Of this latter, while Conscience teaches the obligation, and Reason the expediency, Taste contents herself with displaying the charms, waging war upon Vice solely on the ground of her deformity, her disproportion, her animosity to the fitting, to the appropriate, to the harmonious, in a word, to Beauty.

An immortal instinct deep within the spirit of man is thus plainly a sense of the Beautiful. This it is which administers to his delight in the manifold forms, and sounds, and odors, and sentiments, amid which he exists. And just as the lily is repeated in the lake, or the eyes of Amaryllis in the mirror, so is the mere oral or written repetition of these forms, and sounds, and colors, and odors, and sentiments, a duplicate source of delight. But this mere repetition is not poetry. He who shall simply sing, with however glowing enthusiasm, or with however vivid a truth of description, of the sights, and sounds, and odors, and colors, and sentiments, which greet *him* in common with all mankind—he, I say, has yet failed to prove his divine title. There is still a something in the distance which he has been unable to attain. We have still a thirst unquenchable, to allay which he has not shown us the crystal springs. This thirst belongs to the immortality of Man. It is at once a consequence and an indication of his perennial existence. It is the desire of the moth for the star. It is no mere appreciation of the Beauty before us—but a wild effort to reach the Beauty above. Inspired by an ecstatic prescience of the glories beyond the grave, we struggle by multiform combinations among the things and thoughts of Time to attain a portion of that Loveliness whose very elements, perhaps, appertain to eternity alone. And thus when by Poetry—or when by Music, the most entrancing of the Poetic moods—we find ourselves melted into tears, we weep then—not as the Abbate Gravina supposes—through excess of pleasure, but through a certain, petulant, impatient sorrow at our inability to grasp *now*, wholly, here on earth, at once and forever, those divine and rapturous joys, of which *through* the poem or *through* the music, we attain to but brief and indeterminate glimpses.

The struggle to apprehend the supernal Loveliness—this struggle, on the part of souls fittingly constituted—has given to the world all *that* which it (the world) has ever been enabled at once to understand and to *feel* as poetic.

The Poetic Sentiment, of course, may develop itself in various modes—in Painting, in Sculpture, in Architecture, in the Dance—very especially in Music —and very peculiarly, and with a wide field, in the composition of the Landscape Garden. Our present theme, however, has regard only to its manifestation in words. And here let me speak briefly on the topic of rhythm. Contenting myself with the certainty that Music, in its various modes of metre, rhythm, and rhyme, is of so vast a moment in Poetry as never to be wisely rejected—is so vitally important an adjunct that he is simply silly who declines its assistance —I will not now pause to maintain its absolute essentiality. It is in Music, perhaps, that the soul most nearly attains the great end for which, when inspired by the Poetic Sentiment, it struggles—the creation of supernal Beauty. It *may* be, indeed, that here this sublime end is, now and then, attained in *fact*. We are often made to feel, with a shivering delight, that from an earthly harp are stricken notes which *cannot* have been unfamiliar to the angels. And thus there can be little doubt that in the union of Poetry with Music in its popular sense, we shall find the widest field for the Poetic development. The old Bards and Minnesingers had advantages which we do not possess—and Thomas Moore, singing his own songs, was, in the most legitimate manner, perfecting them as poems.

To recapitulate, then:—I would define, in brief, the Poetry of words as *The Rhythmical Creation of Beauty*. Its sole arbiter is Taste. With the Intellect or with the Conscience, it has only collateral relations. Unless incidentally, it has no concern whatever either with Duty or with Truth.

A few words, however, in explanation. *That* pleasure which is at once the most pure, the most elevating, and the most intense, is derived, I maintain, from the contemplation of the Beautiful. In the contemplation of Beauty we alone find it possible to attain that pleasurable elevation, or excitement, *of the soul*, which we recognize as the Poetic Sentiment, and which is so easily distinguished from Truth, which is the satisfaction of the Reason, or from Passion, which is the excitement of the heart. I make Beauty, therefore,—using the word as inclusive of the sublime,—I make Beauty the province of the poem, simply because it is an obvious rule of Art that effects should be made to spring as directly as possible from their causes:—no one as yet having been weak enough to deny that the peculiar elevation in question is at least *most readily* attainable in the poem. It by no means follows, however, that the incitements of Passion, or the precepts of Duty, or even the lessons of Truth, may not be introduced into a poem, and with advantage; for they may subserve incidentally, in various ways, the general purposes of the work:—but the true artist will always contrive to tone them down in proper subjection to that *Beauty* which is the atmosphere and the real essence of the poem.

I cannot better introduce the few poems which I shall present for your consideration, than by the citation of the Proem to Mr. Longfellow's "Waif":

The day is done, and the darkness
    Falls from the wings of Night,
As a feather is wafted downward
    From an eagle in his flight.

I see the lights of the village
    Gleam through the rain and the mist,
And a feeling of sadness comes o'er me,
    That my soul cannot resist;

A feeling of sadness and longing,
    That is not akin to pain,
And resembles sorrow only
    As the mist resembles the rain.

Come, read to me some poem,
    Some simple and heartfelt lay,
That shall soothe this restless feeling,
    And banish the thoughts of day.

> Not from the grand old masters,
> Not from the bards sublime,
> Whose distant footsteps echo
> Through the corridors of Time.
>
> For, like strains of martial music,
> Their mighty thoughts suggest
> Life's endless toil and endeavor;
> And to-night I long for rest.
>
> Read from some humbler poet,
> Whose songs gushed from his heart,
> As showers from the clouds of summer,
> Or tears from the eyelids start;
>
> Who through long days of labor,
> And nights devoid of ease,
> Still heard in his soul the music
> Of wonderful melodies.
>
> Such songs have power to quiet
> The restless pulse of care,
> And come like the benediction
> That follows after prayer.
>
> Then read from the treasured volume
> The poem of thy choice,
> And lend to the rhyme of the poet
> The beauty of thy voice.
>
> And the night shall be filled with music,
> And the cares, that infest the day,
> Shall fold their tents, like the Arabs,
> And as silently steal away.

With no great range of imagination, these lines have been justly admired for their delicacy of expression. Some of the images are very effective. Nothing can be better than

> The bards sublime
> Whose distant footsteps echo
> Down the corridors of Time.

The idea of the last quatrain is also very effective. The poem, on the whole, however, is chiefly to be admired for the graceful *insouciance* of its metre, so well in accordance with the character of the sentiments, and especially for the *ease* of the general manner. This "ease" or naturalness, in a literary style, it has long been the fashion to regard as ease in appearance alone—as a point of really difficult attainment. But not so:—a natural manner is difficult only to him who should never meddle with it—to the unnatural. It is but the result of writing with the understanding, or with the instinct, that *the tone*, in composition, should always be that which the mass of mankind would adopt—and must perpetually vary, of course, with the occasion. The author who, after the fashion of the "North American Review," should be upon *all* occasions merely "quiet," must necessarily upon *many* occasions be simply silly, or stupid; and has no more right to be considered "easy" or "natural" than a Cockney exquisite, or than the sleeping Beauty in the waxworks.

Among the minor poems of Bryant none has so much impressed me as the one which he entitles "June." I quote only a portion of it:

> There, through the long, long summer hours,
>   The golden light should lie,
> And thick young herbs and groups of flowers
>   Stand in their beauty by.
> The oriole should build and tell
> His love-tale, close beside my cell;
>   The idle butterfly
> Should rest him there, and there be heard
> The housewife-bee and humming bird.
>
> And what if cheerful shouts at noon
>   Come, from the village sent,
> Or songs of maids, beneath the moon,
>   With fairy laughter blent?
> And what if, in the evening light,
> Betrothed lovers walk in sight
>   Of my low monument?
> I would the lovely scene around
> Might know no sadder sight nor sound.
>
> I know, I know I should not see
>   The season's glorious show,
> Nor would its brightness shine for me,
>   Nor its wild music flow;
> But if, around my place of sleep,
> The friends I love should come to weep,
>   They might not haste to go.
> Soft airs, and song, and light and bloom
> Should keep them lingering by my tomb.
>
> These to their softened hearts should bear
>   The thought of what has been,
> And speak of one who cannot share
>   The gladness of the scene;

Whose part, in all the pomp that fills
The circuit of the summer hills,
    Is—that his grave is green;
And deeply would their hearts rejoice
To hear again his living voice.

The rhythmical flow here is even voluptuous—nothing could be more melodious. The poem has always affected me in a remarkable manner. The intense melancholy which seems to well up, perforce, to the surface of all the poet's cheerful sayings about his grave, we find thrilling us to the soul—while there is the truest poetic elevation in the thrill. The impression left is one of a pleasurable sadness. And if, in the remaining compositions which I shall introduce to you, there be more or less of a similar tone always apparent, let me remind you that (how or why we know not) this certain taint of sadness is inseparably connected with all the higher manifestations of true Beauty. It is, nevertheless,

A feeling of sadness and longing
    That is not akin to pain,
And resembles sorrow only
    As the mist resembles the rain.

The taint of which I speak is clearly perceptible even in a poem so full of brilliancy and spirit as the "Health" of Edward Coote Pinkney.

I fill this cup to one made up
    Of loveliness alone,
A woman, of her gentle sex
    The seeming paragon;
To whom the better elements
    And kindly stars have given
A form so fair, that, like the air,
    'Tis less of earth than heaven.

Her every tone is music's own,
    Like those of morning birds,
And something more than melody
    Dwells ever in her words;
The coinage of her heart are they,
    And from her lips each flows
As one may see the burden'd bee
    Forth issue from the rose.

Affections are as thoughts to her,
    The measures of her hours;
Her feelings have the fragrancy,
    The freshness of young flowers;
And lovely passions, changing oft,

So fill her, she appears
The image of themselves by turns,—
The idol of past years!

Of her bright face one glance will trace
A picture on the brain,
And of her voice in echoing hearts
A sound must long remain;
But memory, such as mine of her,
So very much endears,
When death is nigh, my latest sigh
Will not be life's but hers.

I fill this cup to one made up
Of loveliness alone,
A woman, of her gentle sex
The seeming paragon—
Her health! and would on earth there stood
Some more of such a frame,
That life might be all poetry,
And weariness a name.

It was the misfortune of Mr. Pinkney to have been born too far south. Had he been a New Englander, it is probable that he would have been ranked as the first of American lyrists, by that magnanimous cabal which has so long controlled the destinies of American Letters, in conducting the thing called "The North American Review." The poem just cited is especially beautiful; but the poetic elevation which it induces, we must refer chiefly to our sympathy in the poet's enthusiasm. We pardon his hyperboles for the evident earnestness with which they are uttered.

It was by no means my design, however, to expatiate upon the *merits* of what I should read you. These will necessarily speak for themselves. Boccalini, in his "Advertisements from Parnassus," tells us that Zoilus once presented Apollo a very caustic criticism upon a very admirable book:—whereupon the god asked him for the beauties of the work. He replied that he only busied himself about the errors. On hearing this, Apollo, handing him a sack of unwinnowed wheat, bade him pick out *all the chaff* for his reward.

Now this fable answers very well as a hit at the critics—but I am by no means sure that the god was in the right. I am by no means certain that the true limits of the critical duty are not grossly misunderstood. Excellence, in a poem especially, may be considered in the light of an axiom, which need only be properly *put,* to become self-evident. It is *not* excellence if it require to be demonstrated as such:—and thus to point out too particularly the merits of a work of Art, is to admit that they are *not* merits altogether.

Among the "Melodies" of Thomas Moore is one whose distinguished character as a poem proper seems to have been singularly left out of view. I allude to his lines beginning—"Come, rest in this bosom." The intense energy of their expression is not surpassed by anything in Byron. There are two of the lines in which a sentiment is conveyed that embodies the *all in all* of the divine passion of love —a sentiment which, perhaps, has found its echo in more, and in more passionate, human hearts than any other single sentiment ever embodied in words:

> Come, rest in this bosom, my own stricken deer,
> Though the herd have fled from thee, thy home is still here;
> Here still is the smile, that no cloud can o'ercast,
> And a heart and a hand all thy own to the last.
>
> Oh! what was love made for, if 'tis not the same
> Through joy and through torment, through glory and shame?
> I know not, I ask not, if guilt's in that heart,
> I but know that I love thee, whatever thou art.
>
> Thou hast call'd me thy Angel in moments of bliss,
> And thy Angel I'll be, 'mid the horrors of this,—
> Through the furnace, unshrinking, thy steps to pursue,
> And shield thee, and save thee,—or perish there too!

It has been the fashion of late days to deny Moore imagination, while granting him fancy—a distinction originating with Coleridge—than whom no man more fully comprehended the great powers of Moore. The fact is, that the fancy of this poet so far predominates over all his other faculties, and over the fancy of all other men, as to have induced, very naturally, the idea that he is fanciful *only*. But never was there a greater mistake. Never was a grosser wrong done the fame of a true poet. In the compass of the English language I can call to mind no poem more profoundly—more weirdly *imaginative*, in the best sense, than the lines commencing—"I would I were by that dim lake"—which are the composition of Thomas Moore. I regret that I am unable to remember them.

One of the noblest—and, speaking of fancy, one of the most singularly fanciful of modern poets, was Thomas Hood. His "Fair Ines" had always for me an inexpressible charm:

> O saw ye not fair Ines?
>   She's gone into the West,
> To dazzle when the sun is down,
>   And rob the world of rest:
> She took our daylight with her,
>   The smiles that we love best,
> With morning blushes on her cheek,
>   And pearls upon her breast.
>
> O turn again, fair Ines,
>   Before the fall of night,
> For fear the Moon should shine alone,
>   And stars unrivall'd bright;

And blessed will the lover be
That walks beneath their light,
And breathes the love against thy cheek
I dare not even write!

Would I had been, fair Ines,
That gallant cavalier,
Who rode so gaily by thy side,
And whisper'd thee so near!
Were there no bonny dames at home,
Or no true lovers here,
That he should cross the seas to win
The dearest of the dear?

I saw thee, lovely Ines,
Descend along the shore,
With bands of noble gentlemen,
And banners wav'd before;
And gentle youth and maidens gay,
And snowy plumes they wore;
It would have been a beauteous dream,
If it had been no more!

Alas, alas, fair Ines,
She went away with song,
With Music waiting on her steps,
And shoutings of the throng;
But some were sad, and felt no mirth,
But only Music's wrong,
In sounds that sang Farewell, Farewell,
To her you've loved so long.

Farewell, farewell, fair Ines,
That vessel never bore
So fair a lady on its deck,
Nor danced so light before,—
Alas for pleasure on the sea,
And sorrow on the shore!
The smile that blest one lover's heart
Has broken many more!

"The Haunted House," by the same author, is one of the truest poems ever written, one of the *truest*, one of the most unexceptionable, one of the most thoroughly artistic, both in its theme and in its execution. It is, moreover, powerfully ideal—imaginative. I regret that its length renders it unsuitable for the purposes of this Lecture. In place of it, permit me to offer the universally appreciated "Bridge of Sighs."

One more Unfortunate,
Weary of breath,
Rashly importunate,
Gone to her death!

Take her up tenderly,
Lift her with care;—
Fashion'd so slenderly,
Young, and so fair!

Look at her garments
Clinging like cerements;
Whilst the wave constantly
Drips from her clothing;
Take her up instantly,
Loving, not loathing—

Touch her not scornfully;
Think of her mournfully,
Gently and humanly;
Not of the stains of her,
All that remains of her
Now is pure womanly.

Make no deep scrutiny
Into her mutiny
Rash and undutiful;
Past all dishonor,
Death has left on her
Only the beautiful.

Still, for all slips of hers,
One of Eve's family—
Wipe those poor lips of hers
Oozing so clammily.
Loop up her tresses
Escaped from the comb,
Her fair auburn tresses;
Whilst wonderment guesses
Where was her home?

Who was her father?
Who was her mother?
Had she a sister?
Had she a brother?
Or was there a dearer one
Still, and a nearer one
Yet, than all other?

Alas! for the rarity
Of Christian charity
Under the sun!
Oh! it was pitiful!
Near a whole city full,
Home she had none.

Sisterly, brotherly,
Fatherly, motherly
Feelings had changed:
Love, by harsh evidence,
Thrown from its eminence;
Even God's providence
Seeming estranged.

Where the lamps quiver
So far in the river,
With many a light
From window and casement,
From garret to basement,
She stood, with amazement,
Houseless by night.

The bleak wind of March
Made her tremble and shiver;
But not the dark arch,
Or the black flowing river:
Mad from life's history,
Glad to death's mystery,
Swift to be hurl'd—
Anywhere, anywhere
Out of the world!

In she plunged boldly,
No matter how coldly
The rough river ran,—
Over the brink of it,
Picture it,—think of it,
Dissolute Man!
Lave in it, drink of it
Then, if you can!

Take her up tenderly,
Lift her with care,
Fashion'd so slenderly,
Young, and so fair!

Ere her limbs frigidly
Stiffen too rigidly,

Decently,—kindly,—
Smooth, and compose them;
And her eyes, close them,
Staring so blindly!

Dreadfully staring
Through muddy impurity,
As when with the daring
Last look of despairing
Fixed on futurity.

Perishing gloomily,
Spurred by contumely,
Cold inhumanity,
Burning insanity,
Into her rest,—
Cross her hands humbly,
As if praying dumbly,
Over her breast!
Owning her weakness,
Her evil behaviour,
And leaving, with meekness,
Her sins to her Savior!

The vigor of this poem is no less remarkable than its pathos. The versification, although carrying the fanciful to the very verge of the fantastic, is nevertheless admirably adapted to the wild insanity which is the thesis of the poem.

Among the minor poems of Lord Byron is one which has never received from the critics the praise which it undoubtedly deserves:

Though the day of my destiny's over,
    And the star of my fate hath declined,
Thy soft heart refused to discover
    The faults which so many could find;
Though thy soul with my grief was acquainted,
    It shrunk not to share it with me,
And the love which my spirit hath painted
    It never hath found but in *thee*.

Then when nature around me is smiling,
    The last smile which answers to mine,
I do not believe it beguiling,
    Because it reminds me of thine;
And when winds are at war with the ocean,
    As the breasts I believed in with me,
If their billows excite an emotion,
    It is that they bear me from *thee*.

Though the rock of my last hope is shivered,
    And its fragments are sunk in the wave,
Though I feel that my soul is delivered
    To pain—it shall not be its slave.
There is many a pang to pursue me:
    They may crush, but they shall not contemn—
They may torture, but shall not subdue me—
    'Tis of *thee* that I think—not of them.

Though human, thou didst not deceive me,
    Though woman, thou didst not forsake,
Though loved, thou forborest to grieve me,
    Though slandered, thou never couldst shake,—
Though trusted, thou didst not disclaim me,
    Though parted, it was not to fly,
Though watchful, 'twas not to defame me,
    Nor mute, that the world might belie.

Yet I blame not the world, nor despise it,
    Nor the war of the many with one—
If my soul was not fitted to prize it,
    'Twas folly not sooner to shun:
And if dearly that error hath cost me,
    And more than I once could foresee,
I have found that whatever it lost me,
    It could not deprive me of *thee*.

From the wreck of the past, which hath perished,
    Thus much I at least may recall,
It hath taught me that which I most cherished,
    Deserved to be dearest of all:
In the desert a fountain is springing,
    In the wide waste there still is a tree,
And a bird in the solitude singing,
    Which speaks to my spirit of *thee*.

Although the rhythm here is one of the most difficult, the versification could scarcely be improved. No nobler *theme* ever engaged the pen of poet. It is the soul-elevating idea that no man can consider himself entitled to complain of Fate while, in his adversity, he still retains the unwavering love of woman.

From Alfred Tennyson—although in perfect sincerity I regard him as the noblest poet that ever lived—I have left myself time to cite only a very brief specimen. I call him, and think *him* the noblest of poets—*not* because the impressions he produces are at *all* times the most profound—*not* because the poetical excitement which he induces is at *all* times the most intense—but because it *is* at all times the most ethereal—in other words, the most elevating and most pure. What poet is so little of the earth, earthy. What I am about to read is from his last long poem, "The Princess":

Tears, idle tears, I know not what they mean,
Tears from the depth of some divine despair
Rise in the heart, and gather to the eyes,
In looking on the happy Autumn-fields,
And thinking of the days that are no more.

Fresh as the first beam glittering on a sail,
That brings our friends up from the underworld,
Sad as the last which reddens over one
That sinks with all we love below the verge;
So sad, so fresh, the days that are no more.

Ah, sad and strange as in dark summer dawns
The earliest pipe of half-awaken'd birds
To dying ears, when unto dying eyes
The casement slowly grows a glimmering square;
So sad, so strange, the days that are no more.

Dear as remember'd kisses after death,
And sweet as those by hopeless fancy feign'd
On lips that are for others; deep as love,
Deep as first love, and wild with all regret;
O Death in Life, the days that are no more.

Thus, although in a very cursory and imperfect manner, I have endeavoured to convey to you my conception of the Poetic Principle. It has been my purpose to suggest that, while this Principle itself is strictly and simply the Human Aspiration for Supernal Beauty, the manifestation of the Principle is always found in *an elevating excitement of the Soul*, quite independent of that passion which is the intoxication of the Heart, or of that truth which is the satisfaction of the Reason. For in regard to Passion, alas! its tendency is to degrade rather than to elevate the Soul. Love, on the contrary—Love—the true, the divine Eros—the Uranian as distinguished from the Dionaean Venus—is unquestionably the purest and truest of all poetical themes. And in regard to Truth—if, to be sure, through the attainment of a truth we are led to perceive a harmony where none was apparent before, we experience at once the true poetical effect—but this effect is referable to the harmony alone, and not in the least degree to the truth which merely served to render the harmony manifest.

We shall reach, however, more immediately a distinct conception of what the true Poetry is, by mere reference to a few of the simple elements which induce in the Poet himself the true poetical effect. He recognizes the ambrosia which nourishes his soul, in the bright orbs that shine in Heaven—in the volutes of the flower—in the clustering of low shrubberies—in the waving of the grain-fields—in the slanting of tall Eastern trees—in the blue distance of mountains—in the grouping of clouds—in the twinkling of half-hidden brooks—in the gleaming of silver rivers—in the repose of sequestered lakes—in the star-mirroring depths of lonely wells. He perceives it in the songs of birds—in the harp of Aeolus—in the sighing of the night-wind—in the repining voice of the forest—

in the surf that complains to the shore—in the fresh breath of the woods—in the scent of the violet—in the voluptuous perfume of the hyacinth—in the suggestive odor that comes to him at eventide from far-distant, undiscovered islands, over dim oceans, illimitable and unexplored. He owns it in all noble thoughts—in all unworldly motives—in all holy impulses—in all chivalrous, generous, and self-sacrificing deeds. He feels it in the beauty of woman—in the grace of her step—in the lustre of her eye—in the melody of her voice—in her soft laughter—in her sigh—in the harmony of the rustling of her robes. He deeply feels it in her winning endearments—in her burning enthusiasms—in her gentle charities—in her meek and devotional endurances—but above all—ah, far above all—he kneels to it, he worships it in the faith, in the purity, in the strength, in the alto-gether divine majesty—of her *love*.

Let me conclude by the recitation of yet another brief poem—one very differ-ent in character from any that I have before quoted. It is by Motherwell, and is called "The Song of the Cavalier." With our modern and altogether rational ideas of the absurdity and impiety of warfare, we are not precisely in that frame of mind best adapted to sympathize with the sentiments, and thus to appreciate the real excellence of the poem. To do this fully we must identify ourselves in fancy with the soul of the old cavalier.

> Then mounte! then mounte, brave gallants, all,
> And don your helmes amaine:
> Deathe's couriers, Fame and Honour, call
> Us to the field againe.
> No shrewish tears shall fill our eye
> When the sword-hilt's in our hand,—
> Heart-whole we'll part, and no whit sighe
> For the fayrest of the land;
> Let piping swaine, and craven wight,
> Thus weepe and puling crye,
> Our business is like men to fight,
> And hero-like to die!

1850

RALPH WALDO EMERSON ▪▪▪▪▪▪▪▪▪▪▪▪▪

■ ■

Ralph Waldo Emerson (1803–1882) was born in Boston, and educated at the Boston Latin School, Harvard College, and the Harvard Divinity School. He became a Unitarian minister in 1829, but resigned from the ministry three years later because of its cramping effects. His first book, *Nature*, published in 1836, has often been called the bible of New England Transcendentalism. He became suddenly famous as a lecturer and spiritual leader by two addresses at Harvard: "The American Scholar" (1837) and "The Divinity School Address" (1838), both of which presented in more practical and intelligible form the doctrines expounded in *Nature*. Thereafter he was in great demand on lecture platforms not only in New England and in the Middle Atlantic States, but in the Middle West as far as Wisconsin and Illinois. His lectures were published from time to time in such famous collections as *Essays, First Series* (1841), *Essays, Second Series* (1844), *Representative Men* (1850), *The Conduct of Life* (1860). He published two volumes of poems: *Poems* (1847) and *May Day* (1867). Although he advocated staying at home ("The wise man stays at home," he said in "Self-Reliance"), he visited Europe three times: in 1833, 1847, and 1872. He visited Thomas Carlyle at Craigenputtock "amid desolate heathery hills, where the lonely scholar nourished his mighty heart." The meeting marked the beginning of a lifelong friendship, immortalized in two volumes of correspondence. Emerson was famous during his lifetime, and for a good while after, as an inspirer of youth. His influence has fallen off somewhat in the twentieth century, but his position as the chief and most persuasive American expounder of the idealistic philosophy cannot be gainsaid.

The definitive biography is by Ralph Leslie Rusk, published in 1949. Rusk also has edited the *Letters* in six volumes. Emerson's *Journals*, which are among his most interesting writings, were published in ten volumes in 1904. Among the many critical appraisals may be mentioned: W. C. Brownell, *American Prose Masters* (1909); Norman Foerster, *American Criticism* (1928); Vivian C. Hopkins, *Spires of Form* (1951); and Sherman Paul, *Emerson's Angle of Vision* (1952).

THE RHODORA:

On Being Asked, Whence Is the Flower?

In May, when sea-winds pierced our solitudes,
I found the fresh Rhodora in the woods,
Spreading its leafless blooms in a damp nook,
To please the desert and the sluggish brook.
The purple petals, fallen in the pool,
Made the black water with their beauty gay;
Here might the red-bird come his plumes to cool,
And court the flower that cheapens his array.
Rhodora! if the sages ask thee why
10   This charm is wasted on the earth and sky,
Tell them, dear, that if eyes were made for seeing,
Then Beauty is its own excuse for being:
Why thou wert there, O rival of the rose!
I never thought to ask, I never knew:
But, in my simple ignorance, suppose
The self-same Power that brought me there brought you.
1834·1839

EACH AND ALL

Little thinks, in the field, yon red-cloaked clown
Of thee from the hill-top looking down;
The heifer that lows in the upland farm,
Far-heard, lows not thine ear to charm;
The sexton, tolling his bell at noon,
Deems not that great Napoleon
Stops his horse, and lists with delight,
Whilst his files sweep round yon Alpine height;
Nor knowest thou what argument
10   Thy life to thy neighbor's creed has lent.
All are needed by each one;
Nothing is fair or good alone.
I thought the sparrow's note from heaven,
Singing at dawn on the alder bough;
I brought him home, in his nest, at even;
He sings the song, but it cheers not now,
For I did not bring home the river and sky;—
He sang to my ear,—they sang to my eye.
The delicate shells lay on the shore;

The bubbles of the latest wave   20
Fresh pearls to their enamel gave,
And the bellowing of the savage sea
Greeted their safe escape to me.
I wiped away the weeds and foam,
I fetched my sea-born treasures home;
But the poor, unsightly, noisome things
Had left their beauty on the shore
With the sun and the sand and the wild uproar.
The lover watched his graceful maid,
As 'mid the virgin train she strayed,   30
Nor knew her beauty's best attire
Was woven still by the snow-white choir.
At last she came to his hermitage,
Like the bird from the woodlands to the cage;—
The gay enchantment was undone,
A gentle wife, but fairy none.
Then I said, "I covet truth;
Beauty is unripe childhood's cheat;
I leave it behind with the games of youth":—
As I spoke, beneath my feet   40
The ground-pine curled its pretty wreath,
Running over the club-moss burrs;
I inhaled the violet's breath;
Around me stood the oaks and firs;
Pine-cones and acorns lay on the ground;
Over me soared the eternal sky,
Full of light and of deity;
Again I saw, again I heard,
The rolling river, the morning bird;—
Beauty through my senses stole;   50
I yielded myself to the perfect whole.
1834? · 1839

CONCORD HYMN

Sung at the Completion of the Battle Monument, July 4, 1837

By the rude bridge that arched the flood,
    Their flag to April's breeze unfurled,
Here once the embattled farmers stood
    And fired the shot heard round the world.

The foe long since in silence slept;
    Alike the conqueror silent sleeps;

And Time the ruined bridge has swept
    Down the dark stream which seaward creeps.

On this green bank, by this soft stream,
    We set to-day a votive stone;
That memory may their deed redeem,
    When, like our sires, our sons are gone.

Spirit, that made those heroes dare
    To die, and leave their children free,
Bid Time and Nature gently spare
    The shaft we raise to them and thee.
1837

THE PROBLEM

I like a church; I like a cowl;
I love a prophet of the soul;
And on my heart monastic aisles
Fall like sweet strains, or pensive smiles;
Yet not for all his faith can see
Would I that cowlèd churchman be.

Why should the vest on him allure,
Which I could not on me endure?

Not from a vain or shallow thought
His awful Jove young Phidias brought;
Never from lips of cunning fell
The thrilling Delphic oracle;
Out from the heart of nature rolled
The burdens of the Bible old;
The litanies of nations came,
Like the volcano's tongue of flame,
Up from the burning core below,—
The canticles of love and woe:
The hand that rounded Peter's dome
And groined the aisles of Christian Rome
Wrought in a sad sincerity;
Himself from God he could not free;
He builded better than he knew;—
The conscious stone to beauty grew.
Know'st thou what wove yon woodbird's nest
Of leaves, and feathers from her breast?

Or how the fish outbuilt her shell,
Painting with morn each annual cell?
Or how the sacred pine-tree adds
To her old leaves new myriads?   30
Such and so grew these holy piles,
Whilst love and terror laid the tiles.
Earth proudly wears the Parthenon,
As the best gem upon her zone,
And Morning opes with haste her lids
To gaze upon the Pyramids;
O'er England's abbeys bends the sky,
As on its friends, with kindred eye;
For out of Thought's interior sphere
These wonders rose to upper air;   40
And Nature gladly gave them place,
Adopted them into her race,
And granted them an equal date
With Andes and with Ararat.

These temples grew as grows the grass;
Art might obey, but not surpass.
The passive Master lent his hand
To the vast soul that o'er him planned;
And the same power that reared the shrine
Bestrode the tribes that knelt within.   50
Ever the fiery Pentecost
Girds with one flame the countless host,
Trances the heart through chanting choirs,
And through the priest the mind inspires.
The word unto the prophet spoken
Was writ on tables yet unbroken;
The word by seers or sibyls told,
In groves of oak, or fanes of gold,
Still floats upon the morning wind,
Still whispers to the willing mind.   60
One accent of the Holy Ghost
The heedless world hath never lost.
I know what say the fathers wise,—
The Book itself before me lies,
Old *Chrysostom,* best Augustine,
And he who blent both in his line,
The younger *Golden Lips* or mines,
Taylor, the Shakspeare of divines.
His words are music in my ear,
I see his cowlèd portrait dear;   70
And yet, for all his faith could see,
I would not the good bishop be.
1839·1840

THE SNOW-STORM

Announced by all the trumpets of the sky,
Arrives the snow, and, driving o'er the fields,
Seems nowhere to alight: the whited air
Hides hills and woods, the river, and the heaven,
And veils the farm-house at the garden's end.
The sled and traveller stopped, the courier's feet
Delayed, all friends shut out, the housemates sit
Around the radiant fireplace, enclosed
In a tumultuous privacy of storm.

10   Come see the north wind's masonry.
Out of an unseen quarry evermore
Furnished with tile, the fierce artificer
Curves his white bastions with projected roof
Round every windward stake, or tree, or door.
Speeding, the myriad-handed, his wild work
So fanciful, so savage, nought cares he
For number or proportion. Mockingly,
On coop or kennel he hangs Parian wreaths;
A swan-like form invests the hidden thorn;
20   Fills up the farmer's lane from wall to wall,
Maugre the farmer's sighs; and at the gate
A tapering turret overtops the work.
And when his hours are numbered, and the world
Is all his own, retiring, as he were not,
Leaves, when the sun appears, astonished Art
To mimic in slow structures, stone by stone,
Built in an age, the mad wind's nightwork,
The frolic architecture of the snow.
1841

GRACE

How much, preventing God, how much I owe
To the defenses thou hast round me set;
Example, custom, fear, occasion slow,—
These scorned bondmen were my parapet.
I dare not peep over this parapet
To gauge with glance the roaring gulf below,
The depths of sin to which I had descended,
Had not these me against myself defended.
1842

MERLIN

1

Thy trivial harp will never please
Or fill my craving ear;
Its chords should ring as blows the breeze,
Free, peremptory, clear.
No jingling serenader's art,
Nor tinkle of piano strings,
Can make the wild blood start
In its mystic springs.
The kingly bard
Must smite the chords rudely and hard,   10
As with hammer or with mace;
That they may render back
Artful thunder, which conveys
Secrets of the solar track,
Sparks of the supersolar blaze.
Merlin's blows are strokes of fate,
Chiming with the forest tone,
When boughs buffet boughs in the wood;
Chiming with the gasp and moan
Of the ice-imprisoned flood;   20
With the pulse of manly hearts;
With the voice of orators;
With the din of city arts;
With the cannonade of wars;
With the marches of the brave;
And prayers of might from martyrs' cave.

Great is the art,
Great be the manners, of the bard.
He shall not his brain encumber
With the coil of rhythm and number;   30
But, leaving rule and pale forethought,
He shall aye climb
For his rhyme.
"Pass in, pass in," the angels say,
"In to the upper doors,
Nor count compartments of the floors,
But mount to paradise
By the stairway of surprise."

Blameless master of the games,
King of sport that never shames,   40
He shall daily joy dispense
Hid in song's sweet influence.

Forms more cheerly live and go,
What time the subtle mind
Sings aloud the tune whereto
Their pulses beat,
And march their feet,
And their members are combined.

By Sybarites beguiled,
He shall no task decline;
Merlin's mighty line
Extremes of nature reconciled,—
Bereaved a tyrant of his will,
And made the lion mild.
Songs can the tempest still,
Scattered on the stormy air,
Mold the year to fair increase
And bring in poetic peace.

He shall not seek to weave,
In weak, unhappy times,
Efficacious rhymes;
Wait his returning strength.
Bird, that from the nadir's floor
To the zenith's top can soar,
The soaring orbit of the muse exceeds that journey's length.
Nor profane affect to hit
Or compass that, by meddling wit,
Which only the propitious mind
Publishes when 'tis inclined.
There are open hours
When the God's will sallies free,
And the dull idiot might see
The flowing fortunes of a thousand years;—
Sudden, at unawares,
Self-moved, fly-to the doors,
Nor sword of angels could reveal
What they conceal.

2
The rhyme of the poet
Modulates the king's affairs;
Balance-loving Nature
Made all things in pairs.
To every foot its antipode;
Each color with its counter glowed;
To every tone beat answering tones,
Higher or graver;

Flavor gladly blends with flavor;
Leaf answers leaf upon the bough;
And match the paired cotyledons.
Hands to hands, and feet to feet,
In one body grooms and brides;   90
Eldest rite, two married sides
In every mortal meet.
Light's far furnace shines,
Smelting balls and bars,
Forging double stars,
Glittering twins and trines.
The animals are sick with love,
Lovesick with rhyme;
Each with all propitious Time
Into chorus wove.   100

Like the dancers' ordered band,
Thoughts come also hand in hand;
In equal couples mated,
Or else alternated;
Adding by their mutual gage,
One to other, health and age.
Solitary fancies go
Short-lived wandering to and fro,
Most like to bachelors,
Or an ungiven maid,   110
Not ancestors,
With no posterity to make the lie afraid,
Or keep truth undecayed.
Perfect-paired as eagle's wings,
Justice is the rhyme of things;
Trade and counting use
The selfsame tuneful muse;
And Nemesis,
Who with even matches odd,
Who athwart space redresses   120
The partial wrong,
Fills the just period,
And finishes the song.

Subtle rhymes, with ruin rife,
Murmur in the house of life,
Sung by the Sisters as they spin;
In perfect time and measure they
Build and unbuild our echoing clay,
As the two twilights of the day
Fold us music-drunken in.   130
1846·1847

BACCHUS

Bring me wine, but wine which never grew
In the belly of the grape,
Or grew on vine whose tap-roots, reaching through
Under the Andes to the Cape,
Suffered no savor of the earth to scape.

Let its grapes the morn salute
From a nocturnal root,
Which feels the acrid juice
Of Styx and Erebus;
10   And turns the woe of Night,
By its own craft, to a more rich delight.

We buy ashes for bread;
We buy diluted wine;
Give me of the true,—
Whose ample leaves and tendrils curled
Among the silver hills of heaven
Draw everlasting dew;
Wine of wine,
Blood of the world,
20   Form of forms, and mould of statures,
That I intoxicated,
And by the draught assimilated,
May float at pleasure through all natures;
The bird-language rightly spell,
And that which roses say so well.
Wine that is shed
Like the torrents of the sun
Up the horizon walls,
Or like the Atlantic streams, which run
30   When the South Sea calls.
Water and bread,
Food which needs no transmuting,
Rainbow-flowering, wisdom-fruiting,
Wine which is already man,
Food which teach and reason can.

Wine which music is,—
Music and wine are one,—
That I, drinking this,
Shall hear far Chaos talk with me;
40   Kings unborn shall walk with me;
And the poor grass shall plot and plan
What it will do when it is man.

Quickened so, will I unlock
Every crypt of every rock.

I thank the joyful juice
For all I know;—
Winds of remembering
Of the ancient being blow,
And seeming-solid walls of use
Open and flow.   50

Pour, Bacchus! the remembering wine;
Retrieve the loss of me and mine!
Vine for vine be antidote,
And the grape requite the lote!
Haste to cure the old despair,—
Reason in Nature's lotus drenched,
The memory of ages quenched;
Give them again to shine;
Let wine repair what this undid;
And where the infection slid,   60
A dazzling memory revive;
Refresh the faded tints,
Recut the aged prints,
And write my old adventures with the pen
Which on the first day drew,
Upon the tablets blue,
The dancing Pleiads and eternal men.
1846·1847

ODE

Inscribed to W. H. Channing

Though loath to grieve
The evil time's sole patriot,
I cannot leave
My honeyed thought
For the priest's cant
Or statesman's rant.

If I refuse
My study for their politique,
Which at the best is trick,
The angry Muse   10
Puts confusion in my brain.

But who is he that prates
Of the culture of mankind,
Of better arts and life?
Go, blindworm, go,
Behold the famous States
Harrying Mexico
With rifle and with knife!
Or who, with accent bolder,
Dare praise the freedom-loving mountaineer?
I found by thee, O rushing Contoocook!
And in thy valleys, Agiochook!
The jackals of the Negro-holder.

The God who made New Hampshire
Taunted the lofty land
With little men;—
Small bat and wren
House in the oak:—
If earth-fire cleave
The upheaved land, and bury the folk,
The southern crocodile would grieve.
Virtue palters; Right is hence;
Freedom praised, but hid;
Funeral eloquence
Rattles the coffin-lid.

What boots thy zeal,
O glowing friend,
That would indignant rend
The northland from the south?
Wherefore? to what good end?
Boston Bay and Bunker Hill
Would serve things still;—
Things are of the snake.

The horseman serves the horse,
The neatherd serves the neat,
The merchant serves the purse,
The eater serves his meat;
'Tis the day of the chattel,
Web to weave, and corn to grind;
Things are in the saddle,
And ride mankind.

There are two laws discrete,
Not reconciled,—

Law for man, and law for thing;
The last builds town and fleet,
But it runs wild,
And doth the man unking.

'Tis fit the forest fall,
The steep be graded,
The mountain tunnelled,   60
The sand shaded,
The orchard planted,
The glebe tilled,
The prairie granted,
The steamer built.

Let man serve law for man;
Live for friendship, live for love,
For truth's and harmony's behoof;
The state may follow how it can,
As Olympus follows Jove.   70

    Yet do not I implore
The wrinkled shopman to my sounding woods,
Nor bid the unwilling senator
Ask votes of thrushes in the solitudes.
Every one to his chosen work;—
Foolish hands may mix and mar;
Wise and sure the issues are.
Round they roll till dark is light,
Sex to sex, and even to odd;—
The over-god   80
Who marries Right to Might,
Who peoples, unpeoples,—
He who exterminates
Races by stronger races,
Black by white faces,—
Knows to bring honey
Out of the lion;
Grafts gentlest scion
On pirate and Turk.

The Cossack eats Poland,   90
Like stolen fruit;
Her last noble is ruined,
Her last poet mute:

Ode. 86–87. honey . . . lion: Samson found honey in the carcass of the lion that he had slain. See Judges 14:5–9.

Straight, into double band
The victors divide;
Half for freedom strike and stand;—
The astonished Muse finds thousands at her side.
1847

HAMATREYA

Bulkeley, Hunt, Willard, Hosmer, Meriam, Flint
Possessed the land which rendered to their toil
Hay, corn, roots, hemp, flax, apples, wool and wood.
Each of these landlords walked amidst his farm,
Saying, " 'Tis mine, my children's and my name's.
How sweet the west wind sounds in my own trees!
How graceful climb those shadows on my hill!
I fancy these pure waters and the flags
Know me, as does my dog: we sympathize;
10 And, I affirm, my actions smack of the soil."

Where are these men? Asleep beneath their grounds:
And strangers, fond as they, their furrows plough.
Earth laughs in flowers, to see her boastful boys
Earth-proud, proud of the earth which is not theirs;
Who steer the plough, but cannot steer their feet
Clear of the grave.
They added ridge to valley, brook to pond,
And sighed for all that bounded their domain;
"This suits me for a pasture; that's my park;
20 We must have clay, lime, gravel, granite-ledge,
And misty lowland, where to go for peat.
The land is well,—lies fairly to the south.
'Tis good, when you have crossed the sea and back,
To find the sitfast acres where you left them."
Ah! the hot owner sees not Death, who adds
Him to his land, a lump of mould the more.
Hear what the Earth says:—

Earth-song

"Mine and yours;
Mine, not yours.
30 Earth endures;
Stars abide—
Shine down in the old sea;

Old are the shores;
But where are old men?
I who have seen much,
Such have I never seen.

"The lawyer's deed
Ran sure,
In tail,
To them, and to their heirs   40
Who shall succeed,
Without fail,
Forevermore.

"Here is the land,
Shaggy with wood,
With its old valley,
Mound and flood.
But the heritors?—
Fled like the flood's foam.
The lawyer, and the laws,   50
And the kingdom,
Clean swept herefrom.

"They called me theirs,
Who so controlled me;
Yet every one
Wished to stay, and is gone,
How am I theirs,
If they cannot hold me,
But I hold them?"

When I heard the Earth-song   60
I was no longer brave;
My avarice cooled
Like lust in the chill of the grave.
1847

GIVE ALL TO LOVE

Give all to love;
Obey thy heart;
Friends, kindred, days,
Estate, good-fame,
Plans, credit and the Muse,—
Nothing refuse.

'Tis a brave master;
Let it have scope:
Follow it utterly,
Hope beyond hope:
High and more high
It dives into noon,
With wing unspent,
Untold intent;
But it is a god,
Knows its own path
And the outlets of the sky.

It was never for the mean;
It requireth courage stout.
Souls above doubt
Valor unbending,
It will reward,—
They shall return
More than they were,
And ever ascending.

Leave all for love;
Yet, hear me, yet,
One word more thy heart behoved,
One pulse more of firm endeavor,—
Keep thee to-day,
To-morrow, forever,
Free as an Arab
Of thy beloved.

Cling with life to the maid;
But when the surprise,
First vague shadow of surmise
Flits across her bosom young,
Of a joy apart from thee,
Free be she, fancy-free;
Nor thou detain her vesture's hem,
Nor the palest rose she flung
From her summer diadem.

Though thou loved her as thyself,
As a self of purer clay,
Though her parting dims the day,
Stealing grace from all alive;
Heartily know,
When half-gods go,
The gods arrive.
1847

DAYS

Daughters of Time, the hypocritic Days,
Muffled and dumb like barefoot dervishes,
And marching single in an endless file,
Bring diadems and fagots in their hands.
To each they offer gifts after his will,
Bread, kingdoms, stars, and sky that holds them all.
I, in my pleached garden, watched the pomp,
Forgot my morning wishes, hastily
Took a few herbs and apples, and the Day
Turned and departed silent. I, too late,   10
Under her solemn fillet saw the scorn.
1852? · 1857

BRAHMA

If the red slayer think he slays,
    Or if the slain think he is slain,
They know not well the subtle ways
    I keep, and pass, and turn again.

Far or forgot to me is near;
    Shadow and sunlight are the same;
The vanished gods to me appear;
    And one to me are shame and fame.

They reckon ill who leave me out;
    When me they fly, I am the wings;   10
I am the doubter and the doubt,
    And I the hymn the Brahmin sings.

The strong gods pine for my abode,
    And pine in vain the sacred Seven;
But thou, meek lover of the good!
    Find me, and turn thy back on heaven.
1856 · 1857

TERMINUS

It is time to be old,
To take in sail:—
The god of bounds,
Who sets to seas a shore,
Came to me in his fatal rounds,

And said: "No more!
No farther shoot
Thy broad ambitious branches, and thy root.
Fancy departs: no more invent;
Contract thy firmament
To compass of a tent.
There's not enough for this and that,
Make thy option which of two;
Economize the failing river,
Not the less revere the Giver,
Leave the many and hold the few.
Timely wise accept the terms,
Soften the fall with wary foot;
A little while
Still plan and smile,
And,—fault of novel germs,—
Mature the unfallen fruit.
Curse, if thou wilt, thy sires,
Bad husbands of their fires,
Who when they gave thee breath,
Failed to bequeath
The needful sinew stark as once,
The Baresark marrow to thy bones,
But left a legacy of ebbing veins,
Inconstant heat and nerveless reins,—
Amid the Muses, left thee deaf and dumb,
Amid the gladiators, halt and numb."

As the bird trims her to the gale,
I trim myself to the storm of time,
I man the rudder, reef the sail,
Obey the voice at eve obeyed at prime:
"Lowly faithful, banish fear,
Right onward drive unharmed;
The port, well worth the cruise, is near,
And every wave is charmed."
1866·1867

THE POET

A moody child and wildly wise
Pursued the game with joyful eyes,
Which chose, like meteors, their way,
And rived the dark with private ray:
They overleapt the horizon's edge,

Searched with Apollo's privilege;
Through man, and woman, and sea, and star
Saw the dance of nature forward far;
Through worlds, and races, and terms, and times
Saw musical order, and pairing rhymes.

Olympian bards who sung
Divine ideas below,
Which always find us young,
And always keep us so.

Those who are esteemed umpires of taste are often persons who have acquired some knowledge of admired pictures or sculptures, and have an inclination for whatever is elegant; but if you inquire whether they are beautiful souls, and whether their own acts are like fair pictures, you learn that they are selfish and sensual. Their cultivation is local, as if you should rub a log of dry wood in one spot to produce fire, all the rest remaining cold. Their knowledge of the fine arts is some study of rules and particulars, or some limited judgment of color or form, which is exercised for amusement or for show. It is a proof of the shallowness of the doctrine of beauty as it lies in the minds of our amateurs, that men seem to have lost the perception of the instant dependence of form upon soul. There is no doctrine of forms in our philosophy. We were put into our bodies, as fire is put into a pan to be carried about; but there is no accurate adjustment between the spirit and the organ, much less is the latter the germination of the former. So in regard to other forms, the intellectual men do not believe in any essential dependence of the material world on thought and volition. Theologians think it a pretty air-castle to talk of the spiritual meaning of a ship or a cloud, of a city or a contract, but they prefer to come again to the solid ground of historical evidence; and even the poets are contented with a civil and conformed manner of living, and to write poems from the fancy, at a safe distance from their own experience. But the highest minds of the world have never ceased to explore the double meaning, or shall I say the quadruple or the centuple or much more manifold meaning, of every sensuous fact; Orpheus, Empedocles, Heraclitus, Plato, Plutarch, Dante, Swedenborg, and the masters of sculpture, picture and poetry. For we are not pans and barrows, nor even porters of the fire and torch-bearers, but children of the fire, made of it, and only the same divinity transmuted and at two or three removes, when we know least about it. And this hidden truth, that the fountains whence all this river of Time and its creatures floweth are intrinsically ideal and beautiful, draws us to the consideration of the nature and functions of the Poet, or the man of Beauty; to the means and materials he uses, and to the general aspect of the art in the present time.

The breadth of the problem is great, for the poet is representative. He stands among partial men for the complete man, and apprises us not of his wealth, but of the common wealth. The young man reveres men of genius, because, to speak truly, they are more himself than he is. They receive of the soul as he also receives, but they more. Nature enhances her beauty, to the eye of loving men, from their belief that the poet is beholding her shows at the same time. He is isolated among his contemporaries by truth and by his art, but with this consolation in his pursuits, that they will draw all men sooner or later. For all men live by truth and stand in need of expression. In love, in art, in avarice, in politics, in labor, in games, we study to utter our painful secret. The man is only half himself, the other half is his expression.

Notwithstanding this necessity to be published, adequate expression is rare. I know not how it is that we need an interpreter, but the great majority of men seem to be minors, who have not yet come into possession of their own, or mutes, who cannot report the conversation they have had with nature. There is no man who does not anticipate a supersensual utility in the sun and stars, earth and water. These stand and wait to render him a peculiar service. But there is some obstruction or some excess of phlegm in our constitution, which does not suffer them to yield the due effect. Too feeble fall the impressions of nature on us to make us artists. Every touch should thrill. Every man should be so much an artist that he could report in conversation what had befallen him. Yet, in our experience, the rays or appulses have sufficient force to arrive at the senses, but not enough to reach the quick and compel the reproduction of themselves in speech. The poet is the person in whom these powers are in balance, the man without impediment, who sees and handles that which others dream of, traverses the whole scale of experience, and is representative of man, in virtue of being the largest power to receive and to impart.

For the Universe has three children, born at one time, which reappear under different names in every system of thought, whether they be called cause, operation and effect; or, more poetically, Jove, Pluto, Neptune; or, theologically, the Father, the Spirit and the Son; but which we will call here the Knower, the Doer and the Sayer. These stand respectively for the love of truth, for the love of good, and for the love of beauty. These three are equal. Each is that which he is, essentially, so that he cannot be surmounted or analyzed, and each of these three has the power of the others latent in him, and his own patent.

The poet is the sayer, the namer, and represents beauty. He is a sovereign, and stands on the centre. For the world is not painted or adorned, but is from the beginning beautiful; and God has not made some beautiful things, but Beauty is the creator of the universe. Therefore the poet is not any permissive potentate, but is emperor in his own right. Criticism is infested with a cant of materialism, which assumes that manual skill and activity is the first merit of all men, and disparages such as say and do not, overlooking the fact that some men, namely poets, are natural sayers, sent into the world to the end of expression, and confounds them with those whose province is action but who quit it to imitate the sayers. But Homer's words are as costly and admirable to Homer as Agamemnon's victories are to Agamemnon. The poet does not wait for the hero or the sage, but, as they act and think primarily, so he writes primarily what will and must be spoken, reckoning the others, though primaries also, yet, in respect to him, secondaries and servants; as sitters or models in the studio of a painter, or as assistants who bring building-materials to an architect.

For poetry was all written before time was, and whenever we are so finely organized that we can penetrate into that region where the air is music, we hear those primal warblings and attempt to write them down, but we lose ever and anon a word or a verse and substitute something of our own, and thus miswrite the poem. The men of more delicate ear write down these cadences more faithfully, and these transcripts, though imperfect, become the songs of the nations. For nature is as truly beautiful as it is good, or as it is reasonable, and must as much appear as it must be done, or be known. Words and deeds are quite indifferent modes of the divine energy. Words are also actions, and actions are a kind of words.

The sign and credentials of the poet are that he announces that which no man foretold. He is the true and only doctor; he knows and tells; he is the only teller of news, for he was present and privy to the appearance which he describes. He is a beholder of ideas and an utterer of the necessary and causal. For we do not speak now of men of poetical talents, or of industry and skill in metre, but of the true poet. I took part in a conversation the other day concerning a recent writer of lyrics, a man of subtle mind, whose head appeared to be a music-box of delicate tunes and rhythms, and whose skill and command of language we could not sufficiently praise. But when the question arose whether he was not only a lyrist but a poet, we were obliged to confess that he is plainly a contemporary, not an eternal man. He does not stand out of our low limitations, like a Chimborazo under the line, running up from a torrid base through all the climates of the globe, with belts of the herbage of every latitude on its high and mottled sides; but this genius is the landscape-garden of a modern house, adorned with fountains and statues, with well-bred men and women standing and sitting in the walks and terraces. We hear, through all the varied music, the ground-tone of conventional life. Our poets are men of talents who sing, and not the children of music. The argument is secondary, the finish of the verses is primary.

For it is not metres, but a metre-making argument that makes a poem,—a thought so passionate and alive that like the spirit of a plant or an animal it has an architecture of its own, and adorns nature with a new thing. The thought and the form are equal in the order of time, but in the order of genesis the thought is prior to the form. The poet has a new thought; he has a whole new experience to unfold; he will tell us how it was with him, and all men will be the richer in his fortune. For the experience of each new age requires a new confession, and the world seems always waiting for its poet. I remember when I was young how much I was moved one morning by tidings that genius had appeared in a youth who sat near me at table. He had left his work and gone rambling none knew whither, and had written hundreds of lines, but could not tell whether that which was in him was therein told; he could tell nothing but that all was changed,— man, beast, heaven, earth and sea. How gladly we listened! how credulous! Society seemed to be compromised. We sat in the aurora of a sunrise which was to put out all the stars. Boston seemed to be at twice the distance it had the night before, or was much farther than that. Rome,—what was Rome? Plutarch and Shakspeare were in the yellow leaf, and Homer no more should be heard of. It is much to know that poetry has been written this very day, under this very roof, by your side. What! that wonderful spirit has not expired! These stony moments are still sparkling and animated! I had fancied that the oracles were all silent, and nature had spent her fires; and behold! all night, from every pore, these fine auroras have been streaming. Every one has some interest in the advent of the poet, and no one knows how much it may concern him. We know that the secret of the world is profound, but who or what shall be our interpreter, we know not. A mountain ramble, a new style of face, a new person, may put the key into our hands. Of course the value of genius to us is in the veracity of its report. Talent may frolic and juggle; genius realizes and adds. Mankind in good earnest have availed so far in understanding themselves and their work, that the foremost watchman on the peak announces his news. It is the truest word ever spoken, and the phrase will be the fittest, most musical, and the unerring voice of the world for that time.

All that we call sacred history attests that the birth of a poet is the principal event in chronology. Man, never so often deceived, still watches for the arrival of a brother who can hold him steady to a truth until he has made it his own. With what joy I begin to read a poem which I confide in as an inspiration! And now my chains are to be broken; I shall mount above these clouds and opaque airs in which I live,—opaque, though they seem transparent,—and from the heaven of truth I shall see and comprehend my relations. That will reconcile me to life and renovate nature, to see trifles animated by a tendency, and to know what I am doing. Life will no more be a noise; now I shall see men and women, and know the signs by which they may be discerned from fools and satans. This day shall be better than my birthday: then I became an animal; now I am invited into the science of the real. Such is the hope, but the fruition is postponed. Oftener it falls that this winged man, who will carry me into the heaven, whirls me into mists, then leaps and frisks about with me as it were from cloud to cloud, still affirming that he is bound heavenward; and I, being myself a novice, am slow in perceiving that he does not know the way into the heavens, and is merely bent that I should admire his skill to rise like a fowl or a flying fish, a little way from the ground or the water; but the all-piercing, all-feeding and ocular air of heaven that man shall never inhabit. I tumble down again soon into my old nooks, and lead the life of exaggerations as before, and have lost my faith in the possibility of any guide who can lead me thither where I would be.

But, leaving these victims of vanity, let us, with new hope, observe how nature, by worthier impulses, has insured the poet's fidelity to his office of announcement and affirming, namely by the beauty of things, which becomes a new and higher beauty when expressed. Nature offers all her creatures to him as a picture-language. Being used as a type, a second wonderful value appears in the object, far better than its old value; as the carpenter's stretched cord, if you hold your ear close enough, is musical in the breeze. "Things more excellent than every image," says Jamblichus, "are expressed through images." Things admit of being used as symbols because nature is a symbol, in the whole, and in every part. Every line we can draw in the sand has expression; and there is no body without its spirit or genius. All form is an effect of character; all condition, of the quality of the life; all harmony, of health; and for this reason a perception of beauty should be sympathetic, or proper only to the good. The beautiful rests on the foundations of the necessary. The soul makes the body, as the wise Spenser teaches:—

> "So every spirit, as it is more pure,
> And hath in it the more of heavenly light,
> So it the fairer body doth procure

> To habit in, and it more fairly dight,
> With cheerful grace and amiable sight.
> For, of the soul, the body form doth take,
> For soul is form, and doth the body
>   make."[1]

Here we find ourselves suddenly not in a critical speculation but in a holy place, and should go very warily and reverently. We stand before the secret of the world, there where Being passes into Appearance and Unity into Variety.

The Universe is the externization of the soul. Wherever the life is, that bursts into appearance around it. Our science is sensual, and therefore superficial. The earth and the heavenly bodies, physics and chemistry, we sensually treat, as if they were self-existent; but these are the retinue of that Being we have. "The mighty heaven," said Proclus, "exhibits, in its transfigurations, clear images of the splendor of intellectual perceptions; being moved in conjunction with the unapparent periods of intellectual natures." Therefore science always goes abreast with the just elevation of the man, keeping step with religion and metaphysics; or the state of science is an index of our self-knowledge. Since every thing in nature answers to a moral power, if any phenomenon remains brute and dark it is because the corresponding faculty in the observer is not yet active.

No wonder then, if these waters be so deep, that we hover over them with a religious regard. The beauty of the fable proves the importance of the sense; to the poet, and to all others; or, if you please, every man is so far a poet as to be susceptible of these enchantments of nature; for all men have the thoughts whereof the universe is the celebration. I find that the fascination resides in the symbol. Who loves nature? Who does not? Is it only poets, and men of leisure and cultivation, who live with her? No; but also hunters, farmers, grooms and butchers, though they express their affection in their choice of life and not in their choice of words. The writer wonders what the coachman or the hunter values in riding, in horses and dogs. It is not superficial qualities. When you talk with him he holds these at as slight a rate as you. His worship is sympathetic; he has no definitions, but he is commanded in nature by the living power which he feels to be there present. No imitation or playing of these things would content him; he loves the earnest of the north wind, of rain, of stone and wood and iron. A beauty not explicable is dearer than a beauty which we can see to the end of. It is nature the symbol, nature certifying the supernatural, body overflowed by life which he worships with coarse but sincere rites.

The inwardness and mystery of this attachment drive men of every class to the use of emblems. The schools of poets and philosophers are not more intoxicated with their symbols than the populace with theirs. In our political parties, compute the power of badges and emblems. See the great ball which they roll from Baltimore to Bunker Hill! In the political processions, Lowell goes in a loom, and Lynn in a shoe, and Salem in a ship. Witness the cider-barrel, the log-cabin, the hickory-stick, the palmetto, and all the cognizances of party. See the power of national emblems. Some stars, lilies, leopards, a crescent, a lion, an eagle, or other figure which came into credit God knows how, on an old rag of bunting, blowing in the wind on a fort at the ends of the earth, shall make the blood tingle

1. So . . . make: from Edmund Spenser's "An Hymne in Honour of Beautie."

under the rudest or the most conventional exterior. The people fancy they hate poetry, and they are all poets and mystics!

Beyond this universality of the symbolic language, we are apprised of the divineness of this superior use of things, whereby the world is a temple whose walls are covered with emblems, pictures and commandments of the Deity,—in this, that there is no fact in nature which does not carry the whole sense of nature; and the distinctions which we make in events and in affairs, of low and high, honest and base, disappear when nature is used as a symbol. Thought makes everything fit for use. The vocabulary of an omniscient man would embrace words and images excluded from polite conversation. What would be base, or even obscene, to the obscene, becomes illustrious, spoken in a new connection of thought. The piety of the Hebrew prophets purges their grossness. The circumcision is an example of the power of poetry to raise the low and offensive. Small and mean things serve as well as great symbols. The meaner the type by which a law is expressed, the more pungent it is, and the more lasting in the memories of men; just as we choose the smallest box or case in which any needful utensil can be carried. Bare lists of words are found suggestive to an imaginative and excited mind; as it is related of Lord Chatham that he was accustomed to read in Bailey's Dictionary when he was preparing to speak in Parliament. The poorest experience is rich enough for all the purposes of expressing thought. Why covet a knowledge of new facts? Day and night, house and garden, a few books, a few actions, serve us as well as would all trades and all spectacles. We are far from having exhausted the significance of the few symbols we use. We can come to use them yet with a terrible simplicity. It does not need that a poem should be long. Every word was once a poem. Every new relation is a new word. Also we use defects and deformities to a sacred purpose, so expressing our sense that the evils of the world are such only to the evil eye. In the old mythology, mythologists observe, defects are ascribed to divine natures, as lameness to Vulcan, blindness to Cupid, and the like,—to signify exuberances.

For as it is dislocation and detachment from the life of God that makes things ugly, the poet, who re-attaches things to nature and the Whole,—re-attaching even artificial things and violation of nature, to nature, by a deeper insight,—disposes very easily of the most disagreeable facts. Readers of poetry see the factory-village and the railway, and fancy that the poetry of the landscape is broken up by these; for these works of art are not yet consecrated in their reading; but the poet sees them fall within the great Order not less than the beehive or the spider's geometrical web. Nature adopts them very fast into her vital circles, and the gliding train of cars she loves like her own. Besides, in a centred mind, it signifies nothing how many mechanical inventions you exhibit. Though you add millions, and never so surprising, the fact of mechanics has not gained a grain's weight. The spiritual fact remains unalterable, by many or by few particulars; as no mountain is of any appreciable height to break the curve of the sphere. A shrewd country-boy goes to the city for the first time, and the complacent citizen is not satisfied with his little wonder. It is not that he does not see all the fine houses and know that he never saw such before, but he disposes of them as easily as the poet finds place for the railway. The chief value of the new fact is to enhance the great and constant fact of Life, which can dwarf any and every circumstance, and to which the belt of wampum and the commerce of America are alike.

The world being thus put under the mind for verb and noun, the poet is he who can articulate it. For though life is great, and fascinates and absorbs; and though all men are intelligent of the symbols through which it is named; yet they cannot originally use them. We are symbols and inhabit symbols; workmen, work, and tools, words and things, birth and death, all are emblems; but we sympathize with the symbols, and being infatuated with the economical uses of things, we do not know that they are thoughts. The poet, by an ulterior intellectual perception, gives them a power which makes their old use forgotten, and puts eyes and a tongue into every dumb and inanimate object. He perceives the independence of the thought on the symbol, the stability of the thought, the accidency and fugacity of the symbol. As the eyes of Lyncæus were said to see through the earth, so the poet turns the world to glass, and shows us all things in their right series and procession. For through that better perception he stands one step nearer to things, and sees the flowing or metamorphosis; perceives that thought is multiform; that within the form of every creature is a force impelling it to ascend into a higher form; and following with his eyes the life, uses the forms which express that life, and so his speech flows with the flowing of nature. All the facts of the animal economy, sex, nutriment, gestation, birth, growth, are symbols of the passage of the world into the soul of man, to suffer there a change and reappear a new and higher fact. He uses forms according to the life, and not according to the form. This is true science. The poet alone knows astronomy, chemistry, vegetation and animation, for he does not stop at these facts, but employs them as signs. He knows why the plain or meadow of space was strown with these flowers we call suns and moons and stars; why the great deep is adorned with animals, with men, and gods; for in every word he speaks he rides on them as the horses of thought.

By virtue of this science the poet is the Namer or Language-maker, naming things sometimes after their appearance, sometimes after their essence, and giving to every one its own name and not another's, thereby rejoicing the intellect, which delights in detachment or boundary. The poets made all the words, and therefore language is the archives of history, and, if we must say it, a sort of tomb of the muses. For though the origin of most of our words is forgotten, each word was at first a stroke of genius, and obtained currency because for the moment it symbolized the world to the first speaker and to the hearer. The etymologist finds the deadest word to have been once a brilliant picture. Language is fossil poetry. As the limestone of the continent consists of infinite masses of the shells of animalcules, so language is made up of images or tropes, which now, in their secondary use, have long ceased to remind us of their poetic origin. But the poet names the thing because he sees it, or comes one step nearer to it than any other. This expression or naming is not art, but a second nature, grown out of the first, as a leaf out of a tree. What we call nature is a certain self-regulated motion or change; and nature does all things by her own hands, and does not leave another to baptize her but baptizes herself; and this through the metamorphosis again. I remember that a certain poet described it to me thus:—

Genius is the activity which repairs the decays of things, whether wholly or partly of a material and finite kind. Nature, through all her kingdoms, insures herself. Nobody cares for planting the poor fungus; so she shakes down from the gills of one agaric countless spores, any one of which, being preserved, transmits new billions of spores to-morrow or next day. The new agaric of this hour has a chance which the old one had not. This atom of seed is thrown into a new place, not subject to the accidents which destroyed its parent two rods off. She makes a man; and having brought him to ripe age, she will no longer run the risk of losing this wonder at a blow, but she detaches from him a new self, that the kind may be safe from accidents to which the individual is exposed. So when the soul of the poet has come to ripeness of thought, she detaches and sends away from it its poems or songs,—a fearless, sleepless, deathless progeny, which is not exposed to the accidents of the weary kingdom of time; a fearless, vivacious offspring, clad with wings (such was the virtue of the soul out of which they came) which carry them fast and far, and infix them irrecoverably into the hearts of men. These wings are the beauty of the poet's soul. The songs, thus flying immortal from their mortal parent, are pursued by clamorous flights of censures, which swarm in far greater numbers and threaten to devour them; but these last are not winged. At the end of a very short leap they fall plump down and rot, having received from the souls out of which they came no beautiful wings. But the melodies of the poet ascend and leap and pierce into the deeps of infinite time.

So far the bard taught me, using his freer speech. But nature has a higher end, in the production of new individuals, than security, namely *ascension,* or the passage of the soul into higher forms. I knew in my younger days the sculptor who made the statue of the youth which stands in the public garden. He was, as I remember, unable to tell directly what made him happy or unhappy, but by wonderful indirections he could tell. He rose one day, according to his habit, before the dawn, and saw the morning break, grand as the eternity out of which it came, and for many days after, he strove to express this tranquillity, and lo! his chisel had fashioned out of marble the form of a beautiful youth, Phosphorus, whose aspect is such that it is said all persons who look on it become silent. The poet also resigns himself to his mood, and that thought which agitated him is expressed, but *alter idem,*[1] in a manner totally new. The expression is organic, or the new type which things themselves take when liberated. As, in the sun, objects paint their images on the retina of the eye, so they, sharing the aspiration of the whole universe, tend to paint a far more delicate copy of their essence in his mind. Like the metamorphosis of things into higher organic forms is their change into melodies. Over everything stands its dæmon or soul, and, as the form of the thing is reflected by the eye, so the soul of the thing is reflected by a melody. The sea, the mountain-ridge, Niagara, and every flower-bed, pre-exist, or super-exist, in pre-cantations, which sail like odors in the air, and when any man goes by with an ear sufficiently fine, he overhears them and endeavors to write down the notes without diluting or depraving them. And herein is the legitimation of criticism, in the mind's faith that the poems are a corrupt version of some text in nature with which they ought to be made to tally. A rhyme in one of our sonnets should not be less pleasing than the iterated nodes of a seashell, or the resembling difference of a group of flowers. The pairing of the birds is

---

1. alter idem: a second self.

an idyl, not tedious as our idyls are; a tempest is a rough ode, without falsehood or rant; a summer, with its harvest sown, reaped and stored, is an epic song, subordinating how many admirably executed parts. Why should not the symmetry and truth that modulate these, glide into our spirits, and we participate the invention of nature?

This insight, which expresses itself by what is called Imagination, is a very high sort of seeing, which does not come by study, but by the intellect being where and what it sees; by sharing the path or circuit of things through forms, and so making them translucid to others. The path of things is silent. Will they suffer a speaker to go with them? A spy they will not suffer; a lover, a poet, is the transcendency of their own nature;—him they will suffer. The condition of true naming, on the poet's part, is his resigning himself to the divine *aura* which breathes through forms, and accompanying that.

It is a secret which every intellectual man quickly learns, that beyond the energy of his possessed and conscious intellect he is capable of a new energy (as of an intellect doubled on itself), by abandonment to the nature of things; that beside his privacy of power as an individual man, there is a great public power on which he can draw, by unlocking, at all risks, his human doors, and suffering the ethereal tides to roll and circulate through him; then he is caught up into the life of the Universe, his speech is thunder, his thought is law, and his works are universally intelligible as the plants and animals. The poet knows that he speaks adequately then only when he speaks somewhat wildly, or "with the flower of the mind;" not with the intellect used as an organ, but with the intellect released from all service and suffered to take its direction from its celestial life; or as the ancients were wont to express themselves, not with intellect alone but with the intellect inebriated by nectar. As the traveller who has lost his way throws his reins on his horse's neck and trusts to the instinct of the animal to find his road, so must we do with the divine animal who carries us through this world. For if in any manner we can stimulate this instinct, new passages are opened for us into nature; the mind flows into and through things hardest and highest, and the metamorphosis is possible.

This is the reason why bards love wine, mead, narcotics, coffee, tea, opium, the fumes of sandalwood and tobacco, or whatever other procurers of animal exhilaration. All men avail themselves of such means as they can, to add this extraordinary power to their normal powers; and to this end they prize conversation, music, pictures, sculpture, dancing, theatres, travelling, war, mobs, fires, gaming, politics, or love, or science, or animal intoxication,—which are several coarser or finer *quasi*-mechanical substitutes for the true nectar, which is the ravishment of the intellect by coming nearer to the fact. These are auxiliaries to the centrifugal tendency of a man, to his passage out into free space, and they help him to escape the custody of that body in which he is pent up, and of that jail-yard of individual relations in which he is enclosed. Hence a great number of such as were professionally expressers of Beauty, as painters, poets, musicians and actors, have been more than others wont to lead a life of pleasure and indulgence; all but the few who received the true nectar; and, as it was a spurious mode of attaining freedom, as it was an emancipation not into the heavens but into the freedom of baser places, they were punished for that advantage they won, by a dissipation and deterioration. But never can any advantage be taken of nature by a trick. The spirit of the world, the great calm presence of the Creator, comes not forth to the sorceries of opium or of wine. The sublime vision comes to the pure and simple soul in a clean and chaste body. That is not an inspiration, which we owe to narcotics, but some counterfeit excitement and fury. Milton says that the lyric poet may drink wine and live generously, but the epic poet, he who shall sing of the gods and their descent unto men, must drink water out of a wooden bowl. For poetry is not "Devil's wine," but God's wine. It is with this as it is with toys. We fill the hands and nurseries of our children with all manner of dolls, drums and horses; withdrawing their eyes from the plain face and sufficing objects of nature, the sun and moon, the animals, the water and stones, which should be their toys. So the poet's habit of living should be set on a key so low that the common influences should delight him. His cheerfulness should be the gift of the sunlight; the air should suffice for his inspiration, and he should be tipsy with water. That spirit which suffices quiet hearts, which seems to come forth to such from every dry knoll of sere grass, from every pine stump and half-imbedded stone on which the dull March sun shines, comes forth to the poor and hungry, and such as are of simple taste. If thou fill thy brain with Boston and New York, with fashion and covetousness, and wilt stimulate thy jaded senses with wine and French coffee, thou shalt find no radiance of wisdom in the lonely waste of the pine woods.

If the imagination intoxicates the poet, it is not inactive in other men. The metamorphosis excites in the beholder an emotion of joy. The use of symbols has a certain power of emancipation and exhilaration for all men. We seem to be touched by a wand which makes us dance and run about happily, like children. We are like persons who come out of a cave or cellar into the open air. This is the effect on us of tropes, fables, oracles and all poetic forms. Poets are thus liberating gods. Men have really got a new sense, and found within their world another world, or nest of worlds; for, the metamorphosis once seen, we divine that it does not stop. I will not now consider how much this makes the charm of algebra and the mathematics, which also have their tropes, but it is felt in every definition; as when Aristotle defines *space* to be an immovable vessel in which things are contained;—or when Plato defines a *line* to be a flowing point; or *figure* to be a bound of solid; and many the like. What a joyful sense of freedom we have when Vitruvius announces the old opinion of artists that no architect can build any house well who does not know something of anatomy. When Socrates, in Charmides, tells us that the soul is cured of its maladies by certain incantations, and that these incantations are beautiful reasons, from which temperance is generated in souls; when Plato calls the world an animal, and Timæus affirms that the plants also are animals; or affirms a man to be a heavenly tree, growing with his root, which is his head, upward; and, as George Chapman, following him, writes,

> "So in our tree of man, whose nervie root
> Springs in his top;"

when Orpheus speaks of hoariness as "that white flower which marks extreme old age;" when Proclus calls the universe the statue of the intellect; when Chaucer, in his praise of "Gentilesse," compares good blood in mean condition to fire, which, though carried to the darkest house betwixt this and the mount of

Caucasus, will yet hold its natural office and burn as bright as if twenty thousand men did it behold; when John saw, in the Apocalypse, the ruin of the world through evil, and the stars fall from heaven as the fig tree casteth her untimely fruit; when Æsop reports the whole catalogue of common daily relations through the masquerade of birds and beasts;—we take the cheerful hint of the immortality of our essence and its versatile habit and escapes, as when the gypsies say of themselves, "It is in vain to hang them, they cannot die."

The poets are thus liberating gods. The ancient British bards had for the title of their order, "Those who are free throughout the world." They are free, and they make free. An imaginative book renders us much more service at first, by stimulating us through its tropes, than afterward when we arrive at the precise sense of the author. I think nothing is of any value in books excepting the transcendental and extraordinary. If a man is inflamed and carried away by his thought, to that degree that he forgets the authors and the public and heeds only this one dream which holds him like an insanity, let me read his paper, and you may have all the arguments and histories and criticism. All the value which attaches to Pythagoras, Paracelsus, Cornelius Agrippa, Cardan, Kepler, Swedenborg, Schelling, Oken, or any other who introduces questionable facts into his cosmogony, as angels, devils, magic, astrology, palmistry, mesmerism, and so on, is the certificate we have of departure from routine, and that here is a new witness. That also is the best success in conversation, the magic of liberty, which puts the world like a ball in our hands. How cheap even the liberty then seems; how mean to study, when an emotion communicates to the intellect the power to sap and upheave nature; how great the perspective! nations, times, systems, enter and disappear like threads in tapestry of large figure and many colors; dream delivers us to dream, and while the drunkenness lasts we will sell our bed, our philosophy, our religion, in our opulence.

There is good reason why we should prize this liberation. The fate of the poor shepherd, who, blinded and lost in the snow-storm, perishes in a drift within a few feet of his cottage door, is an emblem of the state of man. On the brink of the waters of life and truth, we are miserably dying. The inaccessibleness of every thought but that we are in, is wonderful. What if you come near to it; you are as remote when you are nearest as when you are farthest. Every thought is also a prison; every heaven is also a prison. Therefore we love the poet, the inventor, who in any form, whether in an ode or in an action or in looks and behavior, has yielded us a new thought. He unlocks our chains and admits us to a new scene.

This emancipation is dear to all men, and the power to impart it, as it must come from greater depth and scope of thought, is a measure of intellect. Therefore all books of the imagination endure, all which ascend to that truth that the writer sees nature beneath him, and uses it as his exponent. Every verse or sentence possessing this virtue will take care of its own immortality. The religions of the world are the ejaculations of a few imaginative men.

But the quality of the imagination is to flow, and not to freeze. The poet did not stop at the color or the form, but read their meaning; neither may he rest in this meaning, but he makes the same objects exponents of his new thought. Here is the difference betwixt the poet and the mystic, that the last nails a symbol to one sense, which was a true sense for a moment, but soon becomes old and false. For all symbols are fluxional; all language is vehicular and transitive, and is good, as ferries and horses are, for conveyance, not as farms and houses are, for homestead. Mysticism consists in the mistake of an accidental and individual symbol for an universal one. The morning-redness happens to be the favorite meteor to the eyes of Jacob Behmen, and comes to stand to him for truth and faith; and, he believes, should stand for the same realities to every reader. But the first reader prefers as naturally the symbol of a mother and child, or a gardener and his bulb, or a jeweller polishing a gem. Either of these, or of a myriad more, are equally good to the person to whom they are significant. Only they must be held lightly, and be very willingly translated into the equivalent terms which others use. And the mystic must be steadily told,—All that you say is just as true without the tedious use of that symbol as with it. Let us have a little algebra, instead of this trite rhetoric,—universal signs, instead of these village symbols,—and we shall both be gainers. The history of hierarchies seems to show that all religious error consisted in making the symbol too stark and solid, and was at last nothing but an excess of the organ of language.

Swedenborg, of all men in the recent ages, stands eminently for the translator of nature into thought. I do not know the man in history to whom things stood so uniformly for words. Before him the metamorphosis continually plays. Everything on which his eye rests, obeys the impulses of moral nature. The figs become grapes whilst he eats them. When some of his angels affirmed a truth, the laurel twig which they held blossomed in their hands. The noise which at a distance appeared like gnashing and thumping, on coming nearer was found to be the voice of disputants. The men in one of his visions, seen in heavenly light, appeared like dragons, and seemed in darkness; but to each other they appeared as men, and when the light from heaven shone into their cabin, they complained of the darkness, and were compelled to shut the window that they might see.

There was this perception in him which makes the poet or seer an object of awe and terror, namely that the same man or society of men may wear one aspect to themselves and their companions, and a different aspect to higher intelligences. Certain priests, whom he describes as conversing very learnedly together, appeared to the children who were at some distance, like dead horses; and many the like misappearances. And instantly the mind inquires whether these fishes under the bridge, yonder oxen in the pasture, those dogs in the yard, are immutably fishes, oxen and dogs, or only so appear to me, and perchance to themselves appear upright men; and whether I appear as a man to all eyes. The Brahmins and Pythagoras propounded the same question, and if any poet has witnessed the transformation he doubtless found it in harmony with various experiences. We have all seen changes as considerable in wheat and caterpillars. He is the poet and shall draw us with love and terror, who sees through the flowing vest the firm nature, and can declare it.

I look in vain for the poet whom I describe. We do not with sufficient plainness or sufficient profoundness address ourselves to life, nor dare we chaunt our own times and social circumstance. If we filled the day with bravery, we should not shrink from celebrating it. Time and nature yield us many gifts, but not yet the timely man, the new religion, the reconciler, whom all things await. Dante's praise is that he dared to write his autobiography in colossal cipher, or into universality. We have yet had no genius in America, with tyrannous eye, which knew the value of our incomparable materials, and saw, in the barbarism and materialism of the times, another carnival of the same gods whose picture he so much admires in Homer; then in the Middle Age; then in Calvinism. Banks and tariffs, the newspaper and caucus, Methodism and Unitarianism, are flat and dull to dull people, but rest on the same foundations of wonder as the town of Troy and the temple of Delphi, and are as swiftly passing away. Our log-rolling, our stumps and their politics, our fisheries, our Negroes and Indians, our boasts and our repudiations, the wrath of rogues and the pusillanimity of honest men, the northern trade, the southern planting, the western clearing, Oregon and Texas, are yet unsung. Yet America is a poem in our eyes; its ample geography dazzles the imagination, and it will not wait long for metres. If I have not found that excellent combination of gifts in my countrymen which I seek, neither could I aid myself to fix the idea of the poet by reading now and then in Chalmers's collection of five centuries of English poets. These are wits more than poets, though there have been poets among them. But when we adhere to the ideal of the poet, we have our difficulties even with Milton and Homer. Milton is too literary, and Homer too literal and historical.

But I am not wise enough for a national criticism, and must use the old largeness a little longer, to discharge my errand from the muse to the poet concerning his art.

Art is the path of the creator to his work. The paths or methods are ideal and eternal, though few men ever see them; not the artist himself for years, or for a lifetime, unless he come into the conditions. The painter, the sculptor, the composer, the epic rhapsodist, the orator, all partake one desire, namely to express themselves symmetrically and abundantly, not dwarfishly and fragmentarily. They found or put themselves in certain conditions, as, the painter and sculptor before some impressive human figures; the orator into the assembly of the people; and the others in such scenes as each has found exciting to his intellect; and each presently feels the new desire. He hears a voice, he sees a beckoning. Then he is apprised, with wonder, what herds of dæmons hem him in. He can no more rest; he says, with the old painter, "By God, it is in me and must go forth of me." He pursues a beauty, half seen, which flies before him. The poet pours out verses in every solitude. Most of the things he says are conventional, no doubt; but by and by he says something which is original and beautiful. That charms him. He would say nothing else but such things. In our way of talking we say, "That is yours, this is mine;" but the poet knows well that it is not his; that it is as strange and beautiful to him as to you; he would fain hear the like eloquence at length. Once having tasted this immortal ichor, he cannot have enough of it, and as an admirable creative power exists in these intellections, it is of the last importance that these things get spoken. What a little of all we know is said! What drops of all the sea of our science are bailed up! and by what accident it is that these are exposed, when so many secrets sleep in nature! Hence the necessity of speech and song; hence these throbs and heart-beatings in the orator, at the door of the assembly, to the end namely that thought may be ejaculated as Logos, or Word.

Doubt not, O poet, but persist. Say, "It is in me, and shall out." Stand there, balked and dumb, stuttering and stammering, hissed and hooted, stand and strive, until at last rage draw out of thee that *dream*-power which every night shows thee is thine own; a power transcending all limit and privacy, and by virtue of which a man is the conductor of the whole river of electricity. Nothing walks, or creeps, or grows, or exists, which must not in turn arise and walk before him as exponent of his meaning. Comes he to that power, his genius is no longer exhaustible. All the creatures by pairs and by tribes pour into his mind as into a Noah's ark, to come forth again to people a new world. This is like the stock of air for our respiration or for the combustion of our fireplace; not a measure of gallons, but the entire atmosphere if wanted. And therefore the rich poets, as Homer, Chaucer, Shakspeare, and Raphael, have obviously no limits to their works except the limits of their lifetime, and resemble a mirror carried through the street, ready to render an image of every created thing.

O poet! a new nobility is conferred in groves and pastures, and not in castles or by the sword-blade any longer. The conditions are hard, but equal. Thou shalt leave the world, and know the muse only. Thou shalt not know any longer the times, customs, graces, politics, or opinions of men, but shalt take all from the muse. For the time of towns is tolled from the world by funereal chimes, but in nature the universal hours are counted by succeeding tribes of animals and plants, and by growth of joy on joy. God wills also that thou abdicate a manifold and duplex life, and that thou be content that others speak for thee. Others shall be thy gentlemen and shall represent all courtesy and worldly life for thee; others shall do the great and resounding actions also. Thou shalt lie close hid with nature, and canst not be afforded to the Capitol or the Exchange. The world is full of renunciations and apprenticeships, and this is thine; thou must pass for a fool and a churl for a long season. This is the screen and sheath in which Pan has protected his well-beloved flower, and thou shalt be known only to thine own, and they shall console thee with tenderest love. And thou shalt not be able to rehearse the names of thy friends in thy verse, for an old shame before the holy ideal. And this is the reward; that the ideal shall be real to thee, and the impressions of the actual world shall fall like summer rain, copious, but not troublesome to thy invulnerable essence. Thou shalt have the whole land for thy park and manor, the sea for thy bath and navigation, without tax and without envy; the woods and the rivers thou shalt own, and thou shalt possess that wherein others are only tenants and boarders. Thou true land-lord! sea-lord! air-lord! Wherever snow falls or water flows or birds fly, wherever day and night meet in twilight, wherever the blue heaven is hung by clouds or sown with stars, wherever are forms with transparent boundaries, wherever are outlets into celestial space, wherever is danger, and awe, and love,—there is Beauty, plenteous as rain, shed for thee, and though thou shouldst walk the world over, thou shalt not be able to find a condition inopportune or ignoble.

1844

WALT WHITMAN

WALT WHITMAN ■■■■■■■■■■■■■■■■■■■

Walt Whitman was born on Long Island in 1819, the son of a carpenter, and grew up on Long Island and in Brooklyn. "Self-educated," he followed a variety of occupations in his youth and young manhood: carpentering with his father, teaching school, working on a newspaper (he was connected with several newspapers, the most important being the Brooklyn *Daily Eagle*, which he edited 1846–1847). A leisurely journey to New Orleans in 1848 and the brief sojourn there must be noted in any biographical record however brief: there was possibly a transforming love affair with a "New Orleans woman," though the fact has never been established nor the woman identified. He never married. The first edition of *Leaves of Grass* appeared in 1855; seven other editions appeared during the author's lifetime, each one containing new poems and the old poems in revised form; the author's revisions, never thoroughly analyzed, are a large and complex subject. During the Civil War, he served faithfully and heroically as a nurse in the army hospitals in Washington; in 1865 he was dismissed from a government clerkship on the charge of having written "an indecent book," and was eloquently defended by his friend and admirer W. D. O'Connor in *The Good Gray Poet*. After the War, he lived serenely in Camden, New Jersey. He suffered a paralytic stroke in 1873; thereafter, he continued to write and receive visitors, though in failing health. He died in 1892. His reputation was fostered in this country by enthusiasts like O'Connor, John Burroughs, and Horace Traubel; it had a more solid basis in England in the admiration of Swinburne, the Rossettis, and Edward Dowden. His acceptance by conservative critics in America dates from Bliss Perry's *Whitman* in 1905. Whatever one's opinion of *Leaves of Grass* as poetry, there can be little doubt that the book was a great turning point in modern literature.

Emory Holloway, *Whitman: An Interpretation in Narrative* (1926); Norman Foerster, "Whitman," in *American Criticism* (1928); F. O. Matthiessen, *American Renaissance* (1941); G. W. Allen, *Walt Whitman Handbook* (1946).

SONG OF MYSELF [1]

1

I celebrate myself, and sing myself,
And what I assume you shall assume,
For every atom belonging to me as good belongs to you.

I loafe and invite my soul,
I lean and loafe at my ease observing a spear of summer grass.

My tongue, every atom of my blood, form'd from this soil, this air,
Born here of parents born here from parents the same, and their parents the
     same,
I, now thirty-seven years old in perfect health begin,
Hoping to cease not till death.

10   Creeds and schools in abeyance,
Retiring back a while sufficed at what they are, but never forgotten,
I harbor for good or bad, I permit to speak at every hazard,
Nature without check with original energy.

2

Houses and rooms are full of perfumes, the shelves are crowded with perfumes,
I breathe the fragrance myself and know it and like it,
The distillation would intoxicate me also, but I shall not let it.

The atmosphere is not a perfume, it has no taste of the distillation, it is odorless,
It is for my mouth forever, I am in love with it,
I will go to the bank by the wood and become undisguised and naked,
20   I am mad for it to be in contact with me.

The smoke of my own breath,
Echoes, ripples, buzz'd whispers, love-root, silk-thread, crotch and vine,
My respiration and inspiration, the beating of my heart, the passing of blood and
    air through my lungs,
The sniff of green leaves and dry leaves, and of the shore and dark-color'd sea-
    rocks, and of hay in the barn,
The sound of the belch'd words of my voice loos'd to the eddies of the wind,
A few light kisses, a few embraces, a reaching around of arms,
The play of shine and shade on the trees as the supple boughs wag,
The delight alone or in the rush of the streets, or along the fields and hill-sides,
The feeling of health, the full-noon trill, the song of me rising from bed and meet-
    ing the sun.

---

1. The present form of "Song of Myself" is the result of many revisions, deletions, and additions made between
1855, the date of its first appearance, and 1881. The student can trace these changes by consulting the Variorum
Readings in Emory Holloway's Inclusive Edition of *Leaves of Grass.*

Have you reckon'd a thousand acres much? have you reckon'd the earth much?   30
Have you practis'd so long to learn to read?
Have you felt so proud to get at the meaning of poems?

Stop this day and night with me and you shall possess the origin of all poems,
You shall possess the good of the earth and sun, (there are millions of suns left,)
You shall no longer take things at second or third hand, nor look through the eyes
    of the dead, nor feed on the spectres in books,
You shall not look through my eyes either, nor take things from me,
You shall listen to all sides and filter them from your self.

3
I have heard what the talkers were talking, the talk of the beginning and the end,
But I do not talk of the beginning or the end.

There was never any more inception than there is now,   40
Nor any more youth or age than there is now,
And will never be any more perfection than there is now,
Nor any more heaven or hell than there is now.

Urge and urge and urge,
Always the procreant urge of the world.
Out of the dimness opposite equals advance, always substance and increase,
    always sex,
Always a knit of identity, always distinction, always a breed of life.

To elaborate is no avail, learn'd and unlearn'd feel that it is so.

Sure as the most certain sure, plumb in the uprights, well entretied, braced in the
    beams,
Stout as a horse, affectionate, haughty, electrical,   50
I and this mystery here we stand.

Clear and sweet is my soul, and clear and sweet is all that is not my soul.
Lack one lacks both, and the unseen is proved by the seen,
Till that becomes unseen and receives proof in its turn.

Showing the best and dividing it from the worst age vexes age,
Knowing the perfect fitness and equanimity of things, while they discuss I am
    silent, and go bathe and admire myself.

Welcome is every organ and attribute of me, and of any man hearty and clean,
Not an inch nor a particle of an inch is vile, and none shall be less familiar than
    the rest.

I am satisfied—I see, dance, laugh, sing;
As the hugging and loving bed-fellow sleeps at my side through the night, and
    withdraws at the peep of the day with stealthy tread,   60

Leaving me baskets cover'd with white towels swelling the house with their plenty,
Shall I postpone my acceptation and realization and scream at my eyes,
That they turn from gazing after and down the road,
And forthwith cipher and show me to a cent,
Exactly the value of one and exactly the value of two, and which is ahead?

4
Trippers and askers surround me,
People I meet, the effect upon me of my early life or the ward and city I live in, or the nation,
The latest dates, discoveries, inventions, societies, authors old and new,
My dinner, dress, associates, looks, compliments, dues,
70 The real or fancied indifference of some man or woman I love,
The sickness of one of my folks or of myself, or ill-doing or loss or lack of money, or depressions or exaltations,
Battles, the horrors of fratricidal war, the fever of doubtful news, the fitful events;
These come to me days and nights and go from me again,
But they are not the Me myself.

Apart from the pulling and hauling stands what I am,
Stands amused, complacent, compassionating, idle, unitary,
Looks down, is erect, or bends an arm on an impalpable certain rest,
Looking with side-curved head curious what will come next,
Both in and out of the game and watching and wondering at it.

80 Backward I see in my own days where I sweated through fog with linguists and contenders,
I have no mockings or arguments, I witness and wait.

5
I believe in you my soul, the other I am must not abase itself to you,
And you must not be abased to the other.

Loafe with me on the grass, loose the stop from your throat,
Not words, not music or rhyme I want, not custom or lecture, not even the best,
Only the lull I like, the hum of your valvèd voice.

I mind how once we lay such a transparent summer morning,
How you settled your head athwart my hips and gently turn'd over upon me,
And parted the shirt from my bosom-bone, and plunged your tongue to my bare-stript heart,
90 And reach'd till you felt my beard, and reach'd till you held my feet.

Swiftly arose and spread around me the peace and knowledge that pass all the argument of the earth,
And I know that the hand of God is the promise of my own,
And I know that the spirit of God is the brother of my own,

And that all the men ever born are also my brothers, and the women my sisters
    and lovers,
And that a kelson of the creation is love,
And limitless are leaves stiff or drooping in the fields,
And brown ants in the little wells beneath them,
And mossy scabs of the worm fence, heap'd stones, elder, mullein and poke-weed.

6
A child said *What is the grass?* fetching it to me with full hands,
How could I answer the child? I do not know what it is any more than he.   100

I guess it must be the flag of my disposition, out of hopeful green stuff woven.

Or I guess it is the handkerchief of the Lord,
A scented gift and remembrancer designedly dropt,
Bearing the owner's name someway in the corners, that we may see and remark,
    and say *Whose?*

Or I guess the grass is itself a child, the produced babe of the vegetation.

Or I guess it is a uniform hieroglyphic,
And it means, Sprouting alike in broad zones, and narrow zones,
Growing among black folks as among white,
Kanuck, Tuckahoe, Congressman, Cuff, I give them the same, I receive them the
    same.

And now it seems to me the beautiful uncut hair of graves.   110

Tenderly will I use you curling grass,
It may be you transpire from the breasts of young men,
It may be if I had known them I would have loved them,
It may be you are from old people, or from offspring taken soon out of their
    mothers' laps,
And here you are the mothers' laps.

This grass is very dark to be from the white heads of old mothers,
Darker than the colorless beards of old men,
Dark to come from under the faint red roofs of mouths.
O I perceive after all so many uttering tongues,
And I perceive they do not come from the roofs of mouths for nothing.   120

I wish I could translate the hints about the dead young men and women,
And the hints about old men and mothers, and the offspring taken soon out of
    their laps.

What do you think has become of the young and old men?
And what do you think has become of the women and children?

They are alive and well somewhere,
The smallest sprout shows there is really no death,
And if ever there was it led forward life, and does not wait at the end to arrest it,
And ceas'd the moment life appear'd.

All goes onward and outward, nothing collapses,
130   And to die is different from what any one supposed, and luckier.

7
Has any one supposed it lucky to be born?
I hasten to inform him or her it is just as lucky to die, and I know it.

I pass death with the dying and birth with the new-wash'd babe, and am not
    contain'd between my hat and boots,
And peruse manifold objects, no two alike and every one good,
The earth good and the stars good, and their adjuncts all good.

I am not an earth nor an adjunct of an earth,
I am the mate and companion of people, all just as immortal and fathomless as
    myself,
(They do not know how immortal, but I know.)

Every kind for itself and its own, for me mine male and female,
140   For me those that have been boys and that love women,
For me the man that is proud and feels how it stings to be slighted,
For me the sweet-heart and the old maid, for me mothers and the mothers of
    mothers,
For me lips that have smiled, eyes that have shed tears,
For me children and the begetters of children.

Undrape! you are not guilty to me, nor stale nor discarded,
I see through the broadcloth and gingham whether or no,
And am around, tenacious, acquisitive, tireless, and cannot be shaken away.

8
The little one sleeps in its cradle,
I lift the gauze and look a long time, and silently brush away flies with my hand.

150   The youngster and the red-faced girl turn aside up the bushy hill,
I peeringly view them from the top.

The suicide sprawls on the bloody floor of the bedroom,
I witness the corpse with its dabbled hair, I note where the pistol has fallen.

The blab of the pave, tires of carts, sluff of boot-soles, talk of the promenaders,
The heavy omnibus, the driver with his interrogating thumb, the clank of the
    shod horses on the granite floor,
The snow-sleighs, clinking, shouted jokes, pelts of snow-balls,

The hurrahs for popular favorites, the fury of rous'd mobs,
The flap of the curtain'd litter, a sick man inside borne to the hospital,
The meeting of enemies, the sudden oath, the blows and fall,
The excited crowd, the policeman with his star quickly working his passage to the
    centre of the crowd, 160
The impassive stones that receive and return so many echoes,
What groans of over-fed or half-starv'd who fall sun-struck or in fits,
What exclamations of women taken suddenly who hurry home and give birth to
    babes,
What living and buried speech is always vibrating here, what howls restrain'd by
    decorum,
Arrests of criminals, slights, adulterous offers made, acceptances, rejections with
    convex lips,
I mind them or the show or resonance of them—I come and I depart.

9

The big doors of the country barn stand open and ready,
The dried grass of the harvest-time loads the slow-drawn wagon,
The clear light plays on the brown gray and green intertinged,
The armfuls are pack'd to the sagging mow. 170

I am there, I help, I came stretch'd atop of the load,
I felt its soft jolts, one leg reclined on the other,
I jump from the cross-beams and seize the clover and timothy,
And roll head over heels and tangle my hair full of wisps.

10

Alone far in the wilds and mountains I hunt,
Wandering amazed at my own lightness and glee,
In the late afternoon choosing a safe spot to pass the night,
Kindling a fire and broiling the fresh-kill'd game,
Falling asleep on the gather'd leaves with my dog and gun by my side.

The Yankee clipper is under her sky-sails, she cuts the sparkle and scud, 180
My eyes settle the land, I bend at her prow or shout joyously from the deck.

The boatmen and clam-diggers arose early and stopt for me,
I tuck'd my trowser-ends in my boots and went and had a good time;
You should have been with us that day round the chowder-kettle.

I saw the marriage of the trapper in the open air in the far west, the bride was a
    red girl,
Her father and his friends sat near cross-legged and dumbly smoking, they had
    moccasins to their feet and large thick blankets hanging from their shoulders,
On a bank lounged the trapper, he was drest mostly in skins, his luxuriant beard
    and curls protected his neck, he held his bride by the hand,
She had long eyelashes, her coarse straight locks descended upon her voluptuous
    limbs and reach'd to her feet.

The runaway slave came to my house and stopt outside,
190 I heard his motions crackling the twigs of the woodpile,
Through the swung half-door of the kitchen I saw him limpsy and weak,
And went where he sat on a log and led him in and assured him,
And brought water and fill'd a tub for his sweated body and bruis'd feet,
And gave him a room that enter'd from my own, and gave him some coarse clean
        clothes,
And remember perfectly well his revolving eyes and his awkwardness,
And remember putting plasters on the galls of his neck and ankles;
He staid with me a week before he was recuperated and pass'd north,
I had him sit next me at table, my fire-lock lean'd in the corner.

11
Twenty-eight young men bathe by the shore,
200 Twenty-eight young men and all so friendly;
Twenty-eight years of womanly life and all so lonesome.

She owns the fine house by the rise of the bank,
She hides handsome and richly drest aft the blinds of the window.

Which of the young men does she like the best?
Ah the homeliest of them is beautiful to her.

Where are you off to, lady? for I see you,
You splash in the water there, yet stay stock still in your room.

Dancing and laughing along the beach came the twenty-ninth bather,
The rest did not see her, but she saw them and loved them.

210 The beards of the young men glisten'd with wet, it ran from their long hair,
Little streams pass'd all over their bodies.

An unseen hand also pass'd over their bodies,
It descended tremblingly from their temples and ribs.

The young men float on their backs, their white bellies bulge to the sun, they do
        not ask who seizes fast to them,
They do not know who puffs and declines with pendant and bending arch,
They do not think whom they souse with spray.

12
The butcher-boy puts off his killing-clothes, or sharpens his knife at the stall in
        the market,
I loiter enjoying his repartee and his shuffle and break-down.

Blacksmiths with grimed and hairy chests environ the anvil,
220 Each has his main-sledge, they are all out, there is a great heat in the fire.

From the cinder-strew'd threshold I follow their movements,
The lithe sheer of their waists plays even with their massive arms,
Overhand the hammers swing, overhand so slow, overhand so sure,
They do not hasten, each man hits in his place.

13

The Negro holds firmly the reins of his four horses, the block swags underneath
    on its tied-over chain,
The Negro that drives the long dray of the stone-yard, steady and tall he stands
    pois'd on one leg on the string-piece,
His blue shirt exposes his ample neck and breast and loosens over his hip-band,
His glance is calm and commanding, he tosses the slouch of his hat away from
    his forehead,
The sun falls on his crispy hair and mustache, falls on the black of his polish'd
    and perfect limbs.

I behold the picturesque giant and love him, and I do not stop there,   230
I go with the team also.

In me the caresser of life wherever moving, backward as well as forward sluing,
To niches aside and junior bending, not a person or object missing,
Absorbing all to myself and for this song.

Oxen that rattle the yoke and chain or halt in the leafy shade, what is that you
    express in your eyes?
It seems to me more than all the print I have read in my life.

My tread scares the wood-drake and wood-duck on my distant and day-long
    ramble,
They rise together, they slowly circle around.

I believe in those wing'd purposes,
And acknowledge red, yellow, white, playing within me,   240
And consider green and violet and the tufted crown intentional,
And do not call the tortoise unworthy because she is not something else,
And the jay in the woods never studied the gamut, yet trills pretty well to me,
And the look of the bay mare shames silliness out of me.

14

The wild gander leads his flock through the cool night,
Ya-honk he says, and sounds it down to me like an invitation,
The pert may suppose it meaningless, but I listening close,
Find its purpose and place up there toward the wintry sky.

The sharp-hoof'd moose of the north, the cat on the house-sill, the chickadee, the
    prairie-dog,
The litter of the grunting sow as they tug at her teats,   250

The brood of the turkey-hen and she with her half-spread wings,
I see in them and myself the same old law.

The press of my foot to the earth springs a hundred affections,
They scorn the best I can do to relate them.

I am enamour'd of growing out-doors,
Of men that live among cattle or taste of the ocean or woods,
Of the builders and steerers of ships and the wielders of axes and mauls, and the
    drivers of horses,
I can eat and sleep with them week in and week out.

What is commonest, cheapest, nearest, easiest, is Me,
260   Me going in for my chances, spending for vast returns,
Adorning myself to bestow myself on the first that will take me,
Not asking the sky to come down to my good will,
Scattering it freely forever.

15

The pure contralto sings in the organ loft,
The carpenter dresses his plank, the tongue of his foreplane whistles its wild
    ascending lisp,
The married and unmarried children ride home to their Thanksgiving dinner,
The pilot seizes the king-pin, he heaves down with a strong arm,
The mate stands braced in the whale-boat, lance and harpoon are ready,
The duck-shooter walks by silent and cautious stretches,
270   The deacons are ordain'd with cross'd hands at the altar,
The spinning-girl retreats and advances to the hum of the big wheel,
The farmer stops by the bars as he walks on a First-day loafe and looks at the
    oats and rye,
The lunatic is carried at last to the asylum a confirm'd case,
(He will never sleep any more as he did in the cot in his mother's bed-room;)
The jour printer with gray head and gaunt jaws works at his case,
He turns his quid of tobacco while his eyes blurr with the manuscript;
The malform'd limbs are tied to the surgeon's table,
What is removed drops horribly in a pail;
The quadroon girl is sold at the auction-stand, the drunkard nods by the bar-
    room stove,
280   The machinist rolls up his sleeves, the policeman travels his beat, the gate-keeper
    marks who pass,
The young fellow drives the express-wagon, (I love him, though I do not know
    him;)
The half-breed straps on his light boots to compete in the race,
The western turkey-shooting draws old and young, some lean on their rifles,
    some sit on logs,
Out from the crowd steps the marksman, takes his position, levels his piece;
The groups of newly-come immigrants cover the wharf or levee,

As the woolly-pates hoe in the sugar-field, the overseer views them from his
saddle,
The bugle calls in the ball-room, the gentlemen run for their partners, the dancers
bow to each other,
The youth lies awake in the cedar-roof'd garret and harks to the musical rain,
The Wolverine sets traps on the creek that helps fill the Huron,
The squaw wrapt in her yellow-hemm'd cloth is offering moccasins and bead-bags
for sale,   290
The connoisseur peers along the exhibition-gallery with half-shut eyes bent
sideways,
As the deck-hands make fast the steamboat the plank is thrown for the shore-
going passengers,
The young sister holds out the skein while the elder sister winds it off in a ball,
and stops now and then for the knots,
The one-year wife is recovering and happy having a week ago borne her first
child,
The clean-hair'd Yankee girl works with her sewing-machine or in the factory or
mill,
The paving-man leans on his two-handed rammer, the reporter's lead flies swiftly
over the note-book, the sign painter is lettering with blue and gold,
The canal boy trots on the tow-path, the book-keeper counts at his desk, the shoe-
maker waxes his thread,
The conductor beats time for the band and all the performers follow him,
The child is baptized, the convert is making his first professions,
The regatta is spread on the bay, the race is begun, (how the white sails sparkle!)   300
The drover watching his drove sings out to them that would stray,
The pedler sweats with his pack on his back, (the purchaser higgling about the
odd cent;)
The bride unrumples her white dress, the minute-hand of the clock moves slowly,
The opium-eater reclines with rigid head and just-open'd lips,
The prostitute draggles her shawl, her bonnet bobs on her tipsy and pimpled
neck,
The crowd laugh at her blackguard oaths, the men jeer and wink to each other,
(Miserable! I do not laugh at your oaths nor jeer you;)
The President holding a cabinet council is surrounded by the great Secretaries,
On the piazza walk three matrons stately and friendly with twined arms,
The crew of the fish-smack pack repeated layers of halibut in the hold,   310
The Missourian crosses the plains toting his wares and his cattle,
As the fare-collector goes through the train he gives notice by the jingling of loose
change,
The floor-men are laying the floor, the tinners are tinning the roof, the masons are
calling for mortar,
In single file each shouldering his hod pass onward the laborers;
Seasons pursuing each other the indescribable crowd is gather'd, it is the fourth
of Seventh-month, (what salutes of cannon and small arms!)
Seasons pursuing each other the plougher ploughs, the mower mows, and the
winter-grain falls in the ground;

Off on the lakes the pike-fisher watches and waits by the hole in the frozen
surface,

The stumps stand thick round the clearing, the squatter strikes deep with his
axe,

Flatboatmen make fast towards dusk near the cotton-wood or pecan-trees,

320 Coon-seekers go through the regions of the Red river or through those drain'd
by the Tennessee, or through those of the Arkansas,

Torches shine in the dark that hangs on the Chattahooche or Altamahaw,

Patriarchs sit at supper with sons and grandsons and great grandsons around
them,

In walls of adobie, in canvas tents, rest hunters and trappers after their day's
sport,

The city sleeps and the country sleeps,

The living sleep for their time, the dead sleep for their time,

The old husband sleeps by his wife and the young husband sleeps by his
wife;

And these tend inward to me, and I tend outward to them,

And such as it is to be of these more or less I am,

And of these one and all I weave the song of myself.

16

330 I am of old and young, of the foolish as much as the wise,

Regardless of others, ever regardful of others,

Maternal as well as paternal, a child as well as a man,

Stuff'd with the stuff that is coarse and stuff'd with the stuff that is fine,

One of the Nation of many nations, the smallest the same and the largest the
same,

A Southerner soon as a Northerner, a planter nonchalant and hospitable down by
the Oconee I live,

A Yankee bound my own way ready for trade, my joints the limberest joints on
earth and the sternest joints on earth,

A Kentuckian walking the vale of the Elkhorn in my deer-skin leggings, a
Louisianian or Georgian,

A boatman over lakes or bays or along coasts, a Hoosier, Badger, Buckeye;

At home on Kanadian snow-shoes or up in the bush, or with fishermen off New-
foundland,

340 At home in the fleet of ice-boats, sailing with the rest and tacking,

At home on the hills of Vermont or in the woods of Maine, or the Texan ranch,

Comrade of Californians, comrade of free North-Westerners, (loving their big
proportions,)

Comrade of raftsmen and coalmen, comrade of all who shake hands and welcome
to drink and meat,

A learner with the simplest, a teacher of the thoughtfullest,

A novice beginning yet experient of myriads of seasons,

Of every hue and caste am I, of every rank and religion,

A farmer, mechanic, artist, gentleman, sailor, quaker,

Prisoner, fancy-man, rowdy, lawyer, physician, priest.

I resist any thing better than my own diversity,
Breathe the air but leave plenty after me,   350
And am not stuck up, and am in my place.

(The moth and the fish-eggs are in their place,
The bright suns I see and the dark suns I cannot see are in their place,
The palpable is in its place and the impalpable is in its place.)

17

These are really the thoughts of all men in all ages and lands, they are not
    original with me,
If they are not yours as much as mine they are nothing, or next to nothing,
If they are not the riddle and the untying of the riddle they are nothing,
If they are not just as close as they are distant they are nothing.

This is the grass that grows wherever the land is and the water is,
This the common air that bathes the globe.   360

18

With music strong I come, with my cornets and my drums,
I play not marches for accepted victors only, I play marches for conquer'd and
    slain persons.

Have you heard that it was good to gain the day?
I also say it is good to fall, battles are lost in the same spirit in which they are
    won.

I beat and pound for the dead,
I blow through my embouchures my loudest and gayest for them.

Vivas to those who have fail'd!
And to those whose war-vessels sank in the sea!
And to those themselves who sank in the sea!
And to all generals that lost engagements, and all overcome heroes!   370
And the numberless unknown heroes equal to the greatest heroes known!

19

This is the meal equally set, this the meat for natural hunger,
It is for the wicked just the same as the righteous, I make appointments with all,
I will not have a single person slighted or left away,
The kept-woman, sponger, thief, are hereby invited,
The heavy-lipp'd slave is invited, the venerealee is invited;
There shall be no difference between them and the rest.

This is the press of a bashful hand, this the float and odor of hair,
This the touch of my lips to yours, this the murmur of yearning,

380 This the far-off depth and height reflecting my own face,
This the thoughtful merge of myself, and the outlet again.

Do you guess I have some intricate purpose?
Well I have, for the Fourth-month showers have, and the mica on the side of a
    rock has.

Do you take it I would astonish?
Does the daylight astonish? does the early redstart twittering through the woods?
Do I astonish more than they?
This hour I tell things in confidence,
I might not tell everybody, but I will tell you.

20
Who goes there? hankering, gross, mystical, nude;
390 How is it I extract strength from the beef I eat?

What is a man anyhow? what am I? what are you?

All I mark as my own you shall offset it with your own,
Else it were time lost listening to me.

I do not snivel that snivel the world over,
That months are vacuums and the ground but wallow and filth.

Whimpering and trucking fold with powders for invalids, conformity goes to the
    fourth-remov'd,
I wear my hat as I please indoors or out.

Why should I pray? why should I venerate and be ceremonious?

Having pried through the strata, analyzed to a hair, counsel'd with doctors and
    calculated close,
400 I find no sweeter fat than sticks to my own bones.

In all people I see myself, none more and not one a barley-corn less,
And the good or bad I say of myself I say of them.

I know I am solid and sound,
To me the converging objects of the universe perpetually flow,
All are written to me, and I must get what the writing means.

I know I am deathless,
I know this orbit of mine cannot be swept by a carpenter's compass,
I know I shall not pass like a child's carlacue cut with a burnt stick at night.

I know I am august,
410 I do not trouble my spirit to vindicate itself or be understood,

I see that the elementary laws never apologize,
(I reckon I behave no prouder than the level I plant my house by, after all.)

I exist as I am, that is enough,
If no other in the world be aware I sit content,
And if each and all be aware I sit content.

One world is aware and by far the largest to me, and that is myself,
And whether I come to my own to-day or in ten thousand or ten million
        years,
I can cheerfully take it now, or with equal cheerfulness I can wait.

My foothold is tenon'd and mortis'd in granite,
I laugh at what you call dissolution,   420
And I know the amplitude of time.

21
I am the poet of the Body and I am the poet of the Soul,
The pleasures of heaven are with me and the pains of hell are with me,
The first I graft and increase upon myself, the latter I translate into a new tongue.

I am the poet of the woman the same as the man,
And I say it is as great to be a woman as to be a man,
And I say there is nothing greater than the mother of men.

I chant the chant of dilation or pride,
We have had ducking and deprecating about enough,
I show that size is only development.   430

Have you outstript the rest? are you the President?
It is a trifle, they will more than arrive there every one, and still pass on.

I am he that walks with the tender and growing night,
I call to the earth and sea half-held by the night.

Press close bare-bosom'd night—press close magnetic nourishing night!
Night of south winds—night of the large few stars!
Still nodding night—mad naked summer night.

Smile O voluptuous cool-breath'd earth!
Earth of the slumbering and liquid trees!
Earth of departed sunset—earth of the mountains misty-topt!   440
Earth of the vitreous pour of the full moon just tinged with blue!
Earth of shine and dark mottling the tide of the river!
Earth of the limpid gray of clouds brighter and clearer for my sake!
Far-swooping elbow'd earth—rich apple-blossom'd earth!
Smile, for your lover comes.

Prodigal, you have given me love—therefore I to you give love!
O unspeakable passionate love.

22

You sea! I resign myself to you also—I guess what you mean,
I behold from the beach your crooked inviting fingers,
450   I believe you refuse to go back without feeling of me,
We must have a turn together, I undress, hurry me out of sight of the land,
Cushion me soft, rock me in billowy drowse,
Dash me with amorous wet, I can repay you.

Sea of stretch'd ground-swells,
Sea breathing broad and convulsive breaths,
Sea of the brine of life and of unshovell'd yet always-ready graves,
Howler and scooper of storms, capricious and dainty sea,
I am integral with you, I too am of one phase and of all phases.

Partaker of influx and efflux, I, extoller of hate and conciliation,
460   Extoller of amies and those that sleep in each others' arms,

I am he attesting sympathy,
(Shall I make my list of things in the house and skip the house that supports
      them?)

I am not the poet of goodness only, I do not decline to be the poet of wickedness
    also.

What blurt is this about virtue and about vice?
Evil propels me and reform of evil propels me, I stand indifferent,
My gait is no fault-finder's or rejecter's gait,
I moisten the roots of all that has grown.

Did you fear some scrofula out of the unflagging pregnancy?
Did you guess the celestial laws are yet to be work'd over and rectified?

470   I find one side a balance and the antipodal side a balance,
Soft doctrine as steady help as stable doctrine,
Thoughts and deeds of the present our rouse and early start.

This minute that comes to me over the past decillions,
There is no better than it and now.

What behaved well in the past or behaves well to-day is not such a wonder,
The wonder is always and always how there can be a mean man or an infidel.

23

Endless unfolding of words of ages!
And mine a word of the modern, the word En-Masse.

A word of the faith that never balks,
Here or henceforward it is all the same to me, I accept Time absolutely.   480

It alone is without flaw, it alone rounds and completes all,
That mystic baffling wonder alone completes all.

I accept Reality and dare not question it,
Materialism first and last imbuing.

Hurrah for positive science! long live exact demonstration!
Fetch stonecrop mixt with cedar and branches of lilac,
This is the lexicographer, this the chemist, this made a grammar of the old
    cartouches,
These mariners put the ship through dangerous unknown seas,
This is the geologist, this works with the scalpel, and this is a mathematician.

Gentlemen, to you the first honors always!   490
Your facts are useful, and yet they are not my dwelling,
I but enter by them to an area of my dwelling.

Less the reminders of properties told my words,
And more the reminders they of life untold, and of freedom and extrication,
And make short account of neuters and geldings, and favor men and women fully
    equipt.
And beat the gong of revolt, and stop with fugitives and them that plot and
    conspire.

24
Walt Whitman, a kosmos, of Manhattan the son,
Turbulent, fleshy, sensual, eating, drinking and breeding,
No sentimentalist, no stander above men and women or apart from them,
No more modest than immodest.   500

Unscrew the locks from the doors!
Unscrew the doors themselves from their jambs!
Whoever degrades another degrades me,
And whatever is done or said returns at last to me.

Through me the afflatus surging and surging, through me the current and index.

I speak the pass-word primeval, I give the sign of democracy,
By God! I will accept nothing which all cannot have their counterpart of on the
    same terms.
Through me many long dumb voices,
Voices of the interminable generations of prisoners and slaves,
Voices of the diseas'd and despairing and of thieves and dwarfs,   510
Voices of cycles of preparation and accretion,

And of the threads that connect the stars, and of wombs and of the father-stuff,
And of the rights of them the others are down upon,
Of the deform'd, trivial, flat, foolish, despised,
Fog in the air, beetles rolling balls of dung.

Through me forbidden voices,
Voices of sexes and lusts, voices veil'd and I remove the veil,
Voices indecent by me clarified and transfigur'd.

I do not press my fingers across my mouth,
520   I keep as delicate around the bowels as around the head and heart,
Copulation is no more rank to me than death is.

I believe in the flesh and the appetites,
Seeing, hearing, feeling, are miracles, and each part and tag of me is a miracle.

Divine am I inside and out, and I make holy whatever I touch or am touch'd
      from,
The scent of these arm-pits aroma finer than prayer,
This head more than churches, bibles, and all the creeds.

If I worship one thing more than another it shall be the spread of my own body,
      or any part of it,
Translucent mould of me it shall be you!
Shaded ledges and rests it shall be you!
530   Firm masculine colter it shall be you!
Whatever goes to the tilth of me it shall be you!
You my rich blood! your milky stream pale strippings of my life!
Breast that presses against other breasts it shall be you!
My brain it shall be your occult convolutions!
Root of wash'd sweet-flag! timorous pond-snipe! nest of guarded duplicate eggs!
      it shall be you!
Mix'd tussled hay of head, beard, brawn, it shall be you!
Trickling sap of maple, fibre of manly wheat, it shall be you!
Sun so generous it shall be you!
Vapors lighting and shading my face it shall be you!
540   You sweaty brooks and dews it shall be you!
Winds whose soft-tickling genitals rub against me it shall be you!
Broad muscular fields, branches of live oak, loving lounger in my winding paths,
      it shall be you!
Hands I have taken, face I have kiss'd, mortal I have ever touch'd, it shall be you.

I dote on myself, there is that lot of me and all so luscious,
Each moment and whatever happens thrills me with joy,
I cannot tell how my ankles bend, nor whence the cause of my faintest wish,
Nor the cause of the friendship I emit, nor the cause of the friendship I take
      again.

That I walk up my stoop, I pause to consider if it really be,
A morning-glory at my window satisfies me more than the metaphysics of books.

To behold the day-break!   550
The little light fades the immense and diaphanous shadows,
The air tastes good to my palate.

Hefts of the moving world at innocent gambols silently rising, freshly exuding,
Scooting obliquely high and low.

Something I cannot see puts upward libidinous prongs,
Seas of bright juice suffuse heaven.

The earth by the sky staid with, the daily close of their junction,
The heav'd challenge from the east that moment over my head,
The mocking taunt, See then whether you shall be master!

25
Dazzling and tremendous how quick the sun-rise would kill me,   560
If I could not now and always send sun-rise out of me.

We also ascend dazzling and tremendous as the sun,
We found our own O my soul in the calm and cool of the daybreak.

My voice goes after what my eyes cannot reach,
With the twirl of my tongue I encompass worlds and volumes of worlds.

Speech is the twin of my vision, it is unequal to measure itself,
It provokes me forever, it says sarcastically,
Walt you contain enough, why don't you let it out then?

Come now I will not be tantalized, you conceive too much of articulation,
Do you not know O speech how the buds beneath you are folded?   570
Waiting in gloom, protected by frost,
The dirt receding before my prophetical screams,
I underlying causes to balance them at last,
My knowledge my live parts, it keeping tally with the meaning of all things,
Happiness, (which whoever hears me let him or her set out in search of this day.)

My final merit I refuse you, I refuse putting from me what I really am,
Encompass worlds, but never try to encompass me,
I crowd your sleekest and best by simply looking toward you.

Writing and talk do not prove me,
I carry the plenum of proof and every thing else in my face,   580
With the hush of my lips I wholly confound the skeptic.

26

Now I will do nothing but listen,
To accrue what I hear into this song, to let sounds contribute toward it.

I hear bravuras of birds, bustle of growing wheat, gossip of flames, clack of
    sticks cooking my meals.
I hear the sound I love, the sound of the human voice,
I hear all sounds running together, combined, fused or following,
Sounds of the city and sounds out of the city, sounds of the day and night,
Talkative young ones to those that like them, the loud laugh of work-people at
    their meals,
The angry bases of disjointed friendship, the faint tones of the sick,
590 The judge with hands tight to the desk, his pallid lips pronouncing a death-
    sentence,
The heave'e'yo of stevedores unlading ships by the wharves, the refrain of the
    anchor-lifters,
The ring of alarm-bells, the cry of fire, the whirr of swift-streaking engines and
    hose-carts with premonitory tinkles and color'd lights,
The steam-whistle, the solid roll of the train of approaching cars,
The slow march play'd at the head of the association marching two and two,
(They go to guard some corpse, the flag-tops are draped with black muslin.)

I hear the violoncello, ('tis the young man's heart's complaint,)
I hear the key'd cornet, it glides quickly in through my ears,
It shakes mad-sweet pangs through my belly and breast.

I hear the chorus, it is a grand opera,
600 Ah this indeed is music—this suits me.

A tenor large and fresh as the creation fills me,
The orbic flex of his mouth is pouring and filling me full.

I hear the train'd soprano (what work with hers is this?)
The orchestra whirls me wider than Uranus flies,
It wrenches such ardors from me I did not know I possess'd them,
It sails me, I dab with bare feet, they are lick'd by the indolent waves,
I am cut by bitter and angry hail, I lose my breath,
Steep'd amid honey'd morphine, my windpipe throttled in fakes of
    death,
At length let up again to feel the puzzle of puzzles,
610 And what we call Being.

27

To be in any form, what is that?
(Round and round we go, all of us, and ever come back thither,)
If nothing lay more develop'd the quahaug in its callous shell were
    enough.

Mine is no callous shell,
I have instant conductors all over me whether I pass or stop,
They seize every object and lead it harmlessly through me.

I merely stir, press, feel with my fingers, and am happy,
To touch my person to some one else's is about as much as I can stand.

28
Is this then a touch? quivering me to a new identity,
Flames and ether making a rush for my veins,   620
Treacherous tip of me reaching and crowding to help them,
My flesh and blood playing out lightning to strike what is hardly different from
    myself,
On all sides prurient provokers stiffening my limbs,
Straining the udder of my heart for its withheld drip,
Behaving licentious toward me, taking no denial,
Depriving me of my best as for a purpose,
Unbuttoning my clothes, holding me by the bare waist,
Deluding my confusion with the calm of the sunlight and pasture-fields,
Immodestly sliding the fellow-senses away,
They bribed to swap off with touch and go and graze at the edges of me,   630
No consideration, no regard for my draining strength or my anger,
Fetching the rest of the herd around to enjoy them a while,
Then all uniting to stand on a headland and worry me.

The sentries desert every other part of me,
They have left me helpless to a red marauder,
They all come to the headland to witness and assist against me.

I am given up by traitors,
I talk wildly, I have lost my wits, I and nobody else am the greatest
    traitor,
I went myself first to the headland, my own hands carried me there.

You villain touch! what are you doing? my breath is tight in its throat,   640
Unclench your floodgates, you are too much for me.

29
Blind loving wrestling touch, sheath'd hooded sharp-tooth'd touch!
Did it make you ache so, leaving me?

Parting track'd by arriving, perpetual payment of perpetual loan,
Rich showering rain, and recompense richer afterward.

Sprouts take and accumulate, stand by the curb prolific and vital,
Landscapes projected masculine, full-sized and golden.

30

All truths wait in all things,
They neither hasten their own delivery nor resist it,
650   They do not need the obstetric forceps of the surgeon,
The insignificant is as big to me as any,
(What is less or more than a touch?)

Logic and sermons never convince,
The damp of the night drives deeper into my soul.

(Only what proves itself to every man and woman is so,
Only what nobody denies is so.)

A minute and a drop of me settle my brain,
I believe the soggy clods shall become lovers and lamps,
And a compend of compends is the meat of a man or woman,
660   And a summit and flower there is the feeling they have for each other,
And they are to branch boundlessly out of that lesson until it becomes omnific,
And until one and all shall delight us, and we them.

31

I believe a leaf of grass is no less than the journey-work of the stars,
And the pismire is equally perfect, and a grain of sand, and the egg of the wren,
And the tree-toad is a chef-d'œuvre for the highest,
And the running blackberry would adorn the parlors of heaven,
And the narrowest hinge in my hand puts to scorn all machinery,
And the cow crunching with depress'd head surpasses any statue,
And a mouse is miracle enough to stagger sextillions of infidels.

670   I find I incorporate gneiss, coal, long-threaded moss, fruits, grains, esculent roots,
And am stucco'd with quadrupeds and birds all over,
And have distanced what is behind me for good reasons,
But call any thing back again when I desire it.

In vain the speeding or shyness,
In vain the plutonic rocks send their old heat against my approach,
In vain the mastodon retreats beneath its own powder'd bones,
In vain objects stand leagues off and assume manifold shapes,
In vain the ocean settling in hollows and the great monsters lying low,
In vain the buzzard houses herself with the sky,
680   In vain the snake slides through the creepers and logs,
In vain the elk takes to the inner passes of the woods,
In vain the razor-bill'd auk sails far north to Labrador,
I follow quickly, I ascend to the nest in the fissure of the cliff.

32

I think I could turn and live with animals, they're so placid and self-contain'd,
I stand and look at them long and long.

They do not sweat and whine about their condition,
They do not lie awake in the dark and weep for their sins,
They do not make me sick discussing their duty to God,
Not one is dissatisfied, not one is demented with the mania of owning things,
Not one kneels to another, nor to his kind that lived thousands of years ago,   690
Not one is respectable or unhappy over the whole earth.

So they show their relations to me and I accept them,
They bring me tokens of myself, they evince them plainly in their possession.

I wonder where they get those tokens,
Did I pass that way huge times ago and negligently drop them?

Myself moving forward then and now and forever,
Gathering and showing more always and with velocity,
Infinite and omnigenous, and the like of these among them,
Not too exclusive toward the reachers of my remembrancers,
Picking out here one that I love, and now go with him on brotherly terms.   700

A gigantic beauty of a stallion, fresh and responsive to my caresses,
Head high in the forehead, wide between the ears,
Limbs glossy and supple, tail dusting the ground,
Eyes full of sparkling wickedness, ears finely cut, flexibly moving.

His nostrils dilate as my heels embrace him,
His well-built limbs tremble with pleasure as we race around and return.

I but use you a minute, then I resign you, stallion,
Why do I need your paces when I myself out-gallop them?
Even as I stand or sit passing faster than you.

33
Space and Time! now I see it is true, what I guess'd at,   710
What I guess'd when I loaf'd on the grass,
What I guess'd while I lay alone in my bed,
And again as I walk'd the beach under the paling stars of the morning.

My ties and ballasts leave me, my elbows rest in sea-gaps,
I skirt sierras, my palms cover continents,
I am afoot with my vision.
By the city's quadrangular houses—in log huts, camping with lumbermen,
Along the ruts of the turnpike, along the dry gulch and rivulet bed,
Weeding my onion-patch or hoeing rows of carrots and parsnips, crossing savan-
     nas, trailing in forests,
Prospecting, gold-digging, girdling the trees of a new purchase,   720
Scorch'd ankle-deep by the hot sand, hauling my boat down the shallow river,
Where the panther walks to and fro on a limb overhead, where the buck turns
     furiously at the hunter,

Where the rattlesnake suns his flabby length on a rock, where the otter is feed-
ing on fish,
Where the alligator in his tough pimples sleeps by the bayou,
Where the black bear is searching for roots or honey, where the beaver pats the
mud with his paddle-shaped tail;
Over the growing sugar, over the yellow-flower'd cotton plant, over the rice in
its low moist field,
Over the sharp-peak'd farm house, with its scallop'd scum and slender shoots
from the gutters,
Over the western persimmon, over the long-leav'd corn, over the delicate blue-
flower flax,
Over the white and brown buckwheat, a hummer and buzzer there with the rest,
730 Over the dusky green of the rye as it ripples and shades in the breeze;
Scaling mountains, pulling myself cautiously up, holding on by low scragged
limbs,
Walking the path worn in the grass and beat through the leaves of the brush,
Where the quail is whistling betwixt the woods and the wheat-lot,
Where the bat flies in the Seventh-month eve, where the great gold-bug drops
through the dark,
Where the brook puts out of the roots of the old tree and flows to the meadow,
Where cattle stand and shake away flies with the tremulous shuddering of their
hides,
Where the cheese-cloth hangs in the kitchen, where andirons straddle the hearth-
slab, where cobwebs fall in festoons from the rafters;
Where trip-hammers crash, where the press is whirling its cylinders,
Where the human heart beats with terrible throes under its ribs,
740 Where the pear-shaped balloon is floating aloft, (floating in it myself and look-
ing composedly down,)
Where the life-car is drawn on the slip-noose, where the heat hatches pale-green
eggs in the dented sand,
Where the she-whale swims with her calf and never forsakes it,
Where the steam-ship trails hind-ways its long pennant of smoke,
Where the fin of the shark cuts like a black chip out of the water,
Where the half-burn'd brig is riding on unknown currents,
Where shells grow to her slimy deck, where the dead are corrupting below;
Where the dense-starr'd flag is borne at the head of the regiments,
Approaching Manhattan up by the long-stretching island,
Under Niagara, the cataract falling like a veil over my countenance,
750 Upon a door-step, upon the horse-block of hard wood outside,
Upon the race-course, or enjoying picnics or jigs or a good game of base-ball,
At he-festivals, with blackguard jibes, ironical license, bull-dances, drinking,
laughter,
At the cider-mill tasting the sweets of the brown mash, sucking the juice through
a straw,
At apple-peelings wanting kisses for all the red fruit I find,
At musters, beach-parties, friendly bees, huskings, house-raisings;
Where the mocking-bird sounds his delicious gurgles, cackles, screams, weeps,

Where the hay-rick stands in the barn-yard, where the dry-stalks are scatter'd,
    where the brood-cow waits in the hovel,
Where the bull advances to do his masculine work, where the stud to the mare,
    where the cock is treading the hen,
Where the heifers browse, where geese nip their food with short jerks,
Where sun-down shadows lengthen over the limitless and lonesome prairie,   760
Where herds of buffalo make a crawling spread of the square miles far and near,
Where the humming-bird shimmers, where the neck of the long-lived swan is
    curving and winding,
Where the laughing-gull scoots by the shore, where she laughs her near-human
    laugh,
Where bee-hives range on a gray bench in the garden half hid by the high weeds,
Where band-neck'd partridges roost in a ring on the ground with their heads
    out,
Where burial coaches enter the arch'd gates of a cemetery,
Where winter wolves bark amidst wastes of snow and icicled trees,
Where the yellow-crown'd heron comes to the edge of the marsh at night and
    feeds upon small crabs,
Where the splash of swimmers and divers cools the warm noon,
Where the katy-did works her chromatic reed on the walnut-tree over the well,   770
Through patches of citrons and cucumbers with silver-wired leaves,
Through the salt-lick or orange glade, or under conical firs,
Through the gymnasium, through the curtain'd saloon, through the office or
    public hall;
Pleas'd with the native and pleas'd with the foreign, pleas'd with the new and
    old,
Pleas'd with the homely woman as well as the handsome,
Pleas'd with the quakeress as she puts off her bonnet and talks melodiously,
Pleas'd with the tune of the choir of the whitewash'd church,
Pleas'd with the earnest words of the sweating Methodist preacher, impress'd
    seriously at the camp-meeting;
Looking in at the shop-windows of Broadway the whole forenoon, flatting the
    flesh of my nose on the thick plate glass,
Wandering the same afternoon with my face turn'd up to the clouds, or down a
    lane or along the beach,   780
My right and left arms round the sides of two friends, and I in the middle;
Coming home with the silent and dark-cheek'd bush-boy, (behind me he rides at
    the drape of the day,)
Far from the settlements studying the print of animals' feet, or the moccasin
    print,
By the cot in the hospital reaching lemonade to a feverish patient,
Nigh the coffin'd corpse when all is still, examining with a candle;
Voyaging to every port to dicker and adventure,
Hurrying with the modern crowd as eager and fickle as any,
Hot toward one I hate, ready in my madness to knife him,
Solitary at midnight in my back yard, my thoughts gone from me a long while,
Walking the old hills of Judæa with the beautiful gentle God by my side,   790

Speeding through space, speeding through heaven and the stars,
Speeding amid the seven satellites and the broad ring, and the diameter of eighty
    thousand miles,
Speeding with tail'd meteors, throwing fire-balls like the rest,
Carrying the crescent child that carries its own full mother in its belly,
Storming, enjoying, planning, loving, cautioning,
Backing and filling, appearing and disappearing,
I tread day and night such roads.

I visit the orchards of spheres and look at the product,
And look at quintillions ripen'd and look at quintillions green.

800   I fly those flights of a fluid and swallowing soul,
My course runs below the soundings of plummets.

I help myself to material and immaterial,
No guard can shut me off, no law prevent me.

I anchor my ship for a little while only,
My messengers continually cruise away or bring their returns to me.

I go hunting polar furs and the seal, leaping chasms with a pike-pointed staff,
    clinging to topples of brittle and blue.

I ascend to the foretruck,
I take my place late at night in the crow's nest,
We sail the arctic sea, it is plenty light enough,
810   Through the clear atmosphere I stretch around on the wonderful beauty,
The enormous masses of ice pass me and I pass them, the scenery is plain in all
    directions,
The white-topt mountains show in the distance, I fling out my fancies toward
    them,
We are approaching some great battle-field in which we are soon to be engaged,
We pass the colossal outposts of the encampment, we pass with still feet and
    caution,
Or we are entering by the suburbs some vast and ruin'd city,
The blocks and fallen architecture more than all the living cities of the globe.

I am a free companion, I bivouac by invading watchfires,
I turn the bridegroom out of bed and stay with the bride myself,
I tighten her all night to my thighs and lips.

820   My voice is the wife's voice, the screech by the rail of the stairs,
They fetch my man's body up dripping and drown'd.

I understand the large hearts of heroes,
The courage of present times and all times,

How the skipper saw the crowded and rudderless wreck of the steamship, and
    Death chasing it up and down the storm,
How he knuckled tight and gave not back an inch, and was faithful of days and
    faithful of nights,
And chalk'd in large letters on a board, *Be of good cheer, we will not desert
    you;*
How he follow'd with them and tack'd with them three days and would not give
    it up,
How he saved the drifting company at last,
How the lank loose-gown'd women look'd when boated from the side of their
    prepared graves,
How the silent old-faced infants and the lifted sick, and the sharp-lipp'd un-
    shaven men;   830
All this I swallow, it tastes good, I like it well, it becomes mine,
I am the man, I suffer'd, I was there.

The disdain and calmness of martyrs,
The mother of old, condemn'd for a witch, burnt with dry wood, her children
    gazing on,
The hounded slave that flags in the race, leans by the fence, blowing, cover'd
    with sweat,
The twinges that sting like needles his legs and neck, the murderous buckshot
    and the bullets,
All these I feel or am.

I am the hounded slave, I wince at the bite of the dogs,
Hell and despair are upon me, crack and again crack the marksmen,
I clutch the rails of the fence, my gore dribs, thinn'd with the ooze of my skin,   840
I fall on the weeds and stones,
The riders spur their unwilling horses, haul close,
Taunt my dizzy ears and beat me violently over the head with whip-stocks.

Agonies are one of my changes of garments.
I do not ask the wounded person how he feels, I myself become the wounded
    person,
My hurts turn livid upon me as I lean on a cane and observe.

I am the mash'd fireman with breast-bone broken,
Tumbling walls buried me in their debris,
Heat and smoke I inspired, I heard the yelling shouts of my comrades,
I heard the distant click of their picks and shovels,   850
They have clear'd the beams away, they tenderly lift me forth.
I lie in the night air in my red shirt, the pervading hush is for my sake,
Painless after all I lie exhausted but not so unhappy,
White and beautiful are the faces around me, the heads are bared of their fire-
    caps,
The kneeling crowd fades with the light of the torches.

Distant and dead resuscitate,
They show as the dial or move as the hands of me, I am the clock myself.

I am an old artillerist, I tell of my fort's bombardment,
I am there again.

860   Again the long roll of the drummers,
Again the attacking cannon, mortars,
Again to my listening ears the cannon responsive.

I take part, I see and hear the whole,
The cries, curses, roar, the plaudits for well-aim'd shots,
The ambulanza slowly passing trailing its red drip,
Workmen searching after damages, making indispensable repairs,
The fall of grenades through the rent roof, the fan-shaped explosion,
The whizz of limbs, heads, stone, wood, iron, high in the air.

Again gurgles the mouth of my dying general, he furiously waves with his hand,
870   He gasps through the clot *Mind not me—mind—the entrenchments.*

34

Now I tell what I knew in Texas in my early youth,
(I tell not the fall of Alamo,
Not one escaped to tell the fall of Alamo,
The hundred and fifty are dumb yet at Alamo,)
'Tis the tale of the murder in cold blood of four hundred and twelve young
     men.

Retreating they had form'd in a hollow square with their baggage for breast-
     works,
Nine hundred lives out of the surrounding enemy's, nine times their number,
     was the price they took in advance,
Their colonel was wounded and their ammunition gone,
They treated for an honorable capitulation, receiv'd writing and seal, gave up
     their arms and march'd back prisoners of war.

880   They were the glory of the race of rangers,
Matchless with horse, rifle, song, supper, courtship,
Large, turbulent, generous, handsome, proud, and affectionate,
Bearded, sunburnt, drest in the free costume of hunters,
Not a single one over thirty years of age.

The second First-day morning they were brought out in squads and massacred,
     it was beautiful early summer,
The work commenced about five o'clock and was over by eight.

None obey'd the command to kneel,
Some made a mad and helpless rush, some stood stark and straight,

A few fell at once, shot in the temple or heart, the living and dead lay together,
The maim'd and mangled dug in the dirt, the new-comers saw them there,   890
Some half-kill'd attempted to crawl away,
These were despatch'd with bayonets or batter'd with the blunts of muskets.
A youth not seventeen years old seiz'd his assassin till two more came to release
    him,
The three were all torn and cover'd with the boy's blood.

At eleven o'clock began the burning of the bodies;
That is the tale of the murder of the four hundred and twelve young men.

35

Would you hear of an old-time sea-fight?
Would you learn who won by the light of the moon and stars?
List to the yarn, as my grandmother's father the sailor told it to me.

Our foe was no skulk in his ship I tell you, (said he,)   900
His was the surly English pluck, and there is no tougher or truer, and never
    was, and never will be;
Along the lower'd eve he came horribly raking us.

We closed with him, the yards entangled, the cannon touch'd,
My captain lash'd fast with his own hands.

We had receiv'd some eighteen pound shots under the water,
On our lower-gun-deck two large pieces had burst at the first fire, killing all
    around and blowing up overhead.

Fighting at sun-down, fighting at dark,
Ten o'clock at night, the full moon well up, our leaks on the gain, and five feet
    of water reported,
The master-at-arms loosing the prisoners confined in the after-hold to give them
    a chance for themselves.

The transit to and from the magazine is now stopt by the sentinels,   910
They see so many strange faces they do not know whom to trust.

Our frigate takes fire,
The other asks if we demand quarter?
If our colors are struck and the fighting done?

Now I laugh content, for I hear the voice of my little captain,
We have not struck, he composedly cries, *we have just begun our part of the
    fighting.*

Only three guns are in use,
One is directed by the captain himself against the enemy's main-mast,
Two well serv'd with grape and canister silence his musketry and clear his decks.

920 The tops alone second the fire of this little battery, especially the main-top,
They hold out bravely during the whole of the action.

Not a moment's cease,
The leaks gain fast on the pumps, the fire eats toward the powder-magazine.

One of the pumps has been shot away, it is generally thought we are sinking.

Serene stands the little captain,
He is not hurried, his voice is neither high nor low,
His eyes give more light to us than our battle-lanterns.

Toward twelve there in the beams of the moon they surrender to us.

36

Stretch'd and still lies the midnight,
930 Two great hulls motionless on the breast of the darkness,
Our vessel riddled and slowly sinking, preparations to pass to the one we have
    conquer'd,
The captain on the quarter-deck coldly giving his orders through a countenance
    white as a sheet,
Near by the corpse of the child that serv'd in the cabin,
The dead face of an old salt with long white hair and carefully curl'd whiskers,
The flames spite of all that can be done flickering aloft and below,
The husky voices of the two or three officers yet fit for duty,
Formless stacks of bodies and bodies by themselves, dabs of flesh upon the
    masts and spars,
Cut of cordage, dangle of rigging, slight shock of the soothe of waves,
Black and impassive guns, litter of powder-parcels, strong scent,
940 A few large stars overhead, silent and mournful shining,
Delicate sniffs of sea-breeze, smells of sedgy grass and fields by the shore, death-
    messages given in charge to survivors,
The hiss of the surgeon's knife, the gnawing teeth of his saw,
Wheeze, cluck, swash of falling blood, short wild scream, and long, dull, taper-
    ing groan,
These so, these irretrievable.

37

You laggards there on guard! look to your arms!
In at the conquer'd doors they crowd! I am possess'd!
Embody all presences outlaw'd or suffering,
See myself in prison shaped like another man,
And feel the dull unintermitted pain,

950 For me the keepers of convicts shoulder their carbines and keep watch,
It is I let out in the morning and barr'd at night.

Not a mutineer walks handcuff'd to jail but I am handcuff'd to him and walk by
    his side,
(I am less the jolly one there, and more the silent one with sweat on my twitch-
    ing lips.)

Not a youngster is taken for larceny but I go up too, and am tried and sentenced.

Not a cholera patient lies at the last gasp but I also lie at the last gasp,
My face is ash-color'd, my sinews gnarl, away from me people retreat.

Askers embody themselves in me and I am embodied in them,
I project my hat, sit shame-faced, and beg.

38
Enough! enough! enough!
Somehow I have been stunn'd. Stand back!   960
Give me a little time beyond my cuff'd head, slumbers, dreams, gaping,
I discover myself on the verge of a usual mistake.

That I could forget the mockers and insults!
That I could forget the trickling tears and the blows of the bludgeons and
    hammers!
That I could look with a separate look on my own crucifixion and bloody crown-
    ing!

I remember now,
I resume the overstaid fraction,
The grave of rock multiplies what has been confided to it, or to any graves,
Corpses rise, gashes heal, fastenings roll from me.

I troop forth replenish'd with supreme power, one of an average unending
    procession,   970
Inland and sea-coast we go, and pass all boundary lines,
Our swift ordinances on their way over the whole earth,
The blossoms we wear in our hats the growth of thousands of years.

Eleves, I salute you! come forward!
Continue your annotations, continue your questionings.

39
The friendly and flowing savage, who is he?
Is he waiting for civilization, or past it and mastering it?

Is he some Southwesterner rais'd out-doors? is he Kanadian?
Is he from the Mississippi country? Iowa, Oregon, California?
The mountains? prairie-life, bush-life? or sailor from the sea?   980

Wherever he goes men and women accept and desire him,
They desire he should like them, touch them, speak to them, stay with them.

Behavior lawless as snow-flakes, words simple as grass, uncomb'd head, laughter,
    and naïveté,
Slow-stepping feet, common features, common modes and emanations,
They descend in new forms from the tips of his fingers,
They are wafted with the odor of his body or breath, they fly out of the glance of
    his eyes.

40
Flaunt of the sunshine I need not your bask—lie over!
You light surfaces only, I force surfaces and depths also.

Earth! you seem to look for something at my hands,
990   Say, old top-knot, what do you want?

Man or woman, I might tell how I like you, but cannot,
And might tell what it is in me and what it is in you, but cannot,
And might tell that pining I have, that pulse of my nights and days.

Behold, I do not give lectures or a little charity,
When I give I give myself.

You there, impotent, loose in the knees,
Open your scarf'd chops till I blow grit within you,
Spread your palms and lift the flaps of your pockets,
I am not to be denied, I compel, I have stores plenty and to spare,
1000 And any thing I have I bestow.

I do not ask who you are, that is not important to me,
You can do nothing and be nothing but what I will infold you.

To cotton-field drudge or cleaner of privies I lean,
On his right cheek I put the family kiss,
And in my soul I swear I never will deny him.

On women fit for conception I start bigger and nimbler babes,
(This day I am jetting the stuff of far more arrogant republics.)

To any one dying, thither I speed and twist the knob of the door,
Turn the bed-clothes toward the foot of the bed,
1010 Let the physician and the priest go home.

I seize the descending man and raise him with resistless will,
O despairer, here is my neck,
By God, you shall not go down! hang your whole weight upon me.

I dilate you with tremendous breath, I buoy you up,
Every room of the house do I fill with an arm'd force,
Lovers of me, bafflers of graves.

Sleep—I and they keep guard all night,
Not doubt, not disease shall dare to lay finger upon you,
I have embraced you, and henceforth possess you to myself,
And when you rise in the morning you will find what I tell you is so.   1020

41
I am he bringing help for the sick as they pant on their backs,
And for strong upright men I bring yet more needed help.

I heard what was said of the universe,
Heard it and heard it of several thousand years;
It is middling well as far as it goes—but is that all?

Magnifying and applying come I,
Outbidding at the start the old cautious hucksters,
Taking myself the exact dimensions of Jehovah,
Lithographing Kronos, Zeus his son, and Hercules his grandson,
Buying drafts of Osiris, Isis, Belus, Brahma, Buddha,   1030
In my portfolio placing Manito loose, Allah on a leaf, the crucifix engraved,
With Odin and the hideous-faced Mexitli and every idol and image,
Taking them all for what they are worth and not a cent more,
Admitting they were alive and did the work of their days,
(They bore mites as for unfledg'd birds who have now to rise and fly and sing
    for themselves,)
Accepting the rough deific sketches to fill out better in myself, bestowing them
    freely on each man and woman I see,
Discovering as much or more in a framer framing a house,
Putting higher claims for him there with his roll'd-up sleeves driving the mallet
    and chisel,
Not objecting to special revelations, considering a curl of smoke or a hair on the
    back of my hand just as curious as any revelation,
Lads ahold of fire-engines and hook-and-ladder ropes no less to me than the gods
    of the antique wars,   1040
Minding their voices peal through the crash of destruction,
Their brawny limbs passing safe over charr'd laths, their white foreheads whole
    and unhurt out of the flames;
By the mechanic's wife with her babe at her nipple interceding for every person
    born,
Three scythes at harvest whizzing in a row from three lusty angels with shirts
    bagg'd out at their waists,
The snag-tooth'd hostler with red hair redeeming sins past and to come,
Selling all he possesses, traveling on foot to fee lawyers for his brother and sit by
    him while he is tried for forgery;

What was strewn in the amplest strewing the square rod about me, and not fill-
    ing the square rod then,
The bull and the bug never worshipp'd half enough,
Dung and dirt more admirable than was dream'd,
1050   The supernatural of no account, myself waiting my time to be one of the
    supremes,
The day getting ready for me when I shall do as much good as the best, and be
    as prodigious;
By my life-lumps! becoming already a creator,
Putting myself here and now to the ambush'd womb of the shadows.

42
A call in the midst of the crowd,
My own voice, orotund sweeping and final.

Come my children,
Come my boys and girls, my women, household and intimates,
Now the performer launches his nerve, he has pass'd his prelude on the reeds
    within.

Easily written loose-finger'd chords—I feel the thrum of your climax and close.

1060   My head slues round on my neck,
Music rolls, but not from the organ,
Folks are around me, but they are no household of mine.

Ever the hard unsunk ground,
Ever the eaters and drinkers, ever the upward and downward sun, ever the air
    and the ceaseless tides,
Ever myself and my neighbors, refreshing, wicked, real,
Ever the old inexplicable query, ever that thorn'd thumb, that breath of itches
    and thirsts,
Ever the vexer's *hoot! hoot!* till we find where the sly one hides and bring him
    forth,
Ever love, ever the sobbing liquid of life,
Ever the bandage under the chin, ever the trestles of death.

1070   Here and there with dimes on the eyes walking,
To feed the greed of the belly of the brains liberally spooning,
Tickets buying, taking, selling, but in to the feast never once going,
Many sweating, ploughing, thrashing, and then the chaff for payment receiving,
A few idly owning, and they the wheat continually claiming.

This is the city and I am one of the citizens,
Whatever interests the rest interests me, politics, wars, markets, newspapers,
    schools,
The mayor and councils, banks, tariffs, steamships, factories, stocks, stores, real
    estate and personal estate.

The little plentiful manikins skipping around in collars and tail'd coats,
I am aware who they are, (they are positively not worms or fleas,)
I acknowledge the duplicates of myself, the weakest and shallowest is deathless
     with me,   1080
What I do and say the same waits for them,
Every thought that flounders in me the same flounders in them.

I know perfectly well my own egotism,
Know my omnivorous lines and must not write any less,
And would fetch you whoever you are flush with myself.

Not words of routine this song of mine,
But abruptly to question, to leap beyond yet nearer bring;
This printed and bound book—but the printer and the printing-office boy?
The well-taken photographs—but your wife or friend close and solid in your
     arms?
The black ship mail'd with iron, her mighty guns in her turrets—but the pluck
     of the captain and engineers?   1090
In the houses the dishes and fare and furniture—but the host and hostess, and
     the look out of their eyes?
The sky up there—yet here or next door, or across the way?
The saints and sages in history—but you yourself?
Sermons, creeds, theology—but the fathomless human brain,
And what is reason? and what is love? and what is life?

43

I do not despise you priests, all time, the world over,
My faith is the greatest of faiths and the least of faiths,
Enclosing worship ancient and modern and all between ancient and
     modern,
Believing I shall come again upon the earth after five thousand years,
Waiting responses from oracles, honoring the gods, saluting the sun,   1100
Making a fetich of the first rock or stump, powowing with sticks in the circle
     of obis,
Helping the llama or brahmin as he trims the lamps of the idols,
Dancing yet through the streets in a phallic procession, rapt and austere in the
     woods a gymnosophist,
Drinking mead from the skull-cup, to Shastas and Vedas admirant, minding the
     Koran,
Walking the teokallis, spotted with gore from the stone and knife, beating the
     serpent-skin drum,
Accepting the Gospels, accepting him that was crucified, knowing assuredly that
     he is divine,
To the mass kneeling or the puritan's prayer rising, or sitting patiently in a pew,
Ranting and frothing in my insane crisis, or waiting dead-like till my spirit
     arouses me,
Looking forth on pavement and land, or outside of pavement and land,
Belonging to the winders of the circuit of circuits.   1110

One of that centripetal and centrifugal gang I turn and talk like a man leaving
    charges before a journey.

Down-hearted doubters dull and excluded,
Frivolous, sullen, moping, angry, affected, dishearten'd, atheistical,
I know every one of you, I know the sea of torment, doubt, despair and unbelief.

How the flukes splash!
How they contort rapid as lightning, with spasms and spouts of blood!

Be at peace bloody flukes of doubters and sullen mopers,
I take my place among you as much as among any,
The past is the push of you, me, all, precisely the same,
1120   And what is yet untried and afterward is for you, me, all precisely the same.

I do not know what is untried and afterward,
But I know it will in its turn prove sufficient, and cannot fail.
Each who passes is consider'd, each who stops is consider'd, not a single one can
    it fail.

It cannot fail the young man who died and was buried,
Nor the young woman who died and was put by his side,
Nor the little child that peep'd in at the door and then drew back and was never
    seen again,
Nor the old man who has lived without purpose, and feels it with bitterness
    worse than gall,
Nor him in the poor house tubercled by rum and the bad disorder,
Nor the numberless slaughter'd and wreck'd, nor the brutish koboo call'd the
    ordure of humanity,
1130   Nor the sacs merely floating with open mouths for food to slip in,
Nor any thing in the earth, or down in the oldest graves of the earth,
Nor any thing in the myriads of spheres, nor the myriads of myriads that in-
    habit them,
Nor the present, nor the least wisp that is known.

44
It is time to explain myself—let us stand up.

What is known I strip away,
I launch all men and women forward with me into the Unknown.

The clock indicates the moment—but what does eternity indicate?

We have thus far exhausted trillions of winters and summers,
There are trillions ahead, and trillions ahead of them.

1140   Births have brought us richness and variety,
And other births will bring us richness and variety.

I do not call one greater and one smaller,
That which fills its period and place is equal to any.

Were mankind murderous or jealous upon you, my brother, my sister?
I am sorry for you, they are not murderous or jealous upon me,
All has been gentle with me, I keep no account with lamentation,
(What have I to do with lamentation?)

I am an acme of things accomplish'd, and I an encloser of things to be.

My feet strike an apex of the apices of the stairs,
On every step bunches of ages, and larger bunches between the steps,   1150
All below duly travel'd, and still I mount and mount.

Rise after rise bow the phantoms behind me,
Afar down I see the huge first Nothing, I know I was even there,
I waited unseen and always, and slept through the lethargic mist,
And took my time, and took no hurt from the fetid carbon.

Long I was hugg'd close—long and long.

Immense have been the preparations for me,
Faithful and friendly the arms that have help'd me.

Cycles ferried my cradle, rowing and rowing like cheerful boatmen,
For room to me stars kept aside in their own rings,   1160
They sent influences to look after what was to hold me.

Before I was born out of my mother generations guided me,
My embryo has never been torpid, nothing could overlay it.

For it the nebula cohered to an orb,
The long slow strata piled to rest it on,
Vast vegetables gave it sustenance,
Monstrous sauroids transported it in their mouths and deposited it with care.

All forces have been steadily employ'd to complete and delight me,
Now on this spot I stand with my robust soul.

45
O span of youth! ever-push'd elasticity.   1170
O manhood, balanced, florid and full.

My lovers suffocate me,
Crowding my lips, thick in the pores of my skin,
Jostling me through streets and public halls, coming naked to me at night,
Crying by day *Ahoy!* from the rocks of the river, swinging and chirping over
    my head,

Calling my name from flower-beds, vines, tangled underbrush,
Lighting on every moment of my life,
Bussing my body with soft balsamic busses,
Noiselessly passing handfuls out of their hearts and giving them to be mine.

1180 Old age superbly rising! O welcome, ineffable grace of dying days!

Every condition promulges not only itself, it promulges what grows after and
out of itself,
And the dark hush promulges as much as any.

I open my scuttle at night and see the far-sprinkled systems,
And all I see multiplied as high as I can cipher edge but the rim of the farther
systems.

Wider and wider they spread, expanding, always expanding,
Outward and outward and forever outward.

My sun has his sun and round him obediently wheels,
He joins with his partners a group of superior circuit,
And greater sets follow, making specks of the greatest inside them.

1190 There is no stoppage and never can be stoppage,
If I, you, and the worlds, and all beneath or upon their surfaces, were this mo-
ment reduced back to a pallid float, it would not avail in the long run,
We should surely bring up again where we now stand,
And surely go as much farther, and then farther and farther.

A few quadrillions of eras, a few octillions of cubic leagues, do not hazard the
span or make it impatient,
They are but parts, any thing is but a part.

See ever so far, there is limitless space outside of that,
Count ever so much, there is limitless time around that.

My rendezvous is appointed, it is certain,
The Lord will be there and wait till I come on perfect terms,
1200 The great Camerado, the lover true for whom I pine will be there.

46
I know I have the best of time and space, and was never measured and never
will be measured.

I tramp a perpetual journey, (come listen all!)
My signs are a rain-proof coat, good shoes, and a staff cut from the woods.
No friend of mine takes his ease in my chair,
I have no chair, no church, no philosophy,

I lead no man to a dinner-table, library, exchange,
But each man and each woman of you I lead upon a knoll,
My left hand hooking you around the waist,
My right hand pointing to landscapes of continents and the public road.

Not I, not any one else can travel that road for you,   1210
You must travel it for yourself.

It is not far, it is within reach,
Perhaps you have been on it since you were born and did not know,
Perhaps it is everywhere on water and on land.

Shoulder your duds dear son, and I will mine, and let us hasten forth,
Wonderful cities and free nations we shall fetch as we go.

If you tire, give me both burdens, and rest the chuff of your hand on my hip,
And in due time you shall repay the same service to me,
For after we start we never lie by again.

This day before dawn I ascended a hill and look'd at the crowded heaven,   1220
And I said to my spirit *When we become the enfolders of those orbs, and the
    pleasure and knowledge of every thing in them, shall we be fill'd and satis-
    fied then?*
And my spirit said *No, we but level that lift to pass and continue beyond.*

You are also asking me questions and I hear you,
I answer that I cannot answer, you must find out for yourself.

Sit a while dear son,
Here are biscuits to eat and here is milk to drink,
But as soon as you sleep and renew yourself in sweet clothes, I kiss you with a
    good-by kiss and open the gate for your egress hence.

Long enough have you dream'd contemptible dreams,
Now I wash the gum from your eyes,
You must habit yourself to the dazzle of the light and of every moment of your
    life.   1230

Long have you timidly waded holding a plank by the shore,
Now I will you to be a bold swimmer,
To jump off in the midst of the sea, rise again, nod to me, shout, and laughingly
    dash with your hair.

47

I am the teacher of athletes,
He that by me spreads a wider breast than my own proves the width of my own,
He most honors my style who learns under it to destroy the teacher.

The boy I love, the same becomes a man not through derived power, but in his
    own right,
Wicked rather than virtuous out of conformity or fear,
Fond of his sweetheart, relishing well his steak,
1240   Unrequited love or a slight cutting him worse than sharp steel cuts,
First-rate to ride, to fight, to hit the bull's eye, to sail a skiff, to sing a song, or
    play on the banjo,
Preferring scars and the beard and faces pitted with small-pox over all latherers,
And those well-tann'd to those that keep out of the sun.

I teach straying from me, yet who can stray from me?
I follow you whoever you are from the present hour,
My words itch at your ears till you understand them.

I do not say these things for a dollar or to fill up the time while I wait for a boat,
(It is you talking just as much as myself, I act as the tongue of you,
Tied in your mouth, in mine it begins to be loosen'd.)

1250   I swear I will never again mention love or death inside a house,
And I swear I will never translate myself at all, only to him or her who privately
    stays with me in the open air.

If you would understand me go to the heights or water-shore,
The nearest gnat is an explanation, and a drop or motion of waves a key,
The maul, the oar, the hand-saw, second my words.

No shutter'd room or school can commune with me,
But roughs and little children better than they.

The young mechanic is closest to me, he knows me well,
The woodman that takes his axe and jug with him shall take me with him all
    day,
The farm-boy ploughing in the field feels good at the sound of my voice,
1260   In vessels that sail my words sail, I go with fishermen and seamen and love them.

The soldier camp'd or upon the march is mine,
On the night ere the pending battle many seek me, and I do not fail them,
On that solemn night (it may be their last) those that know me seek me.

My face rubs to the hunter's face when he lies down alone in his blanket,
The driver thinking of me does not mind the jolt of his wagon,
The young mother and old mother comprehend me,
The girl and the wife rest the needle a moment and forget where they are,
They and all would resume what I have told them.

48
I have said that the soul is not more than the body,
1270   And I have said that the body is not more than the soul,

And nothing, not God, is greater to one than one's self is,
And whoever walks a furlong without sympathy walks to his own funeral drest in
  his shroud,
And I or you pocketless of a dime may purchase the pick of the earth,
And to glance with an eye or show a bean in its pod confounds the learning of all
  times,
And there is no trade or employment but the young man following it may be-
  come a hero,
And there is no object so soft but it makes a hub for the wheel'd universe,
And I say to any man or woman, Let your soul stand cool and composed before
  a million universes.

And I say to mankind, Be not curious about God,
For I who am curious about each am not curious about God,
(No array of terms can say how much I am at peace about God and about
  death.)   1280

I hear and behold God in every object, yet understand God not in the least,
Nor do I understand who there can be more wonderful than myself.

Why should I wish to see God better than this day?
I see something of God each hour of the twenty-four, and each moment then,
In the faces of men and women I see God, and in my own face in the glass,
I find letters from God dropt in the street, and every one is sign'd by God's
  name,
And I leave them where they are, for I know that wheresoe'er I go,
Others will punctually come for ever and ever.

49
And as to you Death, and you bitter hug of mortality, it is idle to try to alarm
  me.

To his work without flinching the accoucheur comes,   1290
I see the elder-hand pressing receiving supporting,
I recline by the sills of the exquisite flexible doors,
And mark the outlet, and mark the relief and escape.

And as to you Corpse I think you are good manure, but that does not offend
  me,
I smell the white roses sweet-scented and growing,
I reach to the leafy lips, I reach to the polish'd breasts of melons.

And as to you Life I reckon you are the leavings of many deaths,
(No doubt I have died myself ten thousand times before.)

I hear you whispering there O stars of heaven,
O suns—O grass of graves—O perpetual transfers and promotions,   1300
If you do not say any thing how can I say any thing?

Of the turbid pool that lies in the autumn forest,
Of the moon that descends the steeps of the soughing twilight,
Toss, sparkles of day and dusk—toss on the black stems that decay in the muck,
Toss to the moaning gibberish of the dry limbs.

I ascend from the moon, I ascend from the night,
I perceive that the ghastly glimmer is noonday sunbeams reflected,
And debouch to the steady and central from the offspring great or small.

50
There is that in me—I do not know what it is—but I know it is in me.

1310 Wrench'd and sweaty—calm and cool then my body becomes,
I sleep—I sleep long.

I do not know it—it is without name—it is a word unsaid,
It is not in any dictionary, utterance, symbol.

Something it swings on more than the earth I swing on,
To it the creation is the friend whose embracing awakes me.

Perhaps I might tell more. Outlines! I plead for my brothers and sisters.
Do you see O my brothers and sisters?

It is not chaos or death—it is form, union, plan—it is eternal life—it is Happiness.

51
The past and present wilt—I have fill'd them, emptied them,
1320 And proceed to fill my next fold of the future.

Listener up there! what have you to confide to me?
Look in my face while I snuff the sidle of evening,
(Talk honestly, no one else hears you, and I stay only a minute longer.)

Do I contradict myself?
Very well then I contradict myself,
(I am large, I contain multitudes.)

I concentrate toward them that are nigh, I wait on the door-slab.

Who has done his day's work? who will soonest be through with his supper?
Who wishes to walk with me?

1330 Will you speak before I am gone? will you prove already too late?

52
The spotted hawk swoops by and accuses me, he complains of my gab and my
  loitering.

I too am not a bit tamed, I too am untranslatable,
I sound my barbaric yawp over the roofs of the world.

The last scud of day holds back for me,
It flings my likeness after the rest and true as any on the shadow'd
    wilds,
It coaxes me to the vapor and the dusk.

I depart as air, I shake my white locks at the runaway sun,
I effuse my flesh in eddies, and drift it in lacy jags.

I bequeath myself to the dirt to grow from the grass I love,
If you want me again look for me under your boot-soles.   1340

You will hardly know who I am or what I mean,
But I shall be good health to you nevertheless,
And filter and fibre your blood.

Failing to fetch me at first keep encouraged,
Missing me one place search another,
I stop somewhere waiting for you.
1855·1881

CROSSING BROOKLYN FERRY

1

Flood-tide below me! I see you face to face!
Clouds of the west—sun there half an hour high—I see you also face to face.

Crowds of men and women attired in the usual costumes, how curious you are
    to me!
On the ferry-boats the hundreds and hundreds that cross, returning home, are
    more curious to me than you suppose,
And you that shall cross from shore to shore years hence are more to me, and
    more in my meditations, than you might suppose.

2

The impalpable sustenance of me from all things at all hours of the day,
The simple, compact, well-join'd scheme, myself disintegrated, every one dis-
    integrated yet part of the scheme,
The similitudes of the past and those of the future,
The glories strung like beads on my smallest sights and hearings, on the walk in
    the street and the passage over the river,
The current rushing so swiftly and swimming with me far away,   10

The others that are to follow me, the ties between me and them,
The certainty of others, the life, love, sight, hearing of others.

Others will enter the gates of the ferry and cross from shore to shore,
Others will watch the run of the flood-tide,
Others will see the shipping of Manhattan north and west, and the heights of
    Brooklyn to the south and east,
Others will see the islands large and small;
Fifty years hence, others will see them as they cross, the sun half an hour high,
A hundred years hence, or ever so many hundred years hence, others will see
    them,
Will enjoy the sunset, the pouring-in of the flood-tide, the falling-back to the sea
    of the ebb-tide.

3

20   It avails not, time nor place—distance avails not,
I am with you, you men and women of a generation, or ever so many genera-
    tions hence,
Just as you feel when you look on the river and sky, so I felt,
Just as any of you is one of a living crowd, I was one of a crowd,
Just as you are refresh'd by the gladness of the river and the bright flow, I was
    refresh'd,
Just as you stand and lean on the rail, yet hurry with the swift current, I stood
    yet was hurried,
Just as you look on the numberless masts of ships and the thick-stemm'd pipes of
    steamboats, I look'd.

I too many and many a time cross'd the river of old,
Watched the Twelfth-month sea-gulls, saw them high in the air floating with
    motionless wings, oscillating their bodies,
Saw how the glistening yellow lit up parts of their bodies and left the rest in
    strong shadow,
30   Saw the slow-wheeling circles and the gradual edging toward the south,
Saw the reflection of the summer sky in the water,
Had my eyes dazzled by the shimmering track of beams,
Look'd at the fine centrifugal spokes of light round the shape of my head in the
    sunlit water,
Look'd on the haze on the hills southward and south-westward,
Look'd on the vapor as it flew in fleeces tinged with violet,
Look'd toward the lower bay to notice the vessels arriving,
Saw their approach, saw aboard those that were near me,
Saw the white sails of schooners and sloops, saw the ships at anchor,
The sailors at work in the rigging or out astride the spars,
40   The round masts, the swinging motion of the hulls, the slender serpentine pen-
    nants,
The large and small steamers in motion, the pilots in their pilot-houses,
The white wake left by the passage, the quick tremulous whirl of the wheels,

The flags of all nations, the falling of them at sunset,
The scallop-edged waves in the twilight, the ladled cups, the frolicsome crests
    and glistening,
The stretch afar growing dimmer and dimmer, the gray walls of the granite
    storehouses by the docks,
On the river the shadowy group, the big steam-tug closely flank'd on each side
    by the barges, the hay-boat, the belated lighter,
On the neighboring shore the fires from the foundry chimneys burning high and
    glaringly into the night,
Casting their flicker of black contrasted with wild red and yellow light over the
    tops of houses, and down into the clefts of streets.

4

These and all else were to me the same as they are to you,
I loved well those cities, loved well the stately and rapid river,   50
The men and women I saw were all near to me,
Others the same—others who look back on me because I look'd forward to them,
(The time will come, though I stop here to-day and to-night.)

5

What is it then between us?
What is the count of the scores or hundreds of years between us?

Whatever it is, it avails not—distance avails not, and place avails not,
I too lived, Brooklyn of ample hills was mine,
I too walk'd the streets of Manhattan island, and bathed in the waters around it,
I too felt the curious abrupt questionings stir within me,
In the day among crowds of people sometimes they came upon me,   60
In my walks home late at night or as I lay in my bed they came upon me,
I too had been struck from the float forever held in solution,
I too had receiv'd identity by my body,
That I was I knew was of my body, and what I should be I knew I should be of
    my body.

6

It is not upon you alone the dark patches fall,
The dark threw its patches down upon me also,
The best I had done seem'd to me blank and suspicious,
My great thoughts as I supposed them, were they not in reality meagre?
Nor is it you alone who know what it is to be evil,
I am he who knew what it was to be evil,   70
I too knitted the old knot of contrariety,
Blabb'd, blush'd, resented, lied, stole, grudg'd,
Had guile, anger, lust, hot wishes I dared not speak,
Was wayward, vain, greedy, shallow, sly, cowardly, malignant,
The wolf, the snake, the hog, not wanting in me,
The cheating look, the frivolous word, the adulterous wish, not wanting,

Refusals, hates, postponements, meanness, laziness, none of these wanting,
Was one with the rest, the days and haps of the rest,
Was call'd my nighest name by clear loud voices of young men as they saw me
    approaching or passing,
80   Felt their arms on my neck as I stood, or the negligent leaning of their flesh
    against me as I sat,
Saw many I loved in the street or ferry-boat or public assembly, yet never told
    them a word,
Lived the same life with the rest, the same old laughing, gnawing, sleeping,
Play'd the part that still looks back on the actor or actress,
The same old role, the role that is what we make it, as great as we like,
Or as small as we like, or both great and small.

7

Closer yet I approach you,
What thought you have of me now, I had as much of you—I laid in my stores in
    advance,
I consider'd long and seriously of you before you were born.
Who was to know what should come home to me?
90   Who knows but I am enjoying this?
Who knows, for all the distance, but I am as good as looking at you now, for all
    you cannot see me?

8

Ah, what can ever be more stately and admirable to me than mast-hemm'd Man-
    hattan?
River and sunset and scallop-edg'd waves of flood-tide?
The sea-gulls oscillating their bodies, the hay-boat in the twilight, and the be-
    lated lighter?

What gods can exceed these that clasp me by the hand, and with voices I love call
    me promptly and loudly by my nighest name as I approach?

What is more subtle than this which ties me to the woman or man that looks in
    my face?
Which fuses me into you now, and pours my meaning into you?

We understand then do we not?
What I promis'd without mentioning it, have you not accepted?
100 What the study could not teach—what the preaching could not accomplish is
    accomplish'd, is it not?

9

Flow on, river! flow with the flood-tide, and ebb with the ebb-tide!
Frolic on, crested and scallop-edg'd waves!
Gorgeous clouds of the sunset! drench with your splendor me, or the men and
    women generations after me!

Cross from shore to shore, countless crowds of passengers!
Stand up, tall masts of Mannahatta! stand up, beautiful hills of Brooklyn!
Throb, baffled and curious brain! throw out questions and answers!
Suspend here and everywhere, eternal float of solution!
Gaze, loving and thirsting eyes, in the house or street or public assembly!
Sound out, voices of young men! loudly and musically call me by my nighest
    name!
Live, old life! play the part that looks back on the actor or actress!   110
Play the old role, the role that is great or small according as one makes it!
Consider, you who peruse me, whether I may not in unknown ways be looking
    upon you;
Be firm, rail over the river, to support those who lean idly, yet haste with the
    hasting current;
Fly on, sea-birds! fly sideways, or wheel in large circles high in the air;
Receive the summer sky, you water, and faithfully hold it till all downcast eyes
    have time to take it from you!
Diverge, fine spokes of light, from the shape of my head, or any one's head, in
    the sunlit water!
Come on, ships from the lower bay! pass up or down, white-sail'd schooners,
    sloops, lighters!
Flaunt away, flags of all nations! be duly lower'd at sunset!
Burn high your fires, foundry chimneys! cast black shadows at nightfall! cast
    red and yellow light over the tops of the houses!
Appearances, now or henceforth, indicate what you are,   120
You necessary film, continue to envelop the soul,
About my body for me, and your body for you, be hung our divinest aromas,
Thrive, cities—bring your freight, bring your shows, ample and sufficient rivers,
Expand, being than which none else is perhaps more spiritual,
Keep your places, objects than which none else is more lasting.

You have waited, you always wait, you dumb, beautiful ministers,
We receive you with free sense at last, and are insatiate henceforward,
Not you any more shall be able to foil us, or withhold yourselves from us,
We use you,—and do not cast you aside—we plant you permanently within us,
We fathom you not—we love you—there is perfection in you also,   130
You furnish your parts toward eternity,
Great or small, you furnish your parts toward the soul.
1856·1881

I SING THE BODY ELECTRIC

1
I sing the body electric,
The armies of those I love engirth me and I engirth them,
They will not let me off till I go with them, respond to them,
And discorrupt them, and charge them full with the charge of the soul.

Was it doubted that those who corrupt their own bodies conceal themselves?
And if those who defile the living are as bad as they who defile the dead?
And if the body does not do fully as much as the soul?
And if the body were not the soul, what is the soul?

2
The love of the body of man or woman balks account, the body itself balks ac-
    count,
10   That of the male is perfect, and that of the female is perfect.

The expression of the face balks account,
But the expression of a well-made man appears not only in his face,
It is in his limbs and joints also, it is curiously in the joints of his hips and
    wrists,
It is in his walk, the carriage of his neck, the flex of his waist and knees, dress
    does not hide him,
The strong sweet quality he has strikes through the cotton and broadcloth,
To see him pass conveys as much as the best poem, perhaps more,
You linger to see his back, and the back of his neck and shoulder-side.

The sprawl and fulness of babes, the bosoms and heads of women, the folds of
    their dress, their style as we pass in the street, the contour of their shape
    downwards,
The swimmer naked in the swimming-bath, seen as he swims through the trans-
    parent green-shine, or lies with his face up and rolls silently to and fro in
    the heave of the water,
20   The bending forward and backward of rowers in row-boats, the horseman in his
    saddle,
Girls, mothers, house-keepers, in all their performances,
The group of laborers seated at noon-time with their open dinner kettles, and
    their wives waiting,
The female soothing a child, the farmer's daughter in the garden or cow-yard,
The young fellow hoeing corn, the sleigh-driver driving his six horses through
    the crowd,
The wrestle of wrestlers, two apprentice-boys, quite grown, lusty, good-natured,
    native-born, out on the vacant lot at sundown after work,
The coats and caps thrown down, the embrace of love and resistance,
The upper-hold and under-hold, the hair rumpled over and blinding the eyes;
The march of firemen in their own costumes, the play of masculine muscle
    through clean-setting trowsers and waist-straps,
The slow return from the fire, the pause when the bell strikes suddenly again,
    and the listening on the alert,
30   The natural, perfect, varied attitudes, the bent head, the curv'd neck and the
    counting;
Such-like I love—I loosen myself, pass freely, am at the mother's breast with the
    little child,
Swim with the swimmers, wrestle with wrestlers, march in line with the firemen,
    and pause, listen, count.

3

I knew a man, a common farmer, the father of five sons,
And in them the fathers of sons, and in them the fathers of sons.

This man was of wonderful vigor, calmness, beauty of person,
The shape of his head, the pale yellow and white of his hair and beard, the im-
    measurable meaning of his black eye, the richness and breadth of his man-
    ners,
These I used to go and visit him to see, he was wise also,
He was six feet tall, he was over eighty years old, his sons were massive, clean,
    bearded, tan-faced, handsome,
They and his daughters loved him, all who saw him loved him,
They did not love him by allowance, they loved him with personal love,   40
He drank water only, the blood show'd like scarlet through the clear-brown skin
    of his face,
He was a frequent gunner and fisher, he sail'd his boat himself, he had a fine one
    presented to him by a ship-joiner, he had fowling-pieces presented to him
    by men that loved him,
When he went with his five sons and many grand-sons to hunt or fish, you would
    pick him out as the most beautiful and vigorous of the gang,
You would wish long and long to be with him, you would wish to sit by him in
    the boat that you and he might touch each other.

4

I have perceiv'd that to be with those I like is enough,
To stop in company with the rest at evening is enough,
To be surrounded by beautiful, curious, breathing, laughing flesh is enough,
To pass among them or touch any one, or rest my arm ever so lightly round his
    or her neck for a moment, what is this then?
I do not ask any more delight, I swim in it as in a sea.
There is something in staying close to men and women and looking on them, and
    in the contact and odor of them, that pleases the soul well,   50
All things please the soul, but these please the soul well.

5

This is the female form,
A divine nimbus exhales from it from head to foot,
It attracts with fierce undeniable attraction,
I am drawn by its breath as if I were no more than a helpless vapor, all falls
    aside but myself and it,
Books, art, religion, time, the visible and solid earth, and what was expected of
    heaven or fear'd of hell, are now consumed,
Mad filaments, ungovernable shoots play out of it, the response likewise ungov-
    ernable,
Hair, bosom, hips, bend of legs, negligent falling hands all diffused, mine too
    diffused,
Ebb stung by the flow and flow stung by the ebb, love-flesh swelling and deli-
    ciously aching,

60 Limitless limpid jets of love hot and enormous, quivering jelly of love, white-
blow and delirious juice,
Bridegroom night of love working surely and softly into the prostrate dawn,
Undulating into the willing and yielding day,
Lost in the cleave of the clasping and sweet-flesh'd day.

This the nucleus—after the child is born of woman, man is born of woman,
This the bath of birth, this the merge of small and large, and the outlet again.

Be not ashamed women, your privilege encloses the rest, and is the exit of the
rest,
You are the gates of the body, and you are the gates of the soul.

The female contains all qualities and tempers them,
She is in her place and moves with perfect balance,
70 She is all things duly veil'd, she is both passive and active,
She is to conceive daughters as well as sons, and sons as well as daughters.

As I see my soul reflected in Nature,
As I see through a mist, One with inexpressible completeness, sanity, beauty,
See the bent head and arms folded over the breast, the Female I see.

6
The male is not less the soul nor more, he too is in his place,
He too is all qualities, he is action and power,
The flush of the known universe is in him,
Scorn becomes him well, and appetite and defiance become him well,
The wildest largest passions, bliss that is utmost, sorrow that is utmost become
him well, pride is for him,
80 The full-spread pride of man is calming and excellent to the soul,
Knowledge becomes him, he likes it always, he brings every thing to the test of
himself,
Whatever the survey, whatever the sea and the sail he strikes soundings at last
only here,
(Where else does he strike soundings except here?)

The man's body is sacred and the woman's body is sacred,
No matter who it is, it is sacred—is it the meanest one in the laborers' gang?
Is it one of the dull-faced immigrants just landed on the wharf?
Each belongs here or anywhere just as much as the well-off, just as much as you,
Each has his or her place in the procession.

(All is a procession,
90 The universe is a procession with measured and perfect motion.)

Do you know so much yourself that you call the meanest ignorant?
Do you suppose you have a right to a good sight, and he or she has no right to
a sight?

Do you think matter has cohered together from its diffuse float, and the soil is on
      the surface, and water runs and vegetation sprouts,
For you only, and not for him and her?

7

A man's body at auction,
(For before the war I often go to the slave-mart and watch the sale,)
I help the auctioneer, the sloven does not half know his business.

Gentlemen look on this wonder,
Whatever the bids of the bidders they cannot be high enough for it,
For it the globe lay preparing quintillions of years without one animal or plant,   100
For it the revolving cycles truly and steadily roll'd.

In this head the all-baffling brain,
In it and below it the makings of heroes.

Examine these limbs, red, black, or white, they are cunning in tendon and nerve,
They shall be stript that you may see them.

Exquisite senses, life-lit eyes, pluck, volition,
Flakes of breast-muscle, pliant backbone and neck, flesh not flabby, good-sized
    arms and legs,
And wonders within there yet.

Within there runs blood,
The same old blood! the same red-running blood!   110
There swells and jets a heart, there all passions, desires, reachings, aspirations,
(Do you think they are not there because they are not express'd in parlors and
    lecture-rooms?)

This is not only one man, this the father of those who shall be fathers in their
    turns,
In him the start of populous states and rich republics,
Of him countless immortal lives with countless embodiments and enjoyments.

How do you know who shall come from the offspring of his offspring through
    the centuries?
(Who might you find you have come from yourself, if you could trace back
    through the centuries?)

8

A woman's body at auction,
She too is not only herself, she is the teeming mother of mothers,
She is the bearer of them that shall grow and be mates to the mothers.   120

Have you ever loved the body of a woman?
Have you ever loved the body of a man?

Do you not see that these are exactly the same to all in all nations and times all
over the earth?

If anything is sacred the human body is sacred,
And the glory and sweet of a man is the token of manhood untainted,
And in man or woman a clean, strong, firm-fibred body, is more beautiful than
the most beautiful face.

Have you seen the fool that corrupted his own live body? or the fool that corrupted her own live body?
For they do not conceal themselves, and cannot conceal themselves.

9
O my body! I dare not desert the likes of you in other men and women, nor the
likes of the parts of you,
130   I believe the likes of you are to stand or fall with the likes of the soul, (and that
they are the soul,)
I believe the likes of you shall stand or fall with my poems, and that they are my
poems,
Man's, woman's, child's, youth's, wife's, husband's, mother's, father's, young
man's, young woman's poems,
Head, neck, hair, ears, drop and tympan of the ears,
Eyes, eye-fringes, iris of the eye, eyebrows, and the waking or sleeping of the
lids,
Mouth, tongue, lips, teeth, roof of the mouth, jaws, and the jaw-hinges,
Nose, nostrils of the nose, and the partition,
Cheeks, temples, forehead, chin, throat, back of the neck, neck-slue,
Strong shoulders, manly beard, scapula, hind-shoulders, and the ample side-
round of the chest,
Upper-arm, armpit, elbow-socket, lower-arm, arm-sinews, arm-bones,
140   Wrist and wrist-joints, hand, palm, knuckles, thumb, forefinger, finger-joints,
finger-nails,
Broad breast-front, curling hair of the breast, breast-bone, breast-side,
Ribs, belly, backbone, joints of the backbone,
Hips, hip-sockets, hip-strength, inward and outward round, man-balls, man-root,
Strong set of thighs, well carrying the trunk above,
Leg-fibres, knee, knee-pan, upper-leg, under-leg,
Ankles, instep, foot-ball, toes, toe-joints, the heel;
All attitudes, all the shapeliness, all the belongings of my or your body or of any
one's body, male or female,
The lung-sponges, the stomach-sac, the bowels sweet and clean,
The brain in its folds inside the skull-frame,
150   Sympathies, heart-valves, palate-valves, sexuality, maternity,
Womanhood and all that is a woman, and the man that comes from woman,
The womb, the teats, nipples, breast-milk, tears, laughter, weeping, love-looks,
love-perturbations and risings,
The voice, articulation, language, whispering, shouting aloud,

Food, drink, pulse, digestion, sweat, sleep, walking, swimming,
Poise on the hips, leaping, reclining, embracing, arm-curving and tightening,
The continual changes of the flex of the mouth, and around the eyes,
The skin, the sunburnt shade, freckles, hair,
The curious sympathy one feels when feeling with the hand the naked meat of
    the body,
The circling rivers the breath, and breathing it in and out,
The beauty of the waist, and thence of the hips, and thence downward toward
    the knees,   160
The thin red jellies within you or within me, the bones and the marrow in the
    bones,
The exquisite realization of health;
O I say these are not the parts and poems of the body only, but of the soul,
O I say now these are the soul!
1855·1881

OUT OF THE CRADLE ENDLESSLY ROCKING

Out of the cradle endlessly rocking,
Out of the mocking-bird's throat, the musical shuttle,
Out of the Ninth-month midnight,
Over the sterile sands and the fields beyond, where the child leaving his bed
    wander'd alone, bareheaded, barefoot,
Down from the shower'd halo,
Up from the mystic play of shadows twining and twisting as if they were alive,
Out from the patches of briers and blackberries,
From the memories of the bird that chanted to me,
From your memories sad brother, from the fitful risings and fallings I heard,
From under that yellow half-moon late-risen and swollen as if with tears,   10
From those beginning notes of yearning and love there in the mist,
From the thousand responses of my heart never to cease,
From the myriad thence-arous'd words,
From the word stronger and more delicious than any,
From such as now they start the scene revisiting,
As a flock, twittering, rising, or overhead passing,
Borne hither, ere all eludes me, hurriedly,
A man, yet by these tears a little boy again,
Throwing myself on the sand, confronting the waves,
I, chanter of pains and joys, uniter of here and hereafter,   20
Taking all hints to use them, but swiftly leaping beyond them,
A reminiscence sing.

Once Paumanok,
When the lilac-scent was in the air and Fifth-month grass was growing,
Up this seashore in some briers,

Two feather'd guests from Alabama, two together,
And their nest, and four light-green eggs spotted with brown,
And every day the he-bird to and fro near at hand,
And every day the she-bird crouch'd on her nest, silent, with bright eyes,
30 And every day I, a curious boy, never too close, never disturbing them,
Cautiously peering, absorbing, translating.

Shine! shine! shine!
Pour down your warmth, great sun!
While we bask, we two together.

Two together!
Winds blow south, or winds blow north,
Day come white, or night come black,
Home, or rivers and mountains from home,
Singing all time, minding no time,
40 *While we two keep together.*

Till of a sudden,
May-be kill'd, unknown to her mate,
One forenoon the she-bird crouch'd not on the nest,
Nor return'd that afternoon, nor the next,
Nor ever appear'd again.

And thenceforward all summer in the sound of the sea,
And at night under the full of the moon in calmer weather,
Over the hoarse surging of the sea,
Or flitting from brier to brier by day,
50 I saw, I heard at intervals the remaining one, the he-bird,
The solitary guest from Alabama.

Blow! blow! blow!
Blow up sea-winds along Paumanok's shore;
I wait and I wait till you blow my mate to me.

Yes, when the stars glisten'd,
All night long on the prong of a moss-scallop'd stake,
Down almost amid the slapping waves,
Sat the lone singer wonderful causing tears.

He call'd on his mate,
60 He pour'd forth the meanings which I of all men know.

Yes my brother I know,
The rest might not, but I have treasur'd every note,
For more than once dimly down to the beach gliding,
Silent, avoiding the moonbeams, blending myself with the shadows,

Recalling now the obscure shapes, the echoes, the sounds and sights after their
 sorts,
The white arms out in the breakers tirelessly tossing,
I, with bare feet, a child, the wind wafting my hair,
Listen'd long and long.

Listen'd to keep, to sing, now translating the notes,
Following you my brother.   70

Soothe! soothe! soothe!
Close on its wave soothes the wave behind,
And again another behind embracing and lapping, every one close,
But my love soothes not me, not me.

Low hangs the moon, it rose late,
It is lagging—O I think it is heavy with love, with love.

O madly the sea pushes upon the land,
With love, with love.

O night! do I not see my love fluttering out among the breakers?
What is that little black thing I see there in the white?   80

Loud! loud! loud!
Loud I call to you, my love!
High and clear I shoot my voice over the waves,
Surely you must know who is here, is here,
You must know who I am, my love.

Low-hanging moon!
What is that dusky spot in your brown yellow?
O it is the shape, the shape of my mate!
O moon do not keep her from me any longer.

Land! land! O land!   90
Whichever way I turn, O I think you could give me my mate back again if you
 only would,
For I am almost sure I see her dimly whichever way I look.

O rising stars!
Perhaps the one I want so much will rise, will rise with some of you.

O throat! O trembling throat!
Sound clearer through the atmosphere!
Pierce the woods, the earth,
Somewhere listening to catch you must be the one I want.

Shake out carols!
100 *Solitary here, the night's carols!*
Carols of lonesome love! death's carols!
Carols under that lagging, yellow, waning moon!
O under that moon where she droops almost down into the sea!
O reckless despairing carols.

But soft! sink low!
Soft! let me just murmur,
And do you wait a moment you husky-nois'd sea,
For somewhere I believe I heard my mate responding to me,
So faint, I must be still, be still to listen,
110 *But not altogether still, for then she might not come immediately to me.*

Hither my love!
Here I am! here!
With this just-sustain'd note I announce myself to you,
This gentle call is for you my love, for you.

Do not be decoy'd elsewhere,
That is the whistle of the wind, it is not my voice,
That is the fluttering, the fluttering of the spray,
Those are the shadows of leaves.

O darkness! O in vain!
120 *O I am very sick and sorrowful.*

O brown halo in the sky near the moon, drooping upon the sea!
O troubled reflection in the sea!
O throat! O throbbing heart!
And I singing uselessly, uselessly all the night.

O past! O happy life! O songs of joy!
In the air, in the woods, over fields,
Loved! loved! loved! loved! loved!
But my mate no more, no more with me!
We two together no more.

130 The aria sinking,
All else continuing, the stars shining,
The winds blowing, the notes of the bird continuous echoing,
With angry moans the fierce old mother incessantly moaning,
On the sands of Paumanok's shore gray and rustling,
The yellow half-moon enlarged, sagging down, drooping, the face of the sea al-
    most touching,
The boy ecstatic, with his bare feet the waves, with his hair the atmosphere
    dallying,
The love in the heart long pent, now loose, now at last tumultuously bursting,

The aria's meaning, the ears, the soul, swiftly depositing,
The strange tears down the cheeks coursing,
The colloquy there, the trio, each uttering,   140
The undertone, the savage old mother incessantly crying,
To the boy's soul's questions sullenly timing, some drown'd secret hissing,
To the outsetting bard.

Demon or bird! (said the boy's soul,)
Is it indeed toward your mate you sing? or is it really to me?
For I, that was a child, my tongue's use sleeping, now I have heard you,
Now in a moment I know what I am for, I awake,
And already a thousand singers, a thousand songs, clearer, louder and more sor-
    rowful than yours,
A thousand warbling echoes have started to life within me, never to die.

O you singer solitary, singing by yourself, projecting me,   150
O solitary me listening, never more shall I cease perpetuating you,
Never more shall I escape, never more the reverberations,
Never more the cries of unsatisfied love be absent from me,
Never again leave me to be the peaceful child I was before what there in the
    night,
By the sea under the yellow and sagging moon,
The messenger there arous'd, the fire, the sweet hell within,
The unknown want, the destiny of me.

O give me the clew! (it lurks in the night here somewhere,)
O if I am to have so much, let me have more!

A word then, (for I will conquer it,)   160
The word final, superior to all,
Subtle, sent up—what is it?—I listen;
Are you whispering it, and have been all the time, you sea waves?
Is that it from your liquid rims and wet sands?

Whereto answering, the sea,
Delaying not, hurrying not,
Whisper'd me through the night, and very plainly before daybreak,
Lisp'd to me the low and delicious word death,
And again death, death, death, death,
Hissing melodious, neither like the bird nor like my arous'd child's heart,   170
But edging near as privately for me rustling at my feet,
Creeping thence steadily up to my ears and laving me softly all over,
Death, death, death, death, death.

Which I do not forget,
But fuse the song of my dusky demon and brother,
That he sang to me in the moonlight on Paumanok's gray beach,
With the thousand responsive songs at random,

My own songs awaked from that hour,
And with them the key, the word up from the waves,
180   The word of the sweetest song and all songs,
That strong and delicious word which, creeping to my feet,
(Or like some old crone rocking the cradle, swathed in sweet garments, bending
    aside,)
The sea whisper'd me.
1859·1881

ON THE BEACH AT NIGHT

On the beach at night,
Stands a child with her father,
Watching the east, the autumn sky.

Up through the darkness,
While ravening clouds, the burial clouds, in black masses spreading,
Lower sullen and fast athwart and down the sky,
Amid a transparent clear belt of ether yet left in the east,
Ascends large and calm the lord-star Jupiter,
And nigh at hand, only a very little above,
10   Swim the delicate sisters the Pleiades.

From the beach the child holding the hand of her father,
Those burial clouds that lower victorious soon to devour all,
Watching, silently weeps.

Weep not, child,
Weep not, my darling,
With these kisses let me remove your tears,
The ravening clouds shall not long be victorious,
They shall not long possess the sky, they devour the stars only in apparition,
Jupiter shall emerge, be patient, watch again another night, the Pleiades shall
    emerge,
20   They are immortal, all those stars both silvery and golden shall shine out again,
The great stars and the little ones shall shine out again, they endure,
The vast immortal suns and the long-enduring pensive moons shall again shine.

Then dearest child mournest thou only for Jupiter?
Considerest thou alone the burial of the stars?

Something there is,
(With my lips soothing thee, adding I whisper,
I give thee the first suggestion, the problem and indirection,)
Something there is more immortal even than the stars,
(Many the burials, many the days and nights, passing away,)

Something that shall endure longer even than lustrous Jupiter, 30
Longer than sun or any revolving satellite,
Or the radiant sisters the Pleiades.
1871

CAVALRY CROSSING A FORD

A line in long array where they wind betwixt green islands,
They take a serpentine course, their arms flash in the sun—hark to the musical
    clank,
Behold the silvery river, in it the splashing horses loitering stop to drink,
Behold the brown-faced men, each group, each person a picture, the negligent
    rest on the saddles,
Some emerge on the opposite bank, others are just entering the ford—while,
Scarlet and blue and snowy white,
The guidon flags flutter gayly in the wind.
1865·1871

BIVOUAC ON A MOUNTAIN SIDE

I see before me now a traveling army halting,
Below a fertile valley spread, with barns and the orchards of summer,
Behind, the terraced sides of a mountain, abrupt, in places rising high,
Broken, with rocks, with clinging cedars, with tall shapes dingily seen,
The numerous camp-fires scatter'd near and far, some away up on the mountain,
The shadowy forms of men and horses, looming, large-sized, flickering,
And over all the sky—the sky! far, far out of reach, studded, breaking out, the
    eternal stars.
1865·1871

AN ARMY CORPS ON THE MARCH

With its cloud of skirmishers in advance,
With now the sound of a single shot snapping like a whip, and now an irregular
    volley,
The swarming ranks press on and on, the dense brigades press on,
Glittering dimly, toiling under the sun—the dust-cover'd men,
In columns rise and fall to the undulations of the ground,
With artillery interspers'd—the wheels rumble, the horses sweat,
As the army corps advances.
1865·1871

BY THE BIVOUAC'S FITFUL FLAME

By the bivouac's fitful flame,
A procession winding around me, solemn and sweet and slow—but first I note,
The tents of the sleeping army, the fields' and woods' dim outline,
The darkness lit by spots of kindled fire, the silence,
Like a phantom far or near an occasional figure moving,
The shrubs and trees, (as I lift my eyes they seem to be steathily watching me,)
While wind in procession thoughts, O tender and wondrous thoughts,
Of life and death, of home and the past and loved, and of those that are far
     away;
A solemn and slow procession there as I sit on the ground,
10 By the bivouac's fitful flame.
1865·1867

COME UP FROM THE FIELDS FATHER

Come up from the fields father, here's a letter from our Pete,
And come to the front door mother, here's a letter from thy dear son.

Lo, 'tis autumn,
Lo, where the trees, deeper green, yellower and redder,
Cool and sweeten Ohio's villages with leaves fluttering in the moderate wind,
Where apples ripe in the orchards hang and grapes on the trellis'd vines,
(Smell you the smell of the grapes on the vines?
Smell you the buckwheat where the bees were lately buzzing?)

Above all, lo, the sky so calm, so transparent after the rain, and with wondrous
     clouds,
10 Below too, all calm, all vital and beautiful, and the farm prospers well.

Down in the fields all prospers well,
But now from the fields come father, come at the daughter's call,
And come to the entry mother, to the front door come right away.

Fast as she can she hurries, something ominous, her steps trembling,
She does not tarry to smooth her hair nor adjust her cap.

Open the envelope quickly,
O this is not our son's writing, yet his name is sign'd,
O a strange hand writes for our dear son, O stricken mother's soul!
All swims before her eyes, flashes with black, she catches the main words only,
Sentences broken, *gunshot wound in the breast, cavalry skirmish, taken to hos-*
20   *pital,*
At present low, but will soon be better.

Ah now the single figure to me,
Amid all teeming and wealthy Ohio with all its cities and farms,
Sickly white in the face and dull in the head, very faint,
By the jamb of a door leans.

Grieve not so, dear mother, (the just-grown daughter speaks through her sobs,
The little sisters huddle around speechless and dismay'd,)
See, dearest mother, the letter says Pete will soon be better.

Alas poor boy, he will never be better, (nor may-be needs to be better, that brave
    and simple soul,)
While they stand at home at the door he is dead already,   30
The only son is dead.

But the mother needs to be better,
She with thin form presently drest in black,
By day her meals untouch'd, then at night fitfully sleeping, often waking,
In the midnight waking, weeping, longing with one deep longing,
O that she might withdraw unnoticed, silent from life escape and withdraw,
To follow, to seek, to be with her dear dead son.
1865·1867

VIGIL STRANGE I KEPT ON THE FIELD ONE NIGHT

Vigil strange I kept on the field one night;
When you my son and my comrade dropt at my side that day,
One look I but gave which your dear eyes return'd with a look I shall never
    forget,
One touch of your hand to mine O boy, reach'd up as you lay on the ground,
Then onward I sped in the battle, the even-contested battle,
Till late in the night reliev'd to the place at last again I made my way,
Found you in death so cold dear comrade, found your body son of responding
    kisses, (never again on earth responding,)
Bared your face in the starlight, curious the scene, cool blew the moderate night-
    wind,
Long there and then in vigil I stood, dimly around me the battlefield spreading,
Vigil wondrous and vigil sweet there in the fragrant silent night,   10
But not a tear fell, not even a long-drawn sigh, long, long I gazed,
Then on the earth partially reclining sat by your side leaning my chin in my
    hands,
Passing sweet hours, immortal and mystic hours with you dearest comrade—not
    a tear, not a word,
Vigil of silence, love and death, vigil for you my son and my soldier,
As onward silently stars aloft, eastward new ones upward stole,
Vigil final for you brave boy, (I could not save you, swift was your death,

> I faithfully loved you and cared for you living, I think we shall surely meet
> again,)
> Till at latest lingering of the night, indeed just as the dawn appear'd,
> My comrade I wrapt in his blanket, envelop'd well his form,
> 20 Folded the blanket well, tucking it carefully over head and carefully under feet,
> And there and then and bathed by the rising sun, my son in his grave, in his
> rude-dug grave I deposited,
> Ending my vigil strange with that, vigil of night and battle-field dim,
> Vigil for boy of responding kisses, (never again on earth responding,)
> Vigil for comrade swiftly slain, vigil I never forget, how as day brighten'd,
> I rose from the chill ground and folded my soldier well in his blanket,
> And buried him where he fell.
> 1865·1867

A MARCH IN THE RANKS HARD-PREST, AND THE ROAD UNKNOWN

> A march in the ranks hard-prest, and the road unknown,
> A route through a heavy wood with muffled steps in the darkness,
> Our army foil'd with loss severe, and the sullen remnant retreating,
> Till after midnight glimmer upon us the lights of a dim-lighted building,
> We come to an open space in the woods, and halt by the dim-lighted building,
> 'Tis a large old church at the crossing roads, now an impromptu hospital,
> Entering but for a minute I see a sight beyond all the pictures and poems ever
> made,
> Shadows of deepest, deepest black, just lit by moving candles and lamps,
> And by one great pitchy torch stationary with wild red flame and clouds of
> smoke,
> 10 By these, crowds, groups of forms vaguely I see on the floor, some in the pews
> laid down,
> At my feet more distinctly a soldier, a mere lad, in danger of bleeding to death,
> (he is shot in the abdomen,)
> I stanch the blood temporarily, (the youngster's face is white as a lily,)
> Then before I depart I sweep my eyes o'er the scene fain to absorb it all,
> Faces, varieties, postures beyond description, most in obscurity, some of them
> dead,
> Surgeons operating, attendants holding lights, the smell of ether, the odor of
> blood,
> The crowd, O the crowd of the bloody forms, the yard outside also fill'd,
> Some on the bare ground, some on planks or stretchers, some in the death-spasm
> sweating,
> An occasional scream or cry, the doctor's shouted orders or calls,
> The glisten of the little steel instruments catching the glint of the torches,
> 20 These I resume as I chant, I see again the forms, I smell the odor,
> Then hear outside the orders given, *Fall in, my men, fall in;*

But first I bend to the dying lad, his eyes open, a half-smile gives he me,
Then the eyes close, calmly close, and I speed forth to the darkness,
Resuming, marching, ever in darkness marching, on in the ranks,
The unknown road still marching.
1865·1867

A SIGHT IN CAMP IN THE DAYBREAK GRAY AND DIM

A sight in camp in the daybreak gray and dim,
As from my tent I emerge so early sleepless,
As slow I walk in the cool fresh air the path near by the hospital tent,
Three forms I see on stretchers lying, brought out there untended lying,
Over each the blanket spread, ample brownish woolen blanket,
Gray and heavy blanket, folding, covering all.

Curious I halt and silent stand,
Then with light fingers I from the face of the nearest the first just lift the
    blanket;
Who are you elderly man so gaunt and grim, with well-gray'd hair, and flesh all
    sunken about the eyes?
Who are you my dear comrade?   10

Then to the second I step—and who are you my child and darling?
Who are you sweet boy with cheeks yet blooming?

Then to the third—a face nor child nor old, very calm, as of beautiful yellow-
    white ivory;
Young man I think I know you—I think this face is the face of the Christ him-
    self,
Dead and divine and brother of all, and here again he lies.
1865·1867

AS TOILSOME I WANDER'D VIRGINIA'S WOODS

As toilsome I wander'd Virginia's woods,
To the music of rustling leaves kick'd by my feet, (for 'twas autumn,)
I mark'd at the foot of a tree the grave of a soldier;
Mortally wounded he and buried on the retreat, (easily all could I understand,)
The halt of a mid-day hour, when up! no time to lose—yet this sign left,
On a tablet scrawl'd and nail'd on the tree by the grave,
Bold, cautious, true, and my loving comrade.

Long, long I muse, then on my way go wandering,
Many a changeful season to follow, and many a scene of life,

10   Yet at times through changeful season and scene, abrupt, alone, or in the
        crowded street,
    Comes before me the unknown soldier's grave, comes the inscription rude in
        Virginia's woods,
    Bold, cautious, true, and my loving comrade.
    1865·1867

NOT THE PILOT

Not the pilot has charged himself to bring his ship into port, though beaten back
    and many times baffled;
Not the pathfinder penetrating inland weary and long,
By deserts parch'd, snows chill'd, rivers wet, perseveres till he reaches his desti-
    nation,
More than I have charged myself, heeded or unheeded, to compose a march for
    these States,
For a battle-call, rousing to arms if need be, years, centuries hence.
1860·1881

YEAR THAT TREMBLED AND REEL'D BENEATH ME

Year that trembled and reel'd beneath me!
Your summer wind was warm enough, yet the air I breathed froze me,
A thick gloom fell through the sunshine and darken'd me,
Must I change my triumphant songs? said I to myself,
Must I indeed learn to chant the cold dirges of the baffled?
And sullen hymns of defeat?
1865·1867

THE WOUND-DRESSER

1
An old man bending I come among new faces,
Years looking backward resuming in answer to children,
Come tell us old man, as from young men and maidens that love me,
(Arous'd and angry, I'd thought to beat the alarum, and urge relentless war,
But soon my fingers fail'd me, my face droop'd and I resign'd myself,
To sit by the wounded and soothe them, or silently watch the dead;)
Years hence of these scenes, of these furious passions, these chances,
Of unsurpass'd heroes, (was one side so brave? the other was equally brave;)
Now be witness again, paint the mightiest armies of earth,
10   Of those armies so rapid so wondrous what saw you to tell us?

What stays with you latest and deepest? of curious panics,
Of hard-fought engagements or sieges tremendous what deepest remains?

2

O maidens and young men I love and that love me,
What you ask of my days those the strangest and sudden your talking recalls,
Soldier alert I arrive after a long march cover'd with sweat and dust,
In the nick of time I come, plunge in the fight, loudly shout in the rush of suc-
     cessful charge,
Enter the captur'd works—yet lo, like a swift-running river they fade,
Pass and are gone they fade—I dwell not on soldiers' perils or soldiers' joys,
(Both I remember well—many of the hardships, few the joys, yet I was content.)

But in silence, in dreams' projections,   20
While the world of gain and appearance and mirth goes on,
So soon what is over forgotten, and waves wash the imprints off the sand,
With hinged knees returning I enter the doors, (while for you up there,
Whoever you are, follow without noise and be of strong heart.)

Bearing the bandages, water and sponge,
Straight and swift to my wounded I go,
Where they lie on the ground after the battle brought in,
Where their priceless blood reddens the grass the ground,
Or to the rows of the hospital tent, or under the roof'd hospital,
To the long rows of cots up and down each side I return,   30
To each and all one after another I draw near, not one do I miss,
An attendant follows holding a tray, he carries a refuse pail,
Soon to be fill'd with clotted rags and blood, emptied, and fill'd again.

I onward go, I stop,
With hinged knees and steady hand to dress wounds,
I am firm with each, the pangs are sharp yet unavoidable,
One turns to me his appealing eyes—poor boy! I never knew you,
Yet I think I could not refuse this moment to die for you, if that would save you.

3

On, on I go, (open doors of time! open hospital doors!)
The crush'd head I dress, (poor crazed hand tear not the bandage away,)   40
The neck of the cavalry-man with the bullet through and through I examine,
Hard the breathing rattles, quite glazed already the eye, yet life struggles hard,
(Come sweet death! be persuaded O beautiful death!
In mercy come quickly.)

From the stump of the arm, the amputated hand,
I undo the clotted lint, remove the slough, wash off the matter and blood,
Back on his pillow the soldier bends with curv'd neck and side falling head,
His eyes are closed, his face is pale, he dares not look on the bloody stump,
And has not yet look'd on it.

50   I dress a wound in the side, deep, deep,
But a day or two more, for see the frame all wasted and sinking,
And the yellow-blue countenance see.
I dress the perforated shoulder, the foot with the bullet-wound,
Cleanse the one with a gnawing and putrid gangrene, so sickening, so offensive,
While the attendant stands behind aside me holding the tray and pail.

I am faithful, I do not give out,
The fractur'd thigh, the knee, the wound in the abdomen,
These and more I dress with impassive hand, (yet deep in my breast a fire, a
     burning flame.)

4
Thus in silence in dreams' projections,
60   Returning, resuming, I thread my way through the hospitals,
The hurt and wounded I pacify with soothing hand,
I sit by the restless all the dark night, some are so young,
Some suffer so much, I recall the experience sweet and sad,
(Many a soldier's loving arms about this neck have cross'd and rested,
Many a soldier's kiss dwells on these bearded lips.)
1865·1881

LONG, TOO LONG AMERICA

Long, too long America,
Traveling roads all even and peaceful you learn'd from joys and prosperity only,
But now, ah now, to learn from crises of anguish, advancing, grappling with
    direst fate and recoiling not,
And now to conceive and show to the world what your children en-masse really
    are,
(For who except myself has yet conceiv'd what your children en-masse really
    are?)
1865·1881

OVER THE CARNAGE ROSE PROPHETIC A VOICE

Over the carnage rose prophetic a voice,
Be not dishearten'd, affection shall solve the problems of freedom yet,
Those who love each other shall become invincible,
They shall yet make Columbia victorious.

Sons of the Mother of All, you shall yet be victorious,
You shall yet laugh to scorn the attacks of all the remainder of the earth.

No danger shall balk Columbia's lovers,
If need be a thousand shall sternly immolate themselves for one.

One from Massachusetts shall be a Missourian's comrade,
From Maine and from hot Carolina, and another an Oregonese, shall be friends
    triune,   10
More precious to each other than all the riches of the earth.

To Michigan, Florida perfumes shall tenderly come,
Not the perfumes of flowers, but sweeter, and wafted beyond death.

It shall be customary in the houses and streets to see manly affection,
The most dauntless and rude shall touch face to face lightly,
The dependence of Liberty shall be lovers,
The continuance of Equality shall be comrades.

These shall tie you and band you stronger than hoops of iron,
I, ecstatic, O partners! O lands! with the love of lovers tie you.

(Were you looking to be held together by lawyers?   20
Or by an agreement on a paper? or by arms?
Nay, nor the world, nor any living thing, will so cohere.)
1860·1867

WHEN LILACS LAST IN THE DOORYARD BLOOM'D

1

When lilacs last in the dooryard bloom'd,
And the great star early droop'd in the western sky in the night,
I mourn'd, and yet shall mourn with ever-returning spring.

Ever-returning spring, trinity sure to me you bring,
Lilac blooming perennial and drooping star in the west,
And thought of him I love.

2

O powerful western fallen star!
O shades of night—O moody, tearful night!
O great star disappear'd—O the black murk that hides the star!
O cruel hands that hold me powerless—O helpless soul of me!   10
O harsh surrounding cloud that will not free my soul.

3

In the dooryard fronting an old farm-house near the white-wash'd palings,
Stands the lilac-bush tall-growing with heart-shaped leaves of rich green,

With many a pointed blossom rising delicate, with the perfume strong I love,
With every leaf a miracle—and from this bush in the dooryard,
With delicate-color'd blossoms and heart-shaped leaves of rich green,
A sprig with its flower I break.

4
In the swamp in secluded recesses,
A shy and hidden bird is warbling a song.

20 Solitary the thrush,
The hermit withdrawn to himself, avoiding the settlements,
Sings by himself a song.
Song of the bleeding throat,
Death's outlet song of life, (for well dear brother I know,
If thou wast not granted to sing thou would'st surely die.)

5
Over the breast of the spring, the land, amid cities,
Amid lanes and through old woods, where lately the violets peep'd from the
    ground, spotting the gray debris,
Amid the grass in the fields each side of the lanes, passing the endless grass,
Passing the yellow-spear'd wheat, every grain from its shroud in the dark-brown
    fields uprisen,
30 Passing the apple-tree blows of white and pink in the orchards,
Carrying a corpse to where it shall rest in the grave,
Night and day journeys a coffin.

6
Coffin that passes through lanes and streets,
Through day and night with the great cloud darkening the land,
With the pomp of the inloop'd flags with the cities draped in black,
With the show of the States themselves as of crape-veil'd women standing,
With processions long and winding and the flambeaus of the night,
With the countless torches lit, with the silent sea of faces and the unbared heads,
With the waiting depot, the arriving coffin, and the sombre faces,
40 With dirges through the night, with the thousand voices rising strong and
    solemn,
With all the mournful voices of the dirges pour'd around the coffin,
The dim-lit churches and the shuddering organs—where amid these you journey,
With the tolling tolling bells' perpetual clang,
Here, coffin that slowly passes,
I give you my sprig of lilac.

7
(Nor for you, for one alone,
Blossoms and branches green to coffins all I bring,

For fresh as the morning, thus would I chant a song for you O sane and sacred
    death.
All over bouquets of roses,
O death, I cover you over with roses and early lilies,   50
But mostly and now the lilac that blooms the first,
Copious I break, I break the sprigs from the bushes,
With loaded arms I come, pouring for you,
For you and the coffins all of you O death.)

8
O western orb sailing the heaven,
Now I know what you must have meant as a month since I walk'd,
As I walk'd in silence the transparent shadowy night,
As I saw you had something to tell as you bent to me night after night,
As you droop'd from the sky low down as if to my side, (while the other stars
    all look'd on,)
As we wander'd together the solemn night, (for something I know not what kept
    me from sleep,)   60
As the night advanced, and I saw on the rim of the west how full you were of
    woe,
As I stood on the rising ground in the breeze in the cool transparent night,
As I watch'd where you pass'd and was lost in the netherward black of the night,
As my soul in its trouble dissatisfied sank, as where you sad orb,
Concluded, dropt in the night, and was gone.

9
Sing on there in the swamp,
O singer bashful and tender, I hear your notes, I hear your call,
I hear, I come presently, I understand you,
But a moment I linger, for the lustrous star has detain'd me,
The star my departing comrade holds and detains me.   70

10
O how shall I warble myself for the dead one there I loved?
And how shall I deck my song for the large sweet soul that has gone?
And what shall my perfume be for the grave of him I love?
Sea-winds blown from east and west,
Blown from the Eastern sea and blown from the Western sea, till there on the
    prairies meeting,
These and with these and the breath of my chant,
I'll perfume the grave of him I love.

11
O what shall I hang on the chamber walls?
And what shall the pictures be that I hang on the walls,
To adorn the burial-house of him I love?   80

Pictures of growing spring and farms and homes,
With the Fourth-month eve at sundown, and the gray smoke lucid and bright,
With floods of the yellow gold of the gorgeous, indolent, sinking sun, burning,
    expanding the air,
With the fresh sweet herbage under foot, and the pale green leaves of the trees
    prolific,
In the distance the flowing glaze, the breast of the river, with a wind-dapple
    here and there,
With ranging hills on the banks, with many a line against the sky, and shadows,
And the city at hand with dwellings so dense, and stacks of chimneys,
And all the scenes of life and the workshops, and the workmen homeward
    returning.

12

Lo, body and soul—this land,
90 My own Manhattan with spires, and the sparkling and hurrying tides, and the
    ships,
The varied and ample land, the South and the North in the light, Ohio's shores
    and flashing Missouri,
And ever the far-spreading prairies cover'd with grass and corn.

Lo, the most excellent sun so calm and haughty,
The violet and purple morn with just-felt breezes,
The gentle soft-born measureless light,
The miracle spreading bathing all, the fulfill'd noon,
The coming eve delicious, the welcome night and the stars,
Over my cities shining all, enveloping man and land.

13

Sing on, sing on you gray-brown bird,
100 Sing from the swamps, the recesses, pour your chant from the
    bushes,
Limitless out of the dusk, out of the cedars and pines.

Sing on dearest brother, warble your reedy song,
Loud human song, with voice of uttermost woe.

O liquid and free and tender!
O wild and loose to my soul—O wondrous singer!
You only I hear—yet the star holds me, (but will soon depart,)
Yet the lilac with mastering odor holds me.

14

Now while I sat in the day and look'd forth,
In the close of the day with its light and the fields of spring, and the farmers
    preparing their crops,
110 In the large unconscious scenery of my land with its lakes and forests,

In the heavenly aerial beauty, (after the perturb'd winds and the storms,)
Under the arching heavens of the afternoon swift passing, and the voices of
   children and women,
The many-moving sea-tides, and I saw the ships how they sail'd,
And the summer approaching with richness, and the fields all busy with labor,
And the infinite separate houses, how they all went on, each with its meals and
   minutia of daily usages,
And the streets how their throbbings throbb'd, and the cities pent—lo, then and
   there,
Falling upon them all and among them all, enveloping me with the rest,
Appear'd the cloud, appear'd the long black trail,
And I knew death, its thought, and the sacred knowledge of death.

Then with the knowledge of death as walking one side of me,   120
And the thought of death close-walking the other side of me,
And I in the middle as with companions, and as holding the hands of com-
   panions,
I fled forth to the hiding receiving night that talks not,
Down to the shores of the water, the path by the swamp in the dimness,
To the solemn shadowy cedars and ghostly pines so still.

And the singer so shy to the rest receiv'd me,
The gray-brown bird I know receiv'd us comrades three,
And he sang the carol of death, and a verse for him I love.

From deep secluded recesses,
From the fragrant cedars and the ghostly pines so still,   130
Came the carol of the bird.

And the charm of the carol rapt me,
As I held as if by their hands my comrades in the night,
And the voice of my spirit tallied the song of the bird.

Come lovely and soothing death,
Undulate round the world, serenely arriving, arriving,
In the day, in the night, to all, to each,
Sooner or later delicate death.

Prais'd be the fathomless universe,
For life and joy, and for objects and knowledge curious,   140
And for love, sweet love—but praise! praise! praise!
For the sure-enwinding arms of cool-enfolding death.

Dark mother always gliding near with soft feet,
Have none chanted for thee a chant of fullest welcome?
Then I chant it for thee, I glorify thee above all,
I bring thee a song that when thou must indeed come, come unfalteringly.

Approach strong deliveress,
When it is so, when thou hast taken them I joyously sing the dead,
Lost in the loving floating ocean of thee,
150   *Laved in the flood of thy bliss O death.*

From me to thee glad serenades,
Dances for thee I propose saluting thee, adornments and feastings for thee,
And the sights of the open landscape and the high-spread sky are fitting,
And life and the fields, and the huge and thoughtful night.

The night in silence under many a star,
The ocean shore and the husky whispering wave whose voice I know,
And the soul turning to thee O vast and well-veil'd death,
And the body gratefully nestling close to thee.

Over the tree-tops I float thee a song,
160   *Over the rising and sinking waves, over the myriad fields and the prairies*
      wide,
Over the dense-pack'd cities all and the teeming wharves and ways,
I float this carol with joy, with joy to thee O death.

15
To the tally of my soul,
Loud and strong kept up the gray-brown bird,
With pure deliberate notes spreading filling the night.

Loud in the pines and cedars dim,
Clear in the freshness moist and the swamp-perfume,
And I with my comrades there in the night.

While my sight that was bound in my eyes unclosed,
170   As to long panoramas of visions.

And I saw askant the armies,
I saw as in noiseless dreams hundreds of battle-flags,
Borne through the smoke of the battles and pierc'd with missiles I saw them,
And carried hither and yon through the smoke, and torn and bloody,
And at last but a few shreds left on the staffs, (and all in silence,)
And the staffs all splinter'd and broken.

I saw battle-corpses, myriads of them,
And the white skeletons of young men, I saw them,
I saw the debris and debris of all the slain soldiers of the war,
180   But I saw they were not as was thought,
They themselves were fully at rest, they suffer'd not,
The living remain'd and suffer'd, the mother suffer'd,
And the wife and the child and the musing comrade suffer'd,
And the armies that remain'd suffer'd.

16

Passing the visions, passing the night,
Passing, unloosing the hold of my comrades' hands,
Passing the song of the hermit bird and the tallying song of my soul,
Victorious song, death's outlet song, yet varying ever-altering song,
As low and wailing, yet clear the notes, rising and falling, flooding the night,
Sadly sinking and fainting, as warning and warning, and yet again bursting with
     joy,   190
Covering the earth and filling the spread of the heaven,
As that powerful psalm in the night I heard from recesses,
Passing, I leave thee lilac with heart-shaped leaves,
I leave thee there in the door-yard, blooming, returning with spring.

I cease from my song for thee,
From my gaze on thee in the west, fronting the west, communing with thee,
O comrade lustrous with silver face in the night.

Yet each to keep and all, retrievements out of the night,
The song, the wondrous chant of the gray-brown bird,
And the tallying chant, the echo arous'd in my soul,   200
With the lustrous and drooping star with the countenance full of woe,
With the holders holding my hand nearing the call of the bird,
Comrades mine and I in the midst, and their memory ever to keep, for the dead
    I loved so well,
For the sweetest, wisest soul of all my days and lands—and this for his dear
    sake,
Lilac and star and bird twined with the chant of my soul,
There in the fragrant pines and the cedars dusk and dim.
1865·1881

PASSAGE TO INDIA

1

Singing my days,
Singing the great achievements of the present,
Singing the strong light works of engineers,
Our modern wonders, (the antique ponderous Seven outvied,)
In the Old World the east the Suez canal,
The New by its mighty railroad spann'd,
The seas inlaid with eloquent gentle wires;
Yet first to sound, and ever sound, the cry with thee O soul,
The Past! the Past! the Past!

The Past—the dark unfathom'd retrospect!   10
The teeming gulf—the sleepers and the shadows!

The past—the infinite greatness of the past!
For what is the present after all but a growth out of the past?
(As a projectile form'd, impell'd, passing a certain line, still keeps on,
So the present, utterly form'd, impell'd by the past.)

2

Passage O soul to India!
Eclaircise the myths Asiatic, the primitive fables.

Not you alone proud truths of the world,
Nor you alone ye facts of modern science,
20   But myths and fables of eld, Asia's, Africa's fables,
The far-darting beams of the spirit, the unloos'd dreams,
The deep diving bibles and legends,
The daring plots of the poets, the elder religions;
O you temples fairer than lilies pour'd over by the rising sun!
O you fables spurning the known, eluding the hold of the known, mounting to
        heaven!
You lofty and dazzling towers, pinnacled, red as roses, burnish'd with gold!
Towers of fables immortal fashion'd from mortal dreams!
You too I welcome and fully the same as the rest!
You too with joy I sing.

30   Passage to India!
Lo, soul, seest thou not God's purpose from the first?
The earth to be spann'd, connected by network,
The races, neighbors, to marry and be given in marriage,
The oceans to be cross'd, the distant brought near,
The lands to be welded together.

A worship new I sing,
You captains, voyagers, explorers, yours,
You engineers, you architects, machinists, yours,
You, not for trade or transportation only,
40   But in God's name, and for thy sake O soul.

3

Passage to India!
Lo soul for thee of tableaus twain.
I see in one the Suez canal initiated, open'd,
I see the procession of steamships, the Empress Eugenie's leading the van,
I mark from on deck the strange landscape, the pure sky, the level sand in the
        distance,
I pass swiftly the picturesque groups, the workmen gather'd,
The gigantic dredging machines.

In one again, different, (yet thine, all thine, O soul, the same,)
I see over my own continent the Pacific railroad surmounting every barrier,

I see continual trains of cars winding along the Platte carrying freight and
    passengers, 50
I hear the locomotives rushing and roaring, and the shrill steam-whistle,
I hear the echoes reverberate through the grandest scenery in the world,
I cross the Laramie plains, I note the rocks in grotesque shapes, the buttes,
I see the plentiful larkspur and wild onions, the barren, colorless, sage-deserts,
I see in glimpses afar or towering immediately above me the great mountains,
    I see the Wind river and the Wahsatch mountains,
I see the Monument mountain and the Eagle's Nest, I pass the Promontory, I
    ascend the Nevadas,
I scan the noble Elk mountain and wind around its base,
I see the Humboldt range, I thread the valley and cross the river,
I see the clear waters of lake Tahoe, I see forests of majestic pines,
Or crossing the great desert, the alkaline plains, I behold enchanting mirages of
    waters and meadows, 60
Marking through these and after all, in duplicate slender lines,
Bridging the three or four thousand miles of land travel,
Tying the Eastern to the Western sea,
The road between Europe and Asia.

(Ah Genoese thy dream! thy dream!
Centuries after thou art laid in thy grave,
The shore thou foundest verifies thy dream.)

4
Passage to India!
Struggles of many a captain, tales of many a sailor dead,
Over my mood stealing and spreading they come, 70
Like clouds and cloudlets in the unreach'd sky.

Along all history, down the slopes,
As a rivulet running, sinking now, and now again to the surface rising,
A ceaseless thought, a varied train—lo, soul, to thee, thy sight, they rise,
The plans, the voyages again, the expeditions;
Again Vasco de Gama sails forth,
Again the knowledge gain'd, the mariner's compass,
Lands found and nations born, thou born America,
For purpose vast, man's long probation fill'd,
Thou rondure of the world at last accomplish'd. 80

5
O vast Rondure, swimming in space,
Cover'd all over with visible power and beauty,
Alternate light and day and the teeming spiritual darkness,
Unspeakable high processions of sun and moon and countless stars above,
Below, the manifold grass and waters, animals, mountains, trees,
With inscrutable purpose, some hidden prophetic intention,
Now first it seems my thought begins to span thee.

Down from the gardens of Asia descending radiating,
Adam and Eve appear, then their myriad progeny after them,
90   Wandering, yearning, curious, with restless explorations,
With questionings, baffled, formless, feverish, with never-happy hearts,
With that sad incessant refrain, *Wherefore unsatisfied soul?* and *Whither O mocking life?*

Ah who shall soothe these feverish children?
Who justify these restless explorations?
Who speak the secret of impassive earth?
Who bind it to us? what is this separate Nature so unnatural?
What is this earth to our affections? (unloving earth, without a throb to answer ours,
Cold earth, the place of graves.)

Yet soul be sure the first intent remains, and shall be carried out,
100   Perhaps even now the time has arrived.

After the seas are all cross'd, (as they seem already cross'd,)
After the great captains and engineers have accomplish'd their work,
After the noble inventors, after the scientists, the chemist, the geologist, ethnologist,
Finally shall come the poet worthy of that name,
The true son of God shall come singing his songs.

Then not your deeds only O voyagers, O scientists and inventors, shall be justified,
All these hearts as of fretted children shall be sooth'd,
All affection shall be fully responded to, the secret shall be told,
All these separations and gaps shall be taken up and hook'd and link'd together,
110   The whole earth, this cold, impassive, voiceless earth, shall be completely justified,
Trinitas divine shall be gloriously accomplish'd and compacted by the true son of God, the poet,
(He shall indeed pass the straits and conquer the mountains,
He shall double the cape of Good Hope to some purpose,)
Nature and Man shall be disjoin'd and diffused no more,
The true son of God shall absolutely fuse them.

6
Year at whose wide-flung door I sing!
Year of the purpose accomplish'd!
Year of the marriage of continents, climates and oceans!
(No mere doge of Venice now wedding the Adriatic,)
120   I see O year in you the vast terraqueous globe given and giving all,
Europe to Asia, Africa join'd, and they to the New World,
The lands, geographies, dancing before you, holding a festival garland,
As brides and bridegrooms hand in hand.

Passage to India!
Cooling airs from Caucasus, far, soothing cradle of man,
The river Euphrates flowing, the past lit up again.

Lo soul, the retrospect brought forward,
The old, most populous, wealthiest of earth's lands,
The streams of the Indus and the Ganges and their many affluents,
(I my shores of America walking to-day behold, resuming all,)   130
The tale of Alexander on his warlike marches suddenly dying,
On one side China and on the other Persia and Arabia,
To the south the great seas and the bay of Bengal,
The flowing literatures, tremendous epics, religions, castes,
Old occult Brahma interminably far back, the tender and junior Buddha,
Central and southern empires and all their belongings, possessors,
The wars of Tamerlane, the reign of Aurungzebe,
The traders, rulers, explorers, Moslems, Venetians, Byzantium, the Arabs, Por-
    tuguese,
The first travelers famous yet, Marco Polo, Batouta, the Moor,
Doubts to be solv'd, the map incognita, blanks to be fill'd,   140
The foot of man unstay'd, the hands never at rest,
Thyself O soul that will not brook a challenge.

The mediæval navigators rise before me,
The world of 1492, with its awaken'd enterprise,
Something swelling in humanity now like the sap of the earth in spring,
The sunset splendor of chivalry declining.

And who art thou sad shade?
Gigantic, visionary, thyself a visionary,
With majestic limbs and pious beaming eyes,
Spreading around with every look of thine a golden world,   150
Enhuing it with gorgeous hues.

As the chief histrion,
Down to the footlights walks in some great scena,
Dominating the rest I see the Admiral himself,
(History's type of courage, action, faith,)
Behold him sail from Palos leading his little fleet,
His voyage behold, his return, his great fame,
His misfortunes, calumniators, behold him a prisoner, chain'd,
Behold his dejection, poverty, death.

(Curious in time I stand, noting the efforts of heroes,   160
Is the deferment long? bitter the slander, poverty, death?
Lies the seed unreck'd for centuries in the ground? lo, to God's due
    occasion,
Uprising in the night, it sprouts, blooms,
And fills the earth with use and beauty.)

7

Passage indeed O soul to primal thought,
Not lands and seas alone, thy own clear freshness,
The young maturity of brood and bloom,
To realms of budding bibles.

O soul, repressless, I with thee and thou with me,
170   Thy circumnavigation of the world begin,
Of man, the voyage of his mind's return.
To reason's early paradise,
Back, back to wisdom's birth, to innocent intuitions,
Again with fair creation.

8

O we can wait no longer,
We too take ship O soul,
Joyous we too launch out on trackless seas,
Fearless for unknown shores on waves of ecstasy to sail,
Amid the wafting winds, (thou pressing me to thee, I thee to me, O soul,)
180   Caroling free, singing our song of God,
Chanting our chant of pleasant exploration.

With laugh and many a kiss,
(Let others deprecate, let others weep for sin, remorse, humiliation,)
O soul thou pleasest me, I thee.

Ah more than any priest O soul we too believe in God,
But with the mystery of God we dare not dally.

O soul thou pleasest me, I thee,
Sailing these seas or on the hills, or waking in the night,
Thoughts, silent thoughts, of Time and Space and Death, like waters flowing,
190   Bear me indeed as through the regions infinite,
Whose air I breathe, whose ripples hear, lave me all over,
Bathe me O God in thee, mounting to thee,
I and my soul to range in range of thee.

O Thou transcendent,
Nameless, the fibre and the breath,
Light of the light, shedding forth universes, thou centre of them,
Thou mightier centre of the true, the good, the loving,
Thou moral, spiritual fountain—affection's source—thou reservoir,
(O pensive soul of me—O thirst unsatisfied—waitest not there?
200   Waitest not haply for us somewhere there the Comrade perfect?)
Thou pulse—thou motive of the stars, suns, systems,
That, circling, move in order, safe, harmonious,
Athwart the shapeless vastnesses of space,

How should I think, how breathe a single breath, how speak, if out of
    myself,
I could not launch, to those, superior universes?

Swiftly I shrivel at the thought of God,
At Nature and its wonders, Time and Space and Death,
But that I, turning, call to thee O soul, thou actual Me,
And lo, thou gently masterest the orbs,
Thou matest Time, smilest content at Death,   210
And fillest, swellest full the vastnesses of Space.

Greater than stars or suns,
Bounding O soul thou journeyest forth;
What love than thine and ours could wider amplify?
What aspirations, wishes, outvie thine and ours O soul?
What dreams of the ideal? what plans of purity, perfection, strength,
What cheerful willingness for others' sake to give up all?
For others' sake to suffer all?

Reckoning ahead O soul, when thou, the time achiev'd,
The seas all cross'd, weather'd the capes, the voyage done,   220
Surrounded, copest, frontest God, yieldest, the aim attain'd,
As fill'd with friendship, love complete, the Elder Brother found,
The Younger melts in fondness in his arms.

9
Passage to more than India!
Are thy wings plumed indeed for such far flights?
O soul, voyagest thou indeed on voyages like those?
Disportest thou on waters such as those?
Soundest below the Sanscrit and the Vedas?
Then have thy bent unleash'd.

Passage to you, your shores, ye aged fierce enigmas!   230
Passage to you, to mastership of you, ye strangling problems!
You, strew'd with the wrecks of skeletons, that, living, never reach'd you.

Passage to more than India!
O secret of the earth and sky!
Of you O waters of the sea! O winding creeks and rivers!
Of you O woods and fields! of you strong mountains of my land!
Of you O prairies! of you gray rocks!
O morning red! O clouds! O rain and snows!
O day and night, passage to you!

O sun and moon and all you stars! Sirius and Jupiter!   240
Passage to you!

Passage, immediate passage! the blood burns in my veins!
Away O soul! hoist instantly the anchor!
Cut the hawsers—haul out—shake out every sail!
Have we not stood here like trees in the ground long enough?
Have we not grovel'd here long enough, eating and drinking like mere brutes?
Have we not darken'd and dazed ourselves with books long enough?

Sail forth—steer for the deep waters only,
Reckless O soul, exploring, I with thee, and thou with me,
250   For we are bound where mariner has not yet dared to go,
And we will risk the ship, ourselves and all.

O my brave soul!
O farther farther sail!
O daring joy, but safe! are they not all the seas of God?
O farther, farther, farther sail!
1868·1871

SO LONG!

To conclude, I announce what comes after me.

I remember I said before my leaves sprang at all,
I would raise my voice jocund and strong with reference to consummations.

When America does what was promis'd,
When through these States walk a hundred millions of superb persons,
When the rest part away for superb persons and contribute to them,
When breeds of the most perfect mothers denote America,
Then to me and mine our due fruition.

I have press'd through in my own right,
10   I have sung the body and the soul, war and peace have I sung, and the songs of
life and death,
And the songs of birth, and shown that there are many births.

I have offer'd my style to every one, I have journey'd with confident step;
While my pleasure is yet at the full I whisper *So long!*
And take the young woman's hand and the young man's hand for the last time.

I announce natural persons to arise,
I announce justice triumphant,
I announce uncompromising liberty and equality,
I announce the justification of candor and the justification of pride.

I announce that the identity of these States is a single identity only,
I announce the Union more and more compact, indissoluble,   20
I announce splendors and majesties to make all the previous politics of the earth
    insignificant.

I announce adhesiveness, I say it shall be limitless, unloosen'd,
I say you shall yet find the friend you were looking for.

I announce a man or woman coming, perhaps you are the one, (*So long!*)
I announce the great individual, fluid as Nature, chaste, affectionate, compas-
    sionate, fully arm'd.

I announce a life that shall be copious, vehement, spiritual, bold,
I announce an end that shall lightly and joyfully meet its translation.

I announce myriads of youths, beautiful, gigantic, sweet-blooded,
I announce a race of splendid and savage old men.

O thicker and faster—(*So long!*)   30
O crowding too close upon me,
I foresee too much, it means more than I thought,
It appears to me I am dying.

Hasten throat and sound your last,
Salute me—salute the days once more. Peal the old cry once more.

Screaming electric, the atmosphere using,
At random glancing, each as I notice absorbing,
Swiftly on, but a little while alighting,
Curious envelop'd messages delivering,
Sparkles hot, seed ethereal down in the dirt dropping,   40
Myself unknowing, my commission obeying, to question it never daring,
To ages and ages yet the growth of the seed leaving,
To troops out of the war arising, they the task I have set promulging,
To women certain whispers of myself bequeathing, their affection me more
    clearly explaining,
To young men my problems offering—no dallier I—I the muscle of their brains
    trying,
So I pass, a little time vocal, visible, contrary,
Afterward a melodious echo, passionately bent for, (death making me really
    undying,)
The best of me then when no longer visible, for toward that I have been inces-
    santly preparing.

What is there more, that I lag and pause and crouch extended with unshut
    mouth?
Is there a single final farewell?   50

My songs cease, I abandon them,
From behind the screen where I hid I advance personally solely to you.

Camerado, this is no book,
Who touches this touches a man,
(Is it night? are we here together alone?)
It is I you hold and who holds you,
I spring from the pages into your arms—decease calls me forth.

O how your fingers drowse me,
Your breath falls around me like dew, your pulse lulls the tympans of my ears,
60   I feel immerged from head to foot,
Delicious, enough.

Enough O deed impromptu and secret,
Enough O gliding present—enough O summ'd-up past.

Dear friend whoever you are take this kiss,
I give it especially to you, do not forget me,
I feel like one who has done work for the day to retire awhile,
I receive now again of my many translations, from my avataras ascending,
     while others doubtless await me,
An unknown sphere more real than I dream'd, more direct, darts awakening
     rays about me, *So long!*
Remember my words, I may again return,
70   I love you, I depart from materials,
I am as one disembodied, triumphant, dead.
1860·1881

PREFACE TO 1855 EDITION
OF ''LEAVES OF GRASS''

America does not repel the past or what it has produced under its forms or
amid other politics or the idea of castes or the old religions . . .[1] accepts the
lesson with calmness . . . is not so impatient as has been supposed that the
slough still sticks to opinions and manners and literature while the life which
served its requirements has passed into the new life of the new forms . . .
perceives that the corpse is slowly borne from the eating and sleeping rooms of
the house . . . perceives that it waits a little while in the door . . . that it was
fittest for its days . . . that its action has descended to the stalwart and well-
shaped heir who approaches . . . and that he shall be fittest for his days.
     The Americans of all nations at any time upon the earth have probably the
fullest poetical nature. The United States themselves are essentially the greatest
poem. In the history of the earth hitherto the largest and most stirring appear

1. religions. . . : The dots are Whitman's throughout and do not indicate omissions.

tame and orderly to their ampler largeness and stir. Here at last is something in the doings of man that corresponds with the broadcast doings of the day and night. Here is not merely a nation but a teeming nation of nations. Here is action untied from strings necessarily blind to particulars and details magnificently moving in vast masses. Here is the hospitality which forever indicates heroes. . . . Here are the roughs and beards and space and ruggedness and nonchalance that the soul loves. Here the performance disdaining the trivial unapproached in the tremendous audacity of its crowds and groupings and the push of its perspective spreads with crampless and flowing breadth and showers its prolific and splendid extravagance. One sees it must indeed own the riches of the summer and winter, and need never be bankrupt while corn grows from the ground or the orchards drop apples or the bays contain fish or men beget children upon women.

Other states indicate themselves in their deputies . . . but the genius of the United States is not best or most in its executives or legislatures, nor in its ambassadors or authors or colleges or churches or parlors, nor even in its newspapers or inventors . . . but always most in the common people. Their manners speech dress friendships—the freshness and candor of their physiognomy—the picturesque looseness of their carriage . . . their deathless attachment to freedom—their aversion to anything indecorous or soft or mean—the practical acknowledgment of the citizens of one state by the citizens of all other states —the fierceness of their roused resentment—their curiosity and welcome of novelty—their self-esteem and wonderful sympathy—their susceptibility to a slight—the air they have of persons who never knew how it felt to stand in the presence of superiors—the fluency of their speech—their delight in music, the sure symptom of manly tenderness and native elegance of soul . . . their good temper and open-handedness—the terrible significance of their elections—the President's taking off his hat to them not they to him—these too are unrhymed poetry. It awaits the gigantic and generous treatment worthy of it.

The largeness of nature or the nation were monstrous without a corresponding largeness and generosity of the spirit of the citizen. Not nature nor swarming states nor streets and steamships nor prosperous business nor farms nor capital nor learning may suffice for the ideal of man . . . nor suffice the poet. No reminiscences may suffice either. A live nation can always cut a deep mark and can have the best authority the cheapest . . . namely from its own soul. This is the sum of the profitable uses of individuals or states and of present action and grandeur and of the subjects of poets.—As if it were necessary to trot back generation after generation to the eastern records! As if the beauty and sacredness of the demonstrable must fall behind that of the mythical! As if men do not make their mark out of any times! As if the opening of the western continent by discovery and what has transpired since in North and South America were less than the small theatre of the antique or the aimless sleep-walking of the middle ages! The pride of the United States leaves the wealth and finesse of the cities and all returns of commerce and agriculture and all the magnitude of geography or shows of exterior victory to enjoy the breed of full-sized men or one fullsized man unconquerable and simple.

The American poets are to enclose old and new for America is the race of races. Of them a bard is to be commensurate with a people. To him the other continents arrive as contributions . . . he gives them reception for their sake and his own sake. His spirit responds to his country's spirit . . . he incarnates its geography and natural life and rivers and lakes. Mississippi with annual freshets and changing chutes, Missouri and Columbia and Ohio and Saint Lawrence with the falls and beautiful masculine Hudson, do not embouchure where they spend themselves more than they embouchure into him. The blue breadth over the inland sea of Virginia and Maryland and the sea off Massachusetts and Maine and over Manhattan bay and over Champlain and Erie and over Ontario and Huron and Michigan and Superior, and over the Texan and Mexican and Floridian and Cuban seas and over the seas off California and Oregon, is not tallied by the blue breadth of the waters below more than the breadth of above and below is tallied by him. When the long Atlantic coast stretches longer and the Pacific coast stretches longer he easily stretches with them north or south. He spans between them also from east to west and reflects what is between them. On him rise solid growths that offset the growths of pine and cedar and hemlock and liveoak and locust and chestnut and cypress and hickory and limetree and cottonwood and tuliptree and cactus and wildvine and tamarind and persimmon . . . and tangles as tangled as any canebreak or swamp . . . and forests coated with transparent ice and icicles hanging from the boughs and crackling in the wind . . . and sides and peaks of mountains . . . and pasturage sweet and free as savannah or upland or prairie . . . with flights and songs and screams that answer those of the wildpigeon and highhold and orchard-oriole and coot and surf-duck and redshouldered-hawk and fish-hawk and white-ibis and indian-hen and cat-owl and water-pheasant and qua-bird and pied-sheldrake and black-bird and mockingbird and buzzard and condor and night-heron and eagle. To him the hereditary countenance descends both mother's and father's. To him enter the essences of the real things and past and present events—of the enormous diversity of temperature and agriculture and mines—the tribes of red aborigines—the weather-beaten vessels entering new ports or making landings on rocky coasts—the first settlements north or south—the rapid stature and muscle—the haughty defiance of '76, and the war and peace and formation of the constitution . . . the union always surrounded by blatherers and always calm and impregnable—the perpetual coming of immigrants—the wharfhem'd cities and superior marine—the unsurveyed interior—the loghouses and clearings and wild animals and hunters and trappers . . . the free commerce—the fisheries and whaling and gold-digging—the endless gestation of new states—the convening of Congress every December, the members duly coming up from all climates and the uttermost parts . . . the noble character of the young mechanics and of all free American workmen and workwomen . . . the general ardor and friendliness and enterprise—the perfect equality of the female with the male . . . the large amativeness—the fluid movement of the population—the factories and mercantile life and laborsaving machinery—the Yankee swap—the New-York firemen and the target excursion—the southern plantation life—the character of the northeast and of the northwest and southwest—slavery and the tremulous spreading of hands to protect it, and the stern opposition to it which shall never cease till it ceases or the speaking of tongues and the moving of lips cease.

For such the expression of the American poet is to be transcendant and new. It is to be indirect and not direct or descriptive or epic. Its quality goes through these to much more. Let the age and wars of other nations be chanted and their eras and characters be illustrated and that finish the verse. Not so the great psalm of the republic. Here the theme is creative and has vista. Here comes one among the wellbeloved stonecutters and plans with decision and science and sees the solid and beautiful forms of the future where there are now no solid forms.

Of all nations the United States with veins full of poetical stuff most need poets and will doubtless have the greatest and use them the greatest. Their Presidents shall not be their common referee so much as their poets shall. Of all mankind the great poet is the equable man. Not in him but off from him things are grotesque or eccentric or fail of their sanity. Nothing out of its place is good and nothing in its place is bad. He bestows on every object or quality its fit proportions neither more nor less. He is the arbiter of the diverse and he is the key. He is the equalizer of his age and land . . . he supplies what wants supplying and checks what wants checking. If peace is the routine out of him speaks the spirit of peace, large, rich, thrifty, building vast and populous cities, encouraging agriculture and the arts and commerce—lighting the study of man, the soul, immortality— federal, state or municipal government, marriage, health, freetrade, intertravel by land and sea . . . nothing too close, nothing too far off . . . the stars not too far off. In war he is the most deadly force of the war. Who recruits him recruits horse and foot . . . he fetches parks of artillery the best that engineer ever knew. If the time becomes slothful and heavy he knows how to arouse it . . . he can make every word he speaks draw blood. Whatever stagnates in the flat of custom or obedience or legislation he never stagnates. Obedience does not master him, he masters it. High up out of reach he stands turning a concentrated light . . . he turns the pivot with his finger . . . he baffles the swiftest runners as he stands and easily overtakes and envelops them. The time straying toward infidelity and confections and persiflage he withholds by his steady faith . . . he spreads out his dishes . . . he offers the sweet firmfibred meat that grows men and women. His brain is the ultimate brain. He is no arguer . . . he is judgment. He judges not as the judge judges but as the sun falling around a helpless thing. As he sees the farthest he has the most faith. His thoughts are the hymns of the praise of things. In the talk on the soul and eternity and God off of his equal plane he is silent. He sees eternity less like a play with a prologue and denouement . . . he sees eternity in men and women . . . he does not see men and women as dreams or dots. Faith is the antiseptic of the soul . . . it pervades the common people and preserves them . . . they never give up believing and expecting and trusting. There is that indescribable freshness and unconsciousness about an illiterate person that humbles and mocks the power of the noblest expressive genius. The poet sees for a certainty how one not a great artist may be just as sacred as the greatest artist. . . . The power to destroy or remould is freely used by him but never the power of attack. What is past is past. If he does not expose superior models and prove himself by every step he takes he is not what is wanted. The presence of the greatest poet conquers . . . not parleying or struggling or any prepared attempts. Now he has passed that way see after him! there is not left any vestige of despair or misanthropy

WHITMAN, PREFACE TO 1855 EDITION OF "LEAVES OF

or cunning or exclusiveness or the ignominy of a nativity or color or delusion of hell or the necessity of hell . . . and no man thenceforward shall be degraded for ignorance or weakness or sin.

The greatest poet hardly knows pettiness or triviality. If he breathes into any thing that was before thought small it dilates with the grandeur and life of the universe. He is a seer . . . he is individual . . . he is complete in himself . . . the others are as good as he, only he sees it and they do not. He is not one of the chorus . . . he does not stop for any regulations . . . he is the president of regulation. What the eyesight does to the rest he does to the rest. Who knows the curious mystery of the eyesight? The other senses corroborate themselves, but this is removed from any proof but its own and foreruns the identities of the spiritual world. A single glance of it mocks all the investigations of man and all the instruments and books of the earth and all reasoning. What is marvelous? what is unlikely? what is impossible or baseless or vague? after you have once just opened the space of a peachpit and given audience to far and near and to the sunset and had all things enter with electric swiftness softly and duly without confusion or jostling or jam.

The land and sea, the animals fishes and birds, the sky of heaven and the orbs, the forests mountains and rivers, are not small themes . . . but folks expect of the poet to indicate more than the beauty and dignity which always attach to dumb real objects . . . they expect him to indicate the path between reality and their souls. Men and women perceive the beauty well enough . . . probably as well as he. The passionate tenacity of hunters, woodmen, early risers, cultivators of gardens and orchards and fields, the love of healthy women for the manly form, seafaring persons, drivers of horses, the passion for light and the open air, all is an old varied sign of the unfailing perception of beauty and of a residence of the poetic in outdoor people. They can never be assisted by poets to perceive . . . some may but they never can. The poetic quality is not marshalled in rhyme or uniformity or abstract addresses to things nor in melancholy complaints or good precepts, but is the life of these and much else and is in the soul. The profit of rhyme is that it drops seeds of a sweeter and more luxuriant rhyme, and of uniformity that it conveys itself into its own roots in the ground out of sight. The rhyme and uniformity of perfect poems show the free growth of metrical laws and bud from them as unerringly and loosely as lilacs or roses on a bush, and take shapes as compact as the shapes of chestnuts and oranges and melons and pears, and shed the perfume impalpable to form. The fluency and ornaments of the finest poems or music or orations or recitations are not independent but dependent. All beauty comes from beautiful blood and a beautiful brain. If the greatnesses are in conjunction in a man or woman it is enough . . . the fact will prevail through the universe . . . but the gaggery and gilt of a million years will not prevail. Who troubles himself about his ornaments or fluency is lost. This is what you shall do: Love the earth and sun and the animals, despise riches, give alms to every one that asks, stand up for the stupid and crazy, devote your income and labor to others, hate tyrants, argue not concerning God, have patience and indulgence toward the people, take off your hat to nothing known or unknown or to any man or number of men, go freely with powerful uneducated persons and with the young and with the mothers of families, read these leaves in the open air every season of every year of your life, re-examine all you have been told at school or church or in any book, dismiss whatever insults your own soul, and your very flesh shall be a great poem and have the richest fluency not only in its words but in the silent lines of its lips and face and between the lashes of your eyes and in every motion and joint of your body. . . . The poet shall not spend his time in unneeded work. He shall know that the ground is always ready plowed and manured . . . others may not know it but he shall. He shall go directly to the creation. His trust shall master the trust of everything he touches . . . and shall master all attachment.

The known universe has one complete lover and that is the greatest poet. He consumes an eternal passion and is indifferent which chance happens and which possible contingency of fortune or misfortune and persuades daily and hourly his delicious pay. What balks or breaks others is fuel for his burning progress to contact and amorous joy. Other proportions of the reception of pleasure dwindle to nothing to his proportions. All expected from heaven or from the highest he is rapport with in the sight of the daybreak or a scene of the winterwoods or the presence of children playing or with his arm round the neck of a man or woman. His love above all love has leisure and expanse . . . he leaves room ahead of himself. He is no irresolute or suspicious lover . . . he is sure . . . he scorns intervals. His experience and the showers and thrills are not for nothing. Nothing can jar him . . . suffering and darkness cannot—death and fear cannot. To him complaint and jealousy and envy are corpses buried and rotten in the earth . . . he saw them buried. The sea is not surer of the shore or the shore of the sea than he is of the fruition of his love and of all perfection and beauty.

The fruition of beauty is no chance of hit or miss . . . it is inevitable as life . . . it is exact and plumb as gravitation. From the eyesight proceeds another eyesight and from the hearing proceeds another hearing and from the voice proceeds another voice eternally curious of the harmony of things with man. To these respond perfections not only in the committees that were supposed to stand for the rest but in the rest themselves just the same. These understand the law of perfection in masses and floods . . . that its finish is to each for itself and onward from itself . . . that it is profuse and impartial . . . that there is not a minute of the light or dark nor an acre of the earth or sea without it—nor any direction of the sky nor any trade or employment nor any turn of events. This is the reason that about the proper expression of beauty there is precision and balance . . . one part does not need to be thrust above another. The best singer is not the one who has the most lithe and powerful organ . . . the pleasure of poems is not in them that take the handsomest measure and similes and sound.

Without effort and without exposing in the least how it is done the greatest poet brings the spirit of any or all events and passions and scenes and persons some more and some less to bear on your individual character as you hear or read. To do this well is to compete with the laws that pursue and follow time. What is the purpose must surely be there and the clue of it must be there . . . and the faintest indication is the indication of the best and then becomes the clearest indication. Past and present and future are not disjoined but joined. The greatest poet forms the consistence of what is to be from what has been and is. He drags the dead out of their coffins and stands them again on their feet . . . he says to the past, Rise and walk before me that I may realize you. He learns the lesson . . . he places himself where the future becomes present. The greatest poet does not only dazzle his rays over character and scenes and passions . . . he finally ascends and finishes all . . . he exhibits the pinnacles that no man can tell what they are for or what is beyond . . . he glows a moment on the extremest verge. He is most wonderful in his last half-hidden smile or frown . . . by that flash of the moment of parting the one that sees it shall be encouraged or terrified afterwards for many years. The greatest poet does not moralize or make applications of morals . . . he knows the soul. The soul has that measureless pride which consists in never acknowledging any lessons but its own. But it has sympathy as measureless as its pride and the one balances the other and neither can stretch too far while it stretches in company with the other. The inmost secrets of art sleep with the twain. The greatest poet has lain close betwixt both and they are vital in his style and thoughts.

The art of art, the glory of expression and the sunshine of the light of letters is simplicity. Nothing is better than simplicity . . . nothing can make up for excess or for the lack of definiteness. To carry on the heave of impulse and pierce intellectual depths and give all subjects their articulations are powers neither common nor very uncommon. But to speak in literature with the perfect rectitude and insouciance of the movements of animals and the unimpeachableness of the sentiment of trees in the woods and grass by the roadside is the flawless triumph of art. If you have looked on him who has achieved it you have looked on one of the masters of the artists of all nations and times. You shall not contemplate the flight of the graygull over the bay or the mettlesome action of the blood horse or the tall leaning of sunflowers on their stalk or the appearance of the sun journeying through heaven or the appearance of the moon afterward with any more satisfaction than you shall contemplate him. The greatest poet has less a marked style and is more the channel of thoughts and things without increase or diminution, and is the free channel of himself. He swears to his art, I will not be meddlesome, I will not have in my writing any elegance or effect or originality to hang in the way between me and the rest like curtains. I will have nothing hang in the way, not the richest curtains. What I tell I tell for precisely what it is. Let who may exalt or startle or fascinate or sooth I will have purposes as health or heat or snow has and be as regardless of observation. What I experience or portray shall go from my composition without a shred of my composition. You shall stand by my side and look in the mirror with me.

The old red blood and stainless gentility of great poets will be proved by their unconstraint. A heroic person walks at his ease through and out of that custom or precedent or authority that suits him not. Of the traits of the brotherhood of writers savans musicians inventors and artists nothing is finer than silent defiance advancing from new free forms. In the need of poems philosophy politics mechanism science behaviour, the craft of art, an appropriate native grand-opera, shipcraft, or any craft, he is greatest forever and forever who contributes the greatest original practical example. The cleanest expression is that which finds no sphere worthy of itself and makes one.

The messages of great poets to each man and woman are, Come to us on equal terms, Only then can you understand us, We are no better than you, What we enclose you enclose, What we enjoy you may enjoy. Did you suppose there could be only one Supreme? We affirm there can be unnumbered Supremes, and that one does not countervail another any more than one eyesight countervails another . . . and that men can be good or grand only of the consciousness of their supremacy within them. What do you think is the grandeur of storms and dismemberments and the deadliest battles and wrecks and the wildest fury of the elements and the power of the sea and the motion of nature and of the throes of human desires and dignity and hate and love? It is that something in the soul which says, Rage on, Whirl on, I tread master here and everywhere, Master of the spasms of the sky and of the shatter of the sea, Master of nature and passion and death, And of all terror and all pain.

The American bards shall be marked for generosity and affection and for encouraging competitors. . . . They shall be kosmos . . . without monopoly or secrecy . . . glad to pass any thing to any one . . . hungry for equals night and day. They shall not be careful of riches and privilege . . . they shall be riches and privilege . . . they shall perceive who the most affluent man is. The most affluent man is he that confronts all the shows he sees by equivalents out of the stronger wealth of himself. The American bard shall delineate no class of persons nor one or two out of the strata of interests nor love most nor truth most nor the soul most nor the body most . . . and not be for the eastern states more than the western or the northern states more than the southern.

Exact science and its practical movements are no checks on the greatest poet but always his encouragement and support. The outset and remembrance are there . . . there are the arms that lifted him first and brace him best . . . there he returns after all his goings and comings. The sailor and traveler . . . the atomist chemist astronomer geologist phrenologist spiritualist mathematician historian and lexicographer are not poets, but they are the lawgivers of poets and their construction underlies the structure of every perfect poem. No matter what rises or is uttered they sent the seed of the conception of it . . . of them and by them stand the visible proofs of souls . . . always of their fatherstuff must be begotten the sinewy races of bards. If there shall be love and content between the father and the son and if the greatness of the son is the exuding of the greatness of the father there shall be love between the poet and the man of demonstrable science. In the beauty of poems are the tuft and final applause of science.

Great is the faith of the flush of knowledge and of the investigation of the depths of qualities and things. Cleaving and circling here swells the soul of the poet yet is president of itself always. The depths are fathomless and therefore calm. The innocence and nakedness are resumed . . . they are neither modest nor immodest. The whole theory of the special and supernatural and all that was twined with it or educed out of it departs as a dream. What has ever happened . . . what happens and whatever may or shall happen, the vital laws enclose all . . . they are sufficient for any case and for all cases . . . none to be hurried or retarded . . . any miracle of affairs or persons inadmissible in the vast clear scheme where every motion and every spear of grass and the frames and spirits of men and women and all that concerns them are unspeakably perfect miracles all referring to all and each distinct and in its place. It is also not consistent with the reality of the soul to admit that there is anything in the known universe more divine than men and women.

Men and women and the earth and all upon it are simply to be taken as they are, and the investigation of their past and present and future shall be uninter-

mitted and shall be done with perfect candor. Upon this basis philosophy specu-
lates ever looking toward the poet, ever regarding the eternal tendencies of all
toward happiness never inconsistent with what is clear to the senses and to the
soul. For the eternal tendencies of all toward happiness make the only point of
sane philosophy. Whatever comprehends less than that . . . whatever is less than
the laws of light and of astronomical motion . . . or less than the laws that
follow the thief the liar the glutton and the drunkard through this life and doubtless afterward . . . or less than vast stretches of time or the slow formation of
density or the patient upheaving of strata—is of no account. Whatever would
put God in a poem or system of philosophy as contending against some being or
influence, is also of no account. Sanity and ensemble characterise the great
master . . . spoilt in one principle all is spoilt. The great master has nothing to
do with miracles. He sees health for himself in being one of the mass . . . he
sees the hiatus in singular eminence. To the perfect shape comes common
ground. To be under the general law is great for that is to correspond with it.
The master knows that he is unspeakably great and that all are unspeakably
great . . . that nothing for instance is greater than to conceive children and
bring them up well . . . that to be is just as great as to perceive or tell.

In the make of the great masters the idea of political liberty is indispensable.
Liberty takes the adherence of heroes wherever men and women exist . . . but
never takes any adherence or welcome from the rest more than from poets. They
are the voice and exposition of liberty. They out of ages are worthy the grand
idea . . . to them it is confided and they must sustain it. Nothing has preced-
ence of it and nothing can warp or degrade it. The attitude of great poets is to
cheer up slaves and horrify despots. The turn of their necks, the sound of their
feet, the motions of their wrists, are full of hazard to the one and hope to the
other. Come nigh them awhile and though they neither speak or advise you shall
learn the faithful American lesson. Liberty is poorly served by men whose good
intent is quelled from one failure or two failures or any number of failures, or
from the casual indifference or ingratitude of the people, or from the sharp show
of the tushes of power, or the bringing to bear soldiers and cannon or any penal
statutes. Liberty relies upon itself, invites no one, promises nothing, sits in calmness and light, is positive and composed, and knows no discouragement. The
battle rages with many a loud alarm and frequent advance and retreat . . .
the enemy triumphs . . . the prison, the handcuffs, the iron necklace and anklet,
the scaffold, garrote and leadballs do their work . . . the cause is asleep . . .
the strong throats are choked with their own blood . . . the young men drop
their eyelashes toward the ground when they pass each other . . . and is liberty
gone out of that place? No never. When liberty goes it is not the first to go nor the
second nor third to go . . . it waits for all the rest to go . . . it is the last.
. . . When the memories of the old martyrs are faded utterly away . . . when
the large names of patriots are laughed at in the public halls from the lips of the
orators . . . when the boys are no more christened after the same but christened
after tyrants and traitors instead . . . when the laws of the free are grudgingly
permitted and laws for informers and bloodmoney are sweet to the taste of the
people . . . when I and you walk abroad upon the earth stung with compassion
at the sight of numberless brothers answering our equal friendship and calling
no man master—and when we are elated with noble joy at the sight of slaves

. . . when the soul retires in the cool communion of the night and surveys its experience and has much extasy over the word and deed that put back a helpless innocent person into the gripe of the gripers or into any cruel inferiority . . . when those in all parts of these states who could easier realize the true American character but do not yet—when the swarms of cringers, suckers, doughfaces, lice of politics, planners of sly involutions for their own preferment to city offices or state legislatures or the judiciary or congress or the presidency, obtain a response of love and natural deference from the people whether they get the offices or no . . . when it is better to be a bound booby and rogue in office at a high salary than the poorest free mechanic or farmer with his hat unmoved from his head and firm eyes and a candid and generous heart . . . and when servility by town or state or the federal government or any oppression on a large scale or small scale can be tried on without its own punishment following duly after in exact proportion against the smallest chance of escape . . . or rather when all life and all the souls of men and women are discharged from any part of the earth—then only shall the instinct of liberty be discharged from that part of the earth.

As the attributes of the poets of the kosmos concentre in the real body and soul and in the pleasure of things they possess the superiority of genuineness over all fiction and romance. As they emit themselves facts are showered over with light . . . the daylight is lit with more volatile light . . . also the deep between the setting and rising sun goes deeper many fold. Each precise object or condition or combination or process exhibits a beauty . . . the multiplication table its—old age its—the carpenter's trade its—the grand-opera its . . . the hugehulled cleanshaped New-York clipper at sea under steam or full sail gleams with unmatched beauty . . . the American circles and large harmonies of government gleam with theirs . . . and the commonest definite intentions and actions with theirs. The poets of the kosmos advance through all interpositions and coverings and turmoils and stratagems to first principles. They are of use . . . they dissolve poverty from its need and riches from its conceit. You large proprietor they say shall not realize or perceive more than any one else. The owner of the library is not he who holds a legal title to it having bought and paid for it. Any one and every one is owner of the library who can read the same through all the varieties of tongues and subjects and styles, and in whom they enter with ease and take residence and force toward paternity and maternity, and make supple and powerful and rich and large. . . . These American states strong and healthy and accomplished shall receive no pleasure from violations of natural models and must not permit them. In paintings or mouldings or carvings in mineral or wood, or in the illustrations of books or newspapers, or in any comic or tragic prints, or in the patterns of woven stuffs or anything to beautify rooms or furniture or costumes, or to put upon cornices or monuments or on the prows or sterns of ships, or to put anywhere before the human eye indoors or out, that which distorts honest shapes or which creates unearthly beings or places or contingencies is a nuisance and revolt. Of the human form especially it is so great it must never be made ridiculous. Of ornaments to a work nothing outre can be allowed . . . but those ornaments can be allowed that conform to the perfect facts of the open air and that flow out of the nature of the work and come irrepressibly from it and are necessary to the completion of the work.

Most works are most beautiful without ornament. . . . Exaggerations will be revenged in human physiology. Clean and vigorous children are jetted and conceived only in those communities where the models of natural forms are public every day. . . . Great genius and the people of these states must never be demeaned to romances. As soon as histories are properly told there is no more need of romances.

The great poets are also to be known by the absence in them of tricks and by the justification of perfect personal candor. Then folks echo a new cheap joy and a divine voice leaping from their brains: How beautiful is candor! All faults may be forgiven of him who has perfect candor. Henceforth let no man of us lie, for we have seen that openness wins the inner and outer world and that there is no single exception, and that never since our earth gathered itself in a mass have deceit or subterfuge or prevarication attracted its smallest particle or the faintest tinge of a shade—and that through the enveloping wealth and rank of a state or the whole republic of states a sneak or sly person shall be discovered and despised . . . and that the soul has never been once fooled and never can be fooled . . . and thrift without the loving nod of the soul is only a fœtid puff . . . and there never grew up in any of the continents of the globe nor upon any planet or satellite or star, nor upon the asteroids, nor in any part of ethereal space, nor in the midst of density, nor under the fluid wet of the sea, nor in that condition which precedes the birth of babes, nor at any time during the changes of life, nor in that condition that follows what we term death, nor in any stretch of abeyance or action afterward of vitality, nor in any process of formation or reformation anywhere, a being whose instinct hated the truth.

Extreme caution or prudence, the soundest organic health, large hope and comparison and fondness for women and children, large alimentiveness and destructiveness and causality, with a perfect sense of the oneness of nature and the propriety of the same spirit applied to human affairs . . . these are called up of the float of the brain of the world to be parts of the greatest poet from his birth out of his mother's womb and from her birth out of her mother's. Caution seldom goes far enough. It has been thought that the prudent citizen was the citizen who applied himself to solid gains and did well for himself and his family and completed a lawful life without debt or crime. The greatest poet sees and admits these economies as he sees the economies of food and sleep, but has higher notions of prudence than to think he gives much when he gives a few slight attentions at the latch of the gate. The premises of the prudence of life are not the hospitality of it or the ripeness and harvest of it. Beyond the independence of a little sum laid aside for burial-money, and of a few clapboards around and shingles overhead on a lot of American soil owned, and the easy dollars that supply the year's plain clothing and meals, the melancholy prudence of the abandonment of such a great being as a man is to the toss and pallor of years of moneymaking with all their scorching days and icy nights and all their stifling deceits and underhanded dodgings, or infinitessimals of parlors, or shameless stuffing while others starve . . . and all the loss of the bloom and odor of the earth and of the flowers and atmosphere and of the sea and of the true taste of the women and men you pass or have to do with in youth or middle age, and the issuing sickness and desperate revolt at the close of a life without elevation or naïveté, and the ghastly chatter of a death without serenity or majesty, is the great fraud upon modern civilization and forethought, blotching the surface and system which civilization undeniably drafts, and moistening with tears the immense features it spreads and spreads with such velocity before the reached kisses of the soul. . . . Still the right explanation remains to be made about prudence. The prudence of the mere wealth and respectability of the most esteemed life appears too faint for the eye to observe at all when little and large alike drop quietly aside at the thought of the prudence suitable for immortality. What is wisdom that fills the thinness of a year or seventy or eighty years to wisdom spaced out by ages and coming back at a certain time with strong reinforcements and rich presents and the clear faces of wedding-guests as far as you can look in every direction running gaily toward you? Only the soul is of itself . . . all else has reference to what ensues. All that a person does or thinks is of consequence. Not a move can a man or woman make that affects him or her in a day or a month or any part of the direct lifetime or the hour of death but the same affects him or her onward afterward through the indirect lifetime. The indirect is always as great and real as the direct. The spirit receives from the body just as much as it gives to the body. Not one name of word or deed . . . not of venereal sores or discolorations . . . not the privacy of the onanist . . . not of the putrid veins of gluttons or rum-drinkers . . . not peculation or cunning or betrayal or murder . . . no serpentine poison of those that seduce women . . . not the foolish yielding of women . . . not prostitution . . . not of any depravity of young men . . . not of the attainment of gain by discreditable means . . . not any nastiness of appetite . . . not any harshness of officers to men or judges to prisoners or fathers to sons or sons to fathers or of husbands to wives or bosses to their boys . . . not of greedy looks or malignant wishes . . . nor any of the wiles practised by people upon themselves . . . ever is or ever can be stamped on the programme but it is duly realized and returned, and that returned in further performances . . . and they returned again. Nor can the push of charity or personal force ever be any thing else than the profoundest reason, whether it bring arguments to hand or no. No specification is necessary . . . to add or subtract or divide is in vain. Little or big, learned or unlearned, white or black, legal or illegal, sick or well, from the first inspiration down the windpipe to the last expiration out of it, all that a male or female does that is vigorous and benevolent and clean is so much sure profit to him or her in the unshakable order of the universe and through the whole scope of it forever. If the savage or felon is wise it is well . . . if the greatest poet or savan is wise it is simply the same . . . if the President or chief justice is wise it is the same . . . if the young mechanic or farmer is wise it is no more or less . . . if the prostitute is wise it is no more nor less. The interest will come round . . . all will come round. All the best actions of war and peace . . . all help given to relatives and strangers and the poor and old and sorrowful and young children and widows and the sick, and to all shunned persons . . . all furtherance of fugitives and of the escape of slaves . . . all the self-denial that stood steady and aloof on wrecks and saw others take the seats of the boats . . . all offering of substance or life for the good old cause, or for a friend's sake or opinion's sake . . . all pains of enthusiasts scoffed at by their neighbors . . . all the vast sweet love and precious suffering of mothers . . . all honest men baffled in strifes recorded or unrecorded . . . all the grandeur and good of the few ancient nations whose

fragments of annals we inherit . . . and all the good of the hundreds of far
mightier and more ancient nations unknown to us by name or date or location
. . . all that was ever manfully begun, whether it succeeded or not . . . all that
has at any time been well suggested out of the divine heart of man or by the
divinity of his mouth or by the shaping of his great hands . . . and all that is
well thought or done this day on any part of the surface of the globe . . . or on
any of the wandering stars or fixed stars by those there as we are here . . . or
that is henceforth to be well thought or done by you whoever you are, or by any
one—these singly and wholly inured at their time and inure now and will inure
always to the identities from which they sprung or shall spring. . . . Did you
guess any of them lived only its moment? The world does not so exist . . . no
parts palpable or impalpable so exist . . . no result exists now without being
from its long antecedent result, and that from its antecedent, and so backward
without the farthest mentionable spot coming a bit nearer to the beginning than
any other spot. . . . Whatever satisfies the soul is truth. The prudence of the
greatest poet answers at last the craving and glut of the soul, is not contemptuous
of less ways of prudence if they conform to its ways, puts off nothing, permits no
let-up for its own case or any case, has no particular sabbath or judgment-day,
divides not the living from the dead or the righteous from the unrighteous, is
satisfied with the present, matches every thought or act by its correlative, knows
no possible forgiveness or deputed atonement . . . knows that the young man
who composedly periled his life and lost it has done exceeding well for himself,
while the man who has not periled his life and retains it to old age in riches and
ease has perhaps achieved nothing for himself worth mentioning . . . and that
only that person has no great prudence to learn who has learnt to prefer real
longlived things, and favors body and soul the same, and perceives the indirect
assuredly following the direct, and what evil or good he does leaping onward
and waiting to meet him again—and who in his spirit in any emergency whatever neither hurries or avoids death.

The direct trial of him who would be the greatest poet is today. If he does not
flood himself with the immediate age as with vast oceanic tides . . . and if he
does not attract his own land body and soul to himself and hang on its neck with
incomparable love and plunge his semitic muscle into its merits and demerits
. . . and if he be not himself the age transfigured . . . and if to him is not
opened the eternity which gives similitude to all periods and locations and proc-
esses and animate and inanimate forms, and which is the bond of time, and rises
up from its inconceivable vagueness and infiniteness in the swimming shape of
today, and is held by the ductile anchors of life, and makes the present spot the
passage from what was to what shall be, and commits itself to the representation
of this wave of an hour and this one of the sixty beautiful children of the wave—
let him merge in the general run and wait his development. . . . Still the final
test of poems or any character or work remains. The prescient poet projects himself centuries ahead and judges performer or performance after the changes of
time. Does it live through them? Does it still hold on untired? Will the same
style and the direction of genius to similar points be satisfactory now? Has no
new discovery in science or arrival at superior planes of thought and judgment
and behaviour fixed him or his so that either can be looked down upon? Have
the marches of tens and hundreds and thousands of years made willing detours to

the right hand and the left hand for his sake? Is he beloved long and long after he is buried? Does the young man think often of him? and the young woman think often of him? and do the middle-aged and the old think of him?

A great poem is for ages and ages in common and for all degrees and complexions and all departments and sects and for a woman as much as a man and a man as much as a woman. A great poem is no finish to a man or woman but rather a beginning. Has any one fancied he could sit at last under some due authority and rest satisfied with explanations and realize and be content and full? To no such terminus does the greatest poet bring . . . he brings neither cessation or sheltered fatness and ease. The touch of him tells in action. Whom he takes he takes with firm sure grasp into live regions previously unattained . . . thenceforward is no rest . . . they see the space and ineffable sheen that turn the old spots and lights into dead vacuums. The companion of him beholds the birth and progress of stars and learns one of the meanings. Now there shall be a man cohered out of tumult and chaos . . . the elder encourages the younger and shows him how . . . they too shall launch off fearlessly together till the new world fits an orbit for itself and looks unabashed on the lesser orbits of the stars and sweeps through the ceaseless rings and shall never be quiet again.

There will soon be no more priests. Their work is done. They may wait awhile . . . perhaps a generation or two . . . dropping off by degrees. A superior breed shall take their place . . . the gangs of kosmos and prophets en masse shall take their place. A new order shall arise and they shall be the priests of man, and every man shall be his own priest. The churches built under their umbrage shall be the churches of men and women. Through the divinity of themselves shall the kosmos and the new breed of poets be interpreters of men and women and of all events and things. They shall find their inspiration in real objects today, symptoms of the past and future . . . They shall not deign to defend immortality or God or the perfection of things or liberty or the exquisite beauty and reality of the soul. They shall arise in America and be responded to from the remainder of the earth.

The English language befriends the grand American expression . . . it is brawny enough and limber and full enough. On the tough stock of a race who through all change of circumstances was never without the idea of political liberty, which is the animus of all liberty, it has attracted the terms of daintier and gayer and subtler and more elegant tongues. It is the powerful language of resistance . . . it is the dialect of common sense. It is the speech of the proud and melancholy races and of all who aspire. It is the chosen tongue to express growth faith self-esteem freedom justice equality friendliness amplitude prudence decision and courage. It is the medium that shall well nigh express the inexpressible.

No great literature nor any like style of behaviour or oratory or social intercourse or household arrangements or public institutions or the treatment by bosses of employed people, nor executive detail or detail of the army or navy, nor spirit of legislation or courts or police or tuition or architecture or songs or amusements or the costumes of young men, can long elude the jealous and passionate instinct of American standards. Whether or no the sign appears from the mouths of the people, it throbs a live interrogation in every freeman's and freewoman's heart after that which passes by or this built to remain. Is it uniform with my country? Are its disposals without ignominious distinctions? Is it for the evergrowing communes of brothers and lovers, large, well-united, proud beyond the old models, generous beyond all models? Is it something grown fresh out of the fields or drawn from the sea for use to me today here? I know that what answers for me an American must answer for any individual or nation that serves for a part of my materials. Does this answer? or is it without reference to universal needs? or sprung of the needs of the less developed society of special ranks? or old needs of pleasure overlaid by modern science and forms? Does this acknowledge liberty with audible and absolute acknowledgment, and set slavery at naught for life and death? Will it help breed one goodshaped and wellhung man, and a woman to be his perfect and independent mate? Does it improve manners? Is it for the nursing of the young of the republic? Does it solve readily with the sweet milk of the nipples of the breasts of the mother of many children? Has it too the old ever-fresh forbearance and impartiality? Does it look with the same love on the last born and those hardening toward stature, and on the errant, and on those who disdain all strength of assault outside of their own?

The poems distilled from other poems will probably pass away. The coward will surely pass away. The expectation of the vital and great can only be satisfied by the demeanor of the vital and great. The swarms of the polished deprecating and reflectors and the polite float off and leave no remembrance. America prepares with composure and goodwill for the visitors that have sent word. It is not intellect that is to be their warrant and welcome. The talented, the artist, the ingenious, the editor, the statesman, the erudite . . . they are not unappreciated . . . they fall in their place and do their work. The soul of the nation also does its work. No disguise can pass on it . . . no disguise can conceal from it. It rejects none, it permits all. Only toward as good as itself and toward the like of itself will it advance half-way. An individual is as superb as a nation when he has the qualities which make a superb nation. The soul of the largest and wealthiest and proudest nation may well go half-way to meet that of its poets. The signs are effectual. There is no fear of mistake. If the one is true the other is true. The proof of a poet is that his country absorbs him as affectionately as he has absorbed it.
1855

EMILY DICKINSON ■■■■■■■■■■■■■■■■

A NARROW FELLOW IN THE GRASS

WE NEVER KNOW HOW HIGH

THIS IS MY LETTER TO THE WORLD

I LIKE TO SEE IT LAP THE MILES

THE HUMMING BIRD

TO HEAR AN ORIOLE SING

THE DAY CAME SLOW, TILL FIVE O'CLOCK

I'LL TELL YOU HOW THE SUN ROSE

I TASTE A LIQUOR NEVER BREWED

THE SKY IS LOW, THE CLOUDS ARE MEAN

HE ATE AND DRANK THE PRECIOUS WORDS

I NEVER SAW A MOOR

SUCCESS IS COUNTED SWEETEST

I'M NOBODY! WHO ARE YOU?

MUCH MADNESS IS DIVINEST SENSE

HE PREACHED UPON ''BREADTH''

APPARENTLY WITH NO SURPRISE

THERE'S A CERTAIN SLANT OF LIGHT

I DIED FOR BEAUTY

IF YOU WERE COMING IN THE FALL

BECAUSE I COULD NOT STOP FOR DEATH

THE BUSTLE IN A HOUSE

AS IMPERCEPTIBLY AS GRIEF

TO FIGHT ALOUD IS VERY BRAVE

Emily Dickinson (1830–1886) was born in Amherst, Massachusetts, the daughter of a lawyer of local distinction. For one year she attended Mount Holyoke Female Seminary (now Mount Holyoke College). She never married and became not at once but progressively a recluse. If there was a "disappointment" in love, the man was probably the Reverend Charles Wadsworth, married and successful, whom she met briefly in Philadelphia and who was probably unaware of her devotion. With the exception of a few scattered poems, her poetry has been published posthumously, the first volume having appeared in 1890; augmented and supplementary collections have appeared since then from time to time, the latest volume of new poems being *Bolts of Melody*, published in 1945. The manuscripts of her poems were acquired by Harvard in 1950. Her great reputation dates from the new critical movement of the 1930's and 1940's, which found "metaphysical" virtues in her work.

G. F. Whicher, *This Was a Poet* (1939) and critical essays in the following volumes: Allen Tate, *Reactionary Essays* (1936); Yvor Winters, *Maule's Curse* (1938); R. P. Blackmur, *The Expense of Greatness* (1939).

A NARROW FELLOW IN THE GRASS

A narrow fellow in the grass
Occasionally rides;
You may have met him,—did you not?
His notice sudden is.

The grass divides as with a comb,
A spotted shaft is seen;
And then it closes at your feet
And opens further on.

He likes a boggy acre,
A floor too cool for corn.
Yet when a child, and barefoot,
I more than once, at morn,

Have passed, I thought, a whip-lash
Unbraiding in the sun,—
When, stooping to secure it,
It wrinkled, and was gone.

Several of nature's people
I know, and they know me;
I feel for them a transport
Of cordiality;

But never met this fellow,
Attended or alone,
Without a tighter breathing,
And zero at the bone.
1890

WE NEVER KNOW HOW HIGH

We never know how high we are
Till we are called to rise;
And then, if we are true to plan,
Our statures touch the skies.

The heroism we recite
Would be a daily thing,
Did not ourselves the cubits warp
For fear to be a king.
1890

THIS IS MY LETTER TO THE WORLD

This is my letter to the world,
That never wrote to me,—
The simple news that Nature told,
With tender majesty.

Her message is committed
To hands I cannot see;
For love of her, sweet countrymen,
Judge tenderly of me!
1890

I LIKE TO SEE IT LAP THE MILES

I like to see it lap the miles,
And lick the valleys up,
And stop to feed itself at tanks;
And then, prodigious, step

Around a pile of mountains,
And, supercilious, peer
In shanties by the sides of roads;
And then a quarry pare

To fit its sides, and crawl between,
Complaining all the while   10
In horrid, hooting stanza;
Then chase itself down hill

And neigh like Boanerges;
Then, punctual as a star,
Stop—docile and omnipotent—
At its own stable door.
1891

THE HUMMING BIRD

A route of evanescence
With a revolving wheel;
A resonance of emerald,
A rush of cochineal;
And every blossom on the bush
Adjusts its tumbled head,—
The mail from Tunis, probably,
An easy morning's ride.
1891

TO HEAR AN ORIOLE SING

To hear an oriole sing
May be a common thing,
Or only a divine.

It is not of the bird
Who sings the same, unheard,
As unto crowd.

The fashion of the ear
Attireth that it hear
In dun or fair.

10 So whether it be rune,
Or whether it be none,
Is of within;

The "tune is in the tree,"
The sceptic showeth me;
"No, sir! In thee!"
1891

THE DAY CAME SLOW, TILL FIVE O'CLOCK

The day came slow, till five o'clock,
Then sprang before the hills
Like hindered rubies, or the light
A sudden musket spills.

The purple could not keep the east,
The sunrise shook from fold,
Like breadths of topaz, packed a night,
The lady just unrolled.

The happy winds their timbrels took;
10 The birds, in docile rows,
Arranged themselves around their prince
(The wind is prince of those).

The orchard sparkled like a Jew,—
How mighty 'twas, to stay
A guest in this stupendous place,
The parlor of the day!
1891

I'LL TELL YOU HOW THE SUN ROSE

I'll tell you how the sun rose,—
A ribbon at a time.
The steeples swam in amethyst,
The news like squirrels ran.

The hills untied their bonnets,
The bobolinks begun.

Then I said softly to myself,
"That must have been the sun!"

. . .

But how he set, I know not.
There seemed a purple stile   10
Which little yellow boys and girls
Were climbing all the while

Till when they reached the other side,
A dominie in gray
Put gently up the evening bars,
And led the flock away.
1890

I TASTE A LIQUOR NEVER BREWED

I taste a liquor never brewed,
From tankards scooped in pearl;
Not all the vats upon the Rhine
Yield such an alcohol!

Inebriate of air am I,
And debauchee of dew,
Reeling, through endless summer days,
From inns of molten blue.

When landlords turn the drunken bee
Out of the foxglove's door,   10
When butterflies renounce their drams,
I shall but drink the more!

Till seraphs swing their snowy hats,
And saints to windows run,
To see the little tippler
Leaning against the sun!
1890

THE SKY IS LOW, THE CLOUDS ARE MEAN

The sky is low, the clouds are mean,
A travelling flake of snow
Across a barn or through a rut
Debates if it will go.

A narrow wind complains all day
How some one treated him;
Nature, like us, is sometimes caught
Without her diadem.
1890

HE ATE AND DRANK THE PRECIOUS WORDS

He ate and drank the precious words,
His spirit grew robust;
He knew no more that he was poor,
Nor that his frame was dust.
He danced along the dingy days,
And this bequest of wings
Was but a book. What liberty
A loosened spirit brings!
1890

I NEVER SAW A MOOR

I never saw a moor,
I never saw the sea;
Yet know I how the heather looks,
And what a wave must be.

I never spoke with God,
Nor visited in heaven;
Yet certain am I of the spot
As if the chart were given.
1890

SUCCESS IS COUNTED SWEETEST

Success is counted sweetest
By those who ne'er succeed.
To comprehend a nectar
Requires sorest need.

Not one of all the purple host
Who took the flag to-day
Can tell the definition,
So clear, of victory,

As he, defeated, dying,
On whose forbidden ear 10
The distant strains of triumph
Break, agonized and clear.
1890

I'M NOBODY! WHO ARE YOU?

I'm nobody! Who are you?
Are you nobody, too?
Then there's a pair of us—don't tell!
They'd banish us, you know.

How dreary to be somebody!
How public, like a frog
To tell your name the livelong day
To an admiring bog!
1891

MUCH MADNESS IS DIVINEST SENSE

Much madness is divinest sense
To a discerning eye;
Much sense the starkest madness.
'Tis the majority
In this, as all, prevails.
Assent, and you are sane;
Demur,—you're straightway dangerous,
And handled with a chain.
1890

HE PREACHED UPON ''BREADTH''

He preached upon "breadth" till it argued him narrow,—
The broad are too broad to define;
And of "truth" until it proclaimed him a liar,—
The truth never flaunted a sign.

Simplicity fled from his counterfeit presence
As gold the pyrites would shun.
What confusion would cover the innocent Jesus
To meet so enabled a man!
1891

APPARENTLY WITH NO SURPRISE

Apparently with no surprise
To any happy flower,
The frost beheads it at its play
In accidental power.

The blond assassin passes on,
The sun proceeds unmoved
To measure off another day
For an approving God.
1890

THERE'S A CERTAIN SLANT OF LIGHT

There's a certain slant of light,
On winter afternoons,
That oppresses, like the weight
Of cathedral tunes.

Heavenly hurt it gives us;
We can find no scar,
But internal difference
Where the meanings are.

10

None may teach it anything,
'Tis the seal, despair,—
An imperial affliction
Sent us of the air.

When it comes, the landscape listens,
Shadows hold their breath;
When it goes, 'tis like the distance
On the look of death.
1890

I DIED FOR BEAUTY

I died for beauty, but was scarce
Adjusted in the tomb,
When one who died for truth was lain
In an adjoining room.

He questioned softly why I failed?
"For beauty," I replied.

"And I for truth,—the two are one;
We brethren are," he said.

And so, as kinsmen met a night,
We talked between the rooms,   10
Until the moss had reached our lips,
And covered up our names.
1890

IF YOU WERE COMING IN THE FALL

If you were coming in the fall,
I'd brush the summer by
With half a smile and half a spurn,
As housewives do a fly.

If I could see you in a year,
I'd wind the months in balls,
And put them each in separate drawers,
Until their time befalls.

If only centuries delayed,
I'd count them on my hand,   10
Subtracting till my fingers dropped
Into Van Diemen's land.

If certain, when this life was out,
That yours and mine should be,
I'd toss it yonder like a rind,
And taste eternity.

But now, all ignorant of the length
Of time's uncertain wing,
It goads me, like the goblin bee,
That will not state its sting.   20
1890

BECAUSE I COULD NOT STOP FOR DEATH

Because I could not stop for Death,
He kindly stopped for me;
The carriage held but just ourselves
And Immortality.

We slowly drove, he knew no haste,
And I had put away
My labor, and my leisure too,
For his civility.

We passed the school where children played
At wrestling in a ring;
We passed the fields of gazing grain,
We passed the setting sun.

We paused before a house that seemed
A swelling of the ground;
The roof was scarcely visible,
The cornice but a mound.

Since then 'tis centuries; but each
Feels shorter than the day
I first surmised the horses' heads
Were toward eternity.
1890

THE BUSTLE IN A HOUSE

The bustle in a house
The morning after death
Is solemnest of industries
Enacted upon earth,—

The sweeping up the heart,
And putting love away
We shall not want to use again
Until eternity.
1890

AS IMPERCEPTIBLY AS GRIEF

As imperceptibly as grief
The summer lapsed away,—
Too imperceptible, at last,
To seem like perfidy.

A quietness distilled,
As twilight long begun,

Or Nature, spending with herself
Sequestered afternoon.

The dusk drew earlier in,
The morning foreign shone,—   10
A courteous, yet harrowing grace,
As guest who would be gone.

And thus, without a wing,
Or service of a keel
Our summer made her light escape
Into the beautiful.
1891

TO FIGHT ALOUD IS VERY BRAVE

To fight aloud is very brave,
But gallanter, I know,
Who charge within the bosom,
The cavalry of woe.

Who win, and nations do not see,
Who fall, and none observe,
Whose dying eyes no country
Regards with patriot love.

We trust, in plumed procession,
For such the angels go,   10
Rank after rank, with even feet
And uniforms of snow.
1890

ROBERT FROST ■■■■■■■■■■■■■■■■■■■■■■■

Modern poetry for the most part has not been popular; most contemporary poets have not been widely read. Poets like Eliot and Yeats have been too difficult to reach a large audience. The trend in poetry seems to be continuing in the direction of difficulty, perhaps increasing difficulty. But this was not always so, nor will it necessarily be so in the future. Some of our greatest poets have been "popular" in the best sense of the word. Writing before the invention of printing was to make possible a large number of readers, Chaucer nevertheless had the elements of popular appeal; he could not be accused of being highbrow, or abstruse, or esoteric. Pope's poetry was once popular; Shakespeare's was, and has been, supremely so. In our time, Robert Frost is the outstanding example of the good poet who is much read, quoted, and admired. Popularity is, of course, irrelevant to the question of poetic merit: a great poet's audience may be either large or small without prejudice to his greatness. It is interesting and significant, though, that in an age notorious for a diminishing response to its poets among readers generally, one poet should be able to carry on the valuable and historic tradition of poetry for the many.

POET OF NEW ENGLAND

Robert Frost is not a "literary" poet. He has doubtless read widely, but—unlike the erudite T. S. Eliot—he rarely employs literary allusion. It would be difficult to say very much about literary influences in Frost's poetry because, although they may be present to a degree, they are mostly unapparent. Two poets may be mentioned as having probably exerted an influence. One is Wordsworth, who—notably in a poem like "Michael"—used the language of rustic speech and the natural, uninverted word order of prose. If Frost was not influenced by "Michael," one can at least say that Wordsworth's poem—save that it is humorless—makes one think of Frost. Another poet is Emerson, whom Frost does the unusual honor of quoting directly (in "New Hampshire," for example, he quotes from the "Ode to W. H. Channing"; in "The Masque of Reason," from "Uriel"). Frost seems to unite qualities found in these two poets: the simplicity and earthiness of Wordsworth's rustic poems, and the cryptic or gnomic speech of Emerson. But to suggest possible relationships like these is not to deprive Frost of an iota of originality; he is in no sense an imitator.

His poetry is peculiar to New England; his world is a New England world. More specifically still, it is the world of northern New England, of New Hampshire and Vermont, which is rural and primitive, as contrasted with southern New England, which is urban and industrial (New England not being everywhere the same any more than the South is everywhere the same, or the West). In reading Frost, one gets a vivid impression of what life is like on an upland farm in New Hampshire or Vermont. This is one of his "values": to give a solid impression of a way of life that has been important, and is still important, in the development of our culture. One might call it the agrarian way, for Frost's poetry can stand for agrarianism wherever found.

One aspect of this way of life, obviously, is manual labor on the farm. No poet has written on this subject more authoritatively or beautifully than Frost. His "Mowing" is a classic instance:

> There was never a sound beside the wood but one,
> And that was my long scythe whispering to the ground. . . .

It is honest work for honest wages: there is no "dream . . . of idle hours/ Or easy gold . . ." though farm labor is more handsomely paid now than when Frost wrote this poem. His laborers, too, are skillful, and enjoy their skill; there is an art, requiring talent and long practice, in building a rock wall, in mowing grass, in loading hay on wagons. Silas, the hired man (in "The Death of the Hired Man"), was famous for his skill in loading hay:

> He bundles every forkful in its place,
> And tags and numbers it for future reference,
> So he can find and easily dislodge it
> In the unloading. . . .
> He takes it out in bunches like big birds' nests.
> You never see him standing on the hay
> He's trying to lift, straining to lift himself.

Chopping wood is another example of skill; it is zestfully and lovingly described in "Two Tramps in Mud Time":

> Good blocks of oak it was I split,
> As large around as the chopping block;
> And every piece I squarely hit
> Fell splinterless as a cloven rock.

One gets the impression that certain mental, spiritual, and even literary virtues can be derived from work of this sort. Possibly the idea is peculiar to New England. Whittier thought that "the strong working hand makes strong the working brain," and Thoreau advised the young writer to "learn to split wood," and went on to argue the proposition that "steady labor with the hands, which engrosses the attention also, is unquestionably the best method of removing palaver and sentimentality out of one's style, both of speaking and writing." Frost, clearly, is in line with these earlier New England writers in his respectful, even reverent, treatment of farm chores. The attitude is at variance with that of some other writers about country life who tell only of toil and fatigue.

There is abundant beauty on a hill farm in Vermont or New Hampshire, but it must not be "gushed" over. There is no "gush" about the beauties of nature in Frost (or for that matter in New England poetry generally). In a characteristic poem like "Stopping by Woods on a Snowy Evening," the speaker is almost apologetic for pausing to watch the woods fill up with snow. He takes comfort in the thought that the owner, who lives in the village, will not see him so occupied, and it is made clear that he has not come to this place for the sole purpose of seeing the beauty. The beauty, indeed, is picked up incidentally in the course of a necessary journey:

> . . . I have promises to keep,
> And miles to go before I sleep.

A somewhat similar attitude is expressed by the man in "The Mountain" who had been on the mountain's sides many times, deer hunting and trout fishing, but had never climbed to its top because he had never had any business there. "I've always meant to go," he explained,

> "And look myself, but you know how it is:
> It doesn't seem so much to climb a mountain
> You've worked around the foot of all your life.
> What would I do? Go in my overalls,
> With a big stick, the same as when the cows
> Haven't come down to the bars at milking time?
> Or with a shotgun for a stray black bear?
> 'Twouldn't seem real to climb for climbing it."

In order to climb the mountain, in other words, he would have to invent a necessary journey, or pretend to some practical business on its summit. And yet his remarks on the brook that is "always cold in summer, warm in winter," show that he is sensitive to natural beauty. The attitude, though possibly Puritan, is not antiaesthetic: some such practicality seems necessary to save nature-appreciation from mere dilettantism. There is a good deal to be said for the opinion that the mountain brook is best appreciated (other things

being equal) by the trout fisherman; the snow-filled woods, by the
traveler who stops to look despite the urgency of his journey.

Labor and beauty seen in conjunction with labor are two aspects
of the world that Frost portrays. A third aspect is dark and sinister,
for Frost's world is too real to be free of the tragic and the horrible.
Parts of rural New England declined after the Civil War; many
young people migrated to the more fertile lands of the West. The
abundant well-being portrayed in Whittier's "Snow-Bound" became
less typical. Some New England farms became lonely places. One
suspects, too, that in regions untouched by the immigration movements of the late nineteenth century, inbreeding had a deteriorating
effect upon the native stock. Such, at any rate, would seem to be the
background of a poem like "A Servant to Servants," where the
pathos of loneliness and the horror of madness are starkly portrayed.
Frost is too much of a realist to neglect these aspects of his subject;
too much of a realist also to suppose that loneliness and madness are
peculiar to a New England world in some respects now decadent. In
"The Hill Wife," the wife's breakdown may be owing in part to her
isolated residence; it is owing also to her husband's inadequacy and
her own, and the tragedy is in no exclusive sense provincial. All of
Frost's poems, in fact, should be read in a double sense: first, as
genre pieces, showing an authentic province; and second, as symbolic and allegorical representations of human values wherever they
are cherished.

SOME CHARACTERISTICS OF THE POETRY

Frost's poetry is more regular than that of most contemporary
poets. He himself has said, "I had as soon write free verse as play
tennis with the net down."

Consider the regularity, for example, of "Two Tramps in Mud
Time." The eight-line stanza, rhyming *ababcdcd,* is strictly observed
throughout. The rhymes without exception are exact: *came-aim,*
yard-hard, and so forth. The basic meter is iambic tetrameter, as in

> And every piece I squarely hit. . . .

Sing-song is avoided and an interesting variety achieved by varying
the foot: by an initial trochee in

> Out of the mud two strangers came. . . .

by three anapaests in

> And you're two months back in the middle of March. . . .

and by other similar changes. The amount of variation, though, is obviously small in the overall pattern; the total impression of the poem is one of great, almost stark, regularity. It would be interesting to raise the question of the appropriateness of the extraordinarily regular meter to the action of the poem. The danger in such inquiries is that one should expect or demand neat, obvious correspondences. There does, however, seem to be in this poem an appropriate and effective correlation between prosody and action: the stanza, the regular meter (with only minor variations), and the exact rhyme correspond nicely with the expert woodchopping, which is an exact art, though not mechanically precise, and the correlation might be extended to include the exactly articulated moral:

> My object in living is to unite
> My avocation and my vocation. . . .

Another kind of meter in Frost—one that is perhaps more characteristic and that he handles even more happily—is the unrhymed iambic pentameter or blank verse. Some of his most famous poems ("Mending Wall," "The Death of the Hired Man," "A Servant to Servants," "Birches," "The Axe-Helve," and others) are in this meter. Frost's blank verse has some rather special qualities: a certain freedom, flexibility, colloquial ease, low pitch—not the exalted pitch (of Milton, for example) usually associated with blank verse. Terminating a sentence within the line and adding a syllable at the end of the line (an eleventh syllable in a line normally decasyllabic) are devices that give an air of informality, as in the following excerpt from "Birches":

> But swinging doesn't bend them down to stay
> As ice-storms do. Often you must have seen them
> Loaded with ice a sunny winter morning
> After a rain. . . .

It is interesting to note that Frost employs overflow comparatively little, that the majority of his lines are end-stopped (the lines just quoted, for example, are end-stopped). One result is a clear awareness of the lines as such; another, an effect of tightness and control.

"The best reader," Frost has said, "is one who will read no faster than he can hear the lines and sentences in his mind's ear as if aloud. Frequenting poetry has slowed him down by its metric or measured pace." "Measured pace" is a good description of Frost's prosody and its tempo. One's appreciation of these matters is enhanced by hearing Frost's own reading of his poetry (either in person or in a recording), for which he has long been famous. The vigor and strength of the poet match the vigor and strength of the verse.

Cleanth Brooks has observed that the method of Frost—a poet

often praised for his "directness"—"is essentially *indirect*."[1] Frost himself seems to bear out this view in his comment on good readers of poetry: "The same people will be apt to take poems right," he has said, "as know how to take a hint when there is one and not to take a hint when none is intended. Theirs is the ultimate refinement." Poetry, then, to Frost is a matter of hints; the poet by indirection finds direction out. Behind the apparent casualness and matter-of-factness, the poet may be slyly hinting at a number of important things. His simplicity may be deceptive; the reader must be on his guard against being taken in by the Yankee shrewdness.

"Frost prefers to sidle up to his themes," Brooks says, "and so pursues, at his best, an impeccable artistic method." A good example is "The Axe-Helve," which consists of an anecdote innocent enough, and yet the poem obviously abounds in "hints." The anecdote suggests the superiority of the handmade axe handle over the machine-made; it hints at the desire of the Frenchman, Baptiste, for social acceptance by the Yankee natives, though it is doubtful if his "human rating" or status has been improved by his friendly gesture; the anecdote hints more obscurely at some truth or supposition of truth about "knowledge" and "education," Baptiste apparently regarding his kind of knowledge, which was ingrained and not put on from without, as superior to that acquired in the schools. At the end of the poem, the axe-helve, which has been represented as a thing of beautiful utility, becomes, strangely enough, a symbol of evil, recalling in its appearance the snake in the Garden of Eden. The reader may be a bit puzzled by such a conclusion, though Baptiste, with whom the axe-helve can be identified, may be sly and serpentlike in his wisdom. But to make observations like these is not to exhaust the hints of the poem. Mrs. Baptiste's manner of rocking in her chair, which tells us something about the frustrations of her existence; the sensual connotation of Baptiste's stroking the axe-helve's "long white body," which may quite as much as the slyness account for the impression of evil upon the Puritan narrator—these and many other plausible meanings crowd upon the reader from all sides.

Frost is a symbolic poet. The more one contemplates "The Axe-Helve," for example, the richer and more complex its symbolic content becomes. Most of Frost's poems not only lend themselves to symbolic interpretation but actually require it, for the thoughtful reader is not content with the "story" alone, nor does the poet intend that he should be. Consider the symbolic treatment of the theme of withdrawal and return in "Birches":

> I'd like to go by climbing a birch tree,
> And climb black branches up a snow-white trunk
> *Toward* heaven, till the tree could bear no more,
> But dipped its top and set me down again.
> That would be good both going and coming back.

1. "Poet or Sage?" *Kenyon Review*, I (Summer 1939) 325.

Or consider the expanded metaphor of "After Apple-Picking." The lines

> For I have had too much
> Of apple-picking: I am overtired
> Of the great harvest I myself desired. . . .

sum up the acute nervous exhaustion resulting from long and anxious application to a labor that paradoxically has proved too fruitful, too abundant.

Frost is a witty poet. He himself has said, "Emotions must be . . . harnessed by discipline to the wit mill." It would be interesting to inquire into the nature of Frost's wit. It contains, of course, a good deal of "down-East humor"—dry, homespun, shrewd, sometimes laconic and (as his Yankees abundantly show, though contrary to all reputation) sometimes loquacious and verbose. The wit strikes the reader as basically native; but it often contains, in addition, a toughness and ingenuity that ally it with the intellectual, "metaphysical" wit of the seventeenth century. The observation (in "New Hampshire") that New Hampshire and Vermont

> lie like wedges,
> Thick end to thin end and thin end to thick end,
> And are a figure of the way the strong
> Of mind and strong of arm should fit together. . . .

is a good example of "wit" in the older "conceitful" tradition of English poetry. The poet's statement that he desires to unite avocation and vocation

> As my two eyes made one in sight. . . .

is "witty" in the older sense and worthy of Donne.

Frost's poetry is, moreover, on occasion aphoristic and gnomic. Every reader remembers "Good fences make good neighbours," "Home is the place where, when you have to go there,/ They have to take you in," and other quotable aphorisms scattered through the poems. Here again Frost is allied with an honorable tradition— that of the literature of "wisdom," which contains among many distinguished examples the *Book of Proverbs* and the essays of Emerson. Everything to be sure depends upon the quality of the wisdom and its expression. Frost is obviously no cheap purveyor of saws. He is didactic in the good sense, not preachy. His wisdom is the result of a rich experience that has been deeply meditated upon. His gnomic passages have been aged long and have been brought to a kind of perfection; they often lean to the cryptic.

And not least, Frost is a patriotic poet who believes that life in America has been comparatively fortunate and that the Jeffersonian principles upon which our country was founded are capable of a fuller realization. He tartly twits the leftists who declare that everything is wrong with the American system and point to Russia as a model:

> How are we to write
> The Russian novel in America
> As long as life goes so unterribly?
> There is the pinch from which our only outcry
> In literature to date is heard to come.
> We get what little misery we can
> Out of not having cause for misery.
> It makes the guild of novel writers sick
> To be expected to be Dostoievskis
> On nothing worse than too much luck and comfort.
> This is not sorrow, though; it's just the vapors,
> And recognized as such in Russia itself,
> Under the new régime, and so forbidden.
> If well it is with Russia, then feel free
> To say so or be stood against the wall
> And shot. It's Pollyanna now or death.
> This, then, is the new freedom we hear tell of. . . .

Sensible, forthright, down-to-earth is the Americanism of these lines from "New Hampshire." It would be untrue to say that Frost is complacent about America; he is aware of our imperfections. He knows (see "The Black Cottage") that the equalitarian principle—that "hard mystery of Jefferson's"—has been flouted by many in modern America, but he believes that the grand proposition that "all men are created free and equal," now "out of favour," "will turn true again." In the strife of the mid-twentieth century, Robert Frost's poetry is a valuable asset—who can estimate the value?—to the democratic forces at work in the world because it is a true embodiment of traditional American democracy.

LIFE AND WORKS

Robert Frost was born in San Francisco in 1875, but grew up after the age of ten in New England. He was educated in the high school at Lawrence, Massachusetts, at Dartmouth, which he briefly attended, and (much later) at Harvard, where he stayed two years. He tried teaching and farming in New Hampshire before settling down (in England, with a wife and four children, at the age of thirty-seven) to poetry as his life work. *A Boy's Will* (1913) and *North of Boston* (1914) brought him fame in England immediately, and soon thereafter in the United States, to which he and his family returned in 1915. Since then, he has divided his time between writing, lecturing, and farming—always keeping as a kind of home base a farm in Vermont. His fame has grown from more to more; he is at the mid-twentieth century the most widely known and deeply honored of living American poets. Besides the volumes already named, his works include *Mountain Interval* (1916), *New Hampshire* (1924), *West-Running Brook* (1928), *A Further Range* (1936), and *A Masque of Reason* (1945).

Amy Lowell, *Tendencies in Modern American Poetry* (1917); Lawrance Thompson, *Fire and Ice: The Art and Thought of Robert Frost* (1942).

MOWING

There was never a sound beside the wood but one,
And that was my long scythe whispering to the ground.
What was it it whispered? I knew not well myself;
Perhaps it was something about the heat of the sun,
Something, perhaps, about the lack of sound—
And that was why it whispered and did not speak.
It was no dream of the gift of idle hours,
Or easy gold at the hand of fay or elf:
Anything more than the truth would have seemed too weak
To the earnest love that laid the swale in rows,   10
Not without feeble-pointed spikes of flowers
(Pale orchises), and scared a bright green snake.
The fact is the sweetest dream that labor knows.
My long scythe whispered and left the hay to make.
1913

THE MOUNTAIN

The mountain held the town as in a shadow,
I saw so much before I slept there once:
I noticed that I missed stars in the west,
Where its black body cut into the sky.
Near me it seemed: I felt it like a wall
Behind which I was sheltered from a wind.
And yet between the town and it I found,
When I walked forth at dawn to see new things,
Were fields, a river, and beyond, more fields.
The river at the time was fallen away,   10
And made a widespread brawl on cobblestones;

But the signs showed what it had done in spring;
Good grass-land gullied out, and in the grass
Ridges of sand, and driftwood stripped of bark.
I crossed the river and swung round the mountain.
And there I met a man who moved so slow
With white-faced oxen in a heavy cart,
It seemed no harm to stop him altogether.

"What town is this?" I asked.

20   "This? Lunenburg."

Then I was wrong: the town of my sojourn,
Beyond the bridge, was not that of the mountain,
But only felt at night its shadowy presence.

"Where is your village? Very far from here?"

"There is no village—only scattered farms.
We were but sixty voters last election.
We can't in nature grow to many more:
That thing takes all the room!" He moved his goad.
The mountain stood there to be pointed at.
30   Pasture ran up the side a little way,
And then there was a wall of trees with trunks:
After that only tops of trees, and cliffs
Imperfectly concealed among the leaves.
A dry ravine emerged from under boughs
Into the pasture.

                         "That looks like a path.
Is that the way to reach the top from here?—
Not for this morning, but some other time:
I must be getting back to breakfast now."
40   "I don't advise your trying from this side.
There is no proper path, but those that *have*
Been up, I understand, have climbed from Ladd's.
That's five miles back. You can't mistake the place:
They logged it there last winter some way up.
I'd take you, but I'm bound the other way."

"You've never climbed it?"

                         "I've been on the sides
Deer-hunting and trout-fishing. There's a brook
That starts up on it somewhere—I've heard say
50   Right on the top, tip-top—a curious thing.
But what would interest you about the brook,

It's always cold in summer, warm in winter.
One of the great sights going is to see
It steam in winter like an ox's breath.
Until the bushes all along its banks
Are inch-deep with the frosty spines and bristles—
You know the kind. Then let the sun shine on it!"

"There ought to be a view around the world
From such a mountain—if it isn't wooded
Clear to the top." I saw through leafy screens   60
Great granite terraces in sun and shadow,
Shelves one could rest a knee on getting up—
With depths behind him sheer a hundred feet;
Or turn and sit on and look out and down,
With little ferns in crevices at his elbow.

"As to that I can't say. But there's the spring.
Right on the summit, almost like a fountain.
That ought to be worth seeing."

                    "If it's there.
You never saw it?"   70
                    "I guess there's no doubt
About its being there. I never saw it.
It may not be right on the very top:
It wouldn't have to be a long way down
To have some head of water from above,
And a *good distance* down might not be noticed
By anyone who'd come a long way up.
One time I asked a fellow climbing it
To look and tell me later how it was."

"What did he say?"   80

                    "He said there was a lake
Somewhere in Ireland on a mountain top."

"But a lake's different. What about the spring?"

"He never got up high enough to see.
That's why I don't advise your trying this side.
He tried this side. I've always meant to go
And look myself, but you know how it is:
It doesn't seem so much to climb a mountain
You've worked around the foot of all your life.
What would I do? Go in my overalls,   90
With a big stick, the same as when the cows
Haven't come down to the bars at milking time?

Or with a shotgun for a stray black bear?
'Twouldn't seem real to climb for climbing it."

"I shouldn't climb it if I didn't want to—
Not for the sake of climbing. What's its name?"

"We call it Hor: I don't know if that's right."

"Can one walk around it? Would it be too far?"

"You can drive round and keep in Lunenburg,
But it's as much as ever you can do,
The boundary lines keep in so close to it.
Hor is the township, and the township's Hor—
And a few houses sprinkled round the foot,
Like boulders broken off the upper cliff,
Rolled out a little farther than the rest."

"Warm in December, cold in June, you say?"

"I don't suppose the water's changed at all.
You and I know enough to know it's warm
Compared with cold, and cold compared with warm.
But all the fun's in how you say a thing."

"You've lived here all your life?"

        "Ever since Hor
Was no bigger than a—" What, I did not hear.

He drew the oxen toward him with light touches
Of his slim goad on nose and offside flank,
Gave them their marching orders and was moving.
1914

THE BLACK COTTAGE

We chanced in passing by that afternoon
To catch it in a sort of special picture
Among tar-banded ancient cherry trees,
Set well back from the road in rank lodged grass,
The little cottage we were speaking of,
A front with just a door between two windows,
Fresh painted by the shower a velvet black.
We paused, the minister and I, to look.
He made as if to hold it at arm's length

Or put the leaves aside that framed it in.   10
"Pretty," he said. "Come in. No one will care."
The path was a vague parting in the grass
That led us to a weathered window-sill.
We pressed our faces to the pane. "You see," he said,
"Everything's as she left it when she died.
Her sons won't sell the house or the things in it.
They say they mean to come and summer here
Where they were boys. They haven't come this year.
They live so far away—one is out west—
It will be hard for them to keep their word.   20
Anyway they won't have the place disturbed."
A buttoned hair-cloth lounge spread scrolling arms
Under a crayon portrait on the wall,
Done sadly from an old daguerreotype.
"That was the father as he went to war.
She always, when she talked about the war,
Sooner or later came and leaned, half knelt
Against the lounge beside it, though I doubt
If such unlifelike lines kept power to stir
Anything in her after all the years.   30
He fell at Gettysburg or Fredericksburg,
I ought to know—it makes a difference which:
Fredericksburg wasn't Gettysburg, of course.
But what I'm getting to is how forsaken
A little cottage this has always seemed;
Since she went more than ever, but before—
I don't mean altogether by the lives
That had gone out of it, the father first,
Then the two sons, till she was left alone.
(Nothing could draw her after those two sons.   40
She valued the considerate neglect
She had at some cost taught them after years.)
I mean by the world's having passed it by—
As we almost got by this afternoon.
It always seems to me a sort of mark
To measure how far fifty years have brought us.
Why not sit down if you are in no haste?
These doorsteps seldom have a visitor.
The warping boards pull out their own old nails
With none to tread and put them in their place.   50
She had her own idea of things, the old lady.
And she liked talk. She had seen Garrison
And Whittier, and had her story of them.
One wasn't long in learning that she thought
Whatever else the Civil War was for,
It wasn't just to keep the States together,
Nor just to free the slaves, though it did both.

She wouldn't have believed those ends enough
To have given outright for them all she gave.
Her giving somehow touched the principle
That all men are created free and equal.
And to hear her quaint phrases—so removed
From the world's view to-day of all those things.
That's a hard mystery of Jefferson's.
What did he mean? Of course the easy way
Is to decide it simply isn't true.
It may not be. I heard a fellow say so.
But never mind, the Welshman got it planted
Where it will trouble us a thousand years.
Each age will have to reconsider it.
You couldn't tell her what the West was saying,
And what the South to her serene belief.
She had some art of hearing and yet not
Hearing the latter wisdom of the world.
White was the only race she ever knew.
Black she had scarcely seen, and yellow never.
But how could they be made so very unlike
By the same hand working in the same stuff?
She had supposed the war decided that.
What are you going to do with such a person?
Strange how such innocence gets its own way.
I shouldn't be surprised if in this world
It were the force that would at last prevail.
Do you know but for her there was a time
When to please younger members of the church,
Or rather say non-members in the church,
Whom we all have to think of nowadays,
I would have changed the Creed a very little?
Not that she ever had to ask me not to;
It never got so far as that; but the bare thought
Of her old tremulous bonnet in the pew,
And of her half asleep was too much for me.
Why, I might wake her up and startle her.
It was the words 'descended into Hades'
That seemed too pagan to our liberal youth.
You know they suffered from a general onslaught.
And well, if they weren't true why keep right on
Saying them like the heathen? We could drop them.
Only—there was the bonnet in the pew.
Such a phrase couldn't have meant much to her.
But suppose she had missed it from the Creed
As a child misses the unsaid Good-night,
And falls asleep with heartache—how should *I* feel?
I'm just as glad she made me keep hands off,
For, dear me, why abandon a belief

Merely because it ceases to be true.
Cling to it long enough, and not a doubt
It will turn true again, for so it goes.
Most of the change we think we see in life
Is due to truths being in and out of favour.   110
As I sit here, and oftentimes, I wish
I could be monarch of a desert land
I could devote and dedicate forever
To the truths we keep coming back and back to.
So desert it would have to be, so walled
By mountain ranges half in summer snow,
No one would covet it or think it worth
The pains of conquering to force change on.
Scattered oases where men dwelt, but mostly
Sand dunes held loosely in tamarisk   120
Blown over and over themselves in idleness.
Sand grains should sugar in the natal dew
The babe born to the desert, the sand storm
Retard mid-waste my cowering caravans—
There are bees in this wall." He struck the clapboards,
Fierce heads looked out; small bodies pivoted.
We rose to go. Sunset blazed on the windows.
1914

A SERVANT TO SERVANTS

I didn't make you know how glad I was
To have you come and camp here on our land.
I promised myself to get down some day
And see the way you lived, but I don't know!
With a houseful of hungry men to feed
I guess you'd find. . . . It seems to me
I can't express my feelings any more
Than I can raise my voice or want to lift
My hand (oh, I can lift it when I have to).
Did ever you feel so? I hope you never.   10
It's got so I don't even know for sure
Whether I *am* glad, sorry, or anything.
There's nothing but a voice-like left inside
That seems to tell me how I ought to feel,
And would feel if I wasn't all gone wrong.
You take the lake. I look and look at it.
I see it's a fair, pretty sheet of water.
I stand and make myself repeat out loud
The advantages it has, so long and narrow,
Like a deep piece of some old running river   20

Cut short off at both ends. It lies five miles
Straight away through the mountain notch
From the sink window where I wash the plates,
And all our storms come up toward the house,
Drawing the slow waves whiter and whiter and whiter.
It took my mind off doughnuts and soda biscuit
To step outdoors and take the water dazzle
A sunny morning, or take the rising wind
About my face and body and through my wrapper,
30   When a storm threatened from the Dragon's Den,
And a cold chill shivered across the lake.
I see it's a fair, pretty sheet of water,
Our Willoughby! How did you hear of it?
I expect, though, everyone's heard of it.
In a book about ferns? Listen to that!
You let things more like feathers regulate
Your going and coming. And you like it here?
I can see how you might. But I don't know!
It would be different if more people came,
40   For then there would be business. As it is,
The cottages Len built, sometimes we rent them,
Sometimes we don't. We've a good piece of shore
That ought to be worth something, and may yet.
But I don't count on it as much as Len.
He looks on the bright side of everything,
Including me. He thinks I'll be all right
With doctoring. But it's not medicine—
Lowe is the only doctor's dared to say so—
It's rest I want—there, I have said it out—
50   From cooking meals for hungry hired men
And washing dishes after them—from doing
Things over and over that just won't stay done.
By good rights I ought not to have so much
Put on me, but there seems no other way.
Len says one steady pull more ought to do it.
He says the best way out is always through.
And I agree to that, or in so far
As that I can see no way out but through—
Leastways for me—and then they'll be convinced.
60   It's not that Len don't want the best for me.
It was his plan our moving over in
Beside the lake from where that day I showed you
We used to live—ten miles from anywhere.
We didn't change without some sacrifice,
But Len went at it to make up the loss.
His work's a man's, of course, from sun to sun,
But he works when he works as hard as I do—
Though there's small profit in comparisons.

(Women and men will make them all the same.)
But work ain't all. Len undertakes too much.   70
He's into everything in town. This year
It's highways, and he's got too many men
Around him to look after that make waste.
They take advantage of him shamefully,
And proud, too, of themselves for doing so.
We have four here to board, great good-for-nothings,
Sprawling about the kitchen with their talk
While I fry their bacon. Much they care!
No more put out in what they do or say
Than if I wasn't in the room at all.   80
Coming and going all the time, they are:
I don't learn what their names are, let alone
Their characters, or whether they are safe
To have inside the house with doors unlocked.
I'm not afraid of them, though, if they're not
Afraid of me. There's two can play at that.
I have my fancies: it runs in the family.
My father's brother wasn't right. They kept him
Locked up for years back there at the old farm.
I've been away once—yes, I've been away.   90
The State Asylum. I was prejudiced;
I wouldn't have sent anyone of mine there;
You know the old idea—the only asylum
Was the poorhouse, and those who could afford,
Rather than send their folks to such a place,
Kept them at home; and it does seem more human.
But it's not so: the place is the asylum.
There they have every means proper to do with,
And you aren't darkening other people's lives—
Worse than no good to them, and they no good   100
To you in your condition; you can't know
Affection or the want of it in that state.
I've heard too much of the old-fashioned way.
My father's brother, he went mad quite young.
Some thought he had been bitten by a dog,
Because his violence took on the form
Of carrying his pillow in his teeth;
But it's more likely he was crossed in love,
Or so the story goes. It was some girl.
Anyway all he talked about was love.   110
They soon saw he would do someone a mischief
If he wa'n't kept strict watch of, and it ended
In father's building him a sort of cage,
Or room within a room, of hickory poles,
Like stanchions in the barn, from floor to ceiling,—
A narrow passage all the way around.

Anything they put in for furniture
He'd tear to pieces, even a bed to lie on.
So they made the place comfortable with straw,

120   Like a beast's stall, to ease their consciences.
Of course they had to feed him without dishes.
They tried to keep him clothed, but he paraded
With his clothes on his arm—all of his clothes.
Cruel—it sounds. I'spose they did the best
They knew. And just when he was at the height,
Father and mother married, and mother came,
A bride, to help take care of such a creature,
And accommodate her young life to his.
That was what marrying father meant to her.

130   She had to lie and hear love things made dreadful
By his shouts in the night. He'd shout and shout
Until the strength was shouted out of him,
And his voice died down slowly from exhaustion.
He'd pull his bars apart like bow and bowstring,
And let them go and make them twang until
His hands had worn them smooth as any oxbow.
And then he'd crow as if he thought that child's play
The only fun he had. I've heard them say, though,
They found a way to put a stop to it.

140   He was before my time—I never saw him;
But the pen stayed exactly as it was
There in the upper chamber in the ell,
A sort of catch-all full of attic clutter.
I often think of the smooth hickory bars.
It got so I would say—you know, half fooling—
'It's time I took my turn upstairs in jail'—
Just as you will till it becomes a habit.
No wonder I was glad to get away.
Mind you, I waited till Len said the word.

150   I didn't want the blame if things went wrong.
I was glad though, no end, when we moved out,
And I looked to be happy, and I was,
As I said, for a while—but I don't know!
Somehow the change wore out like a prescription.
And there's more to it than just window-views
And living by a lake. I'm past such help—
Unless Len took the notion, which he won't,
And I won't ask him—it's not sure enough.
I'spose I've got to go the road I'm going:

160   Other folks have to, and why shouldn't I?
I almost think if I could do like you,
Drop everything and live out on the ground—
But it might be, come night, I shouldn't like it,
Or a long rain. I should soon get enough,

And be glad of a good roof overhead.
I've lain awake thinking of you, I'll warrant,
More than you have yourself, some of these nights.
The wonder was the tents weren't snatched away
From over you as you lay in your beds.
I haven't courage for a risk like that. 170
Bless you, of course, you're keeping me from work,
But the thing of it is, I need to *be* kept.
There's work enough to do—there's always that;
But behind's behind. The worst that you can do
Is set me back a little more behind.
I sha'n't catch up in this world, anyway.
I'd *rather* you'd not go unless you must.
1914

AFTER APPLE-PICKING

My long two-pointed ladder's sticking through a tree
Toward heaven still,
And there's the barrel that I didn't fill
Beside it, and there may be two or three
Apples I didn't pick upon some bough.
But I am done with apple-picking now.
Essence of winter sleep is on the night,
The scent of apples: I am drowsing off.
I cannot rub the strangeness from my sight
I got from looking through a pane of glass 10
I skimmed this morning from the drinking trough
And held against the world of hoary grass.
It melted, and I let it fall and break.
But I was well
Upon my way to sleep before it fell,
And I could tell
What form my dreaming was about to take.
Magnified apples appear and disappear,
Stem end and blossom end,
And every fleck of russet showing clear. 20
My instep arch not only keeps the ache,
It keeps the pressure of a ladder-round.
I feel the ladder sway as the boughs bend.
And I keep hearing from the cellar bin
The rumbling sound
Of load on load of apples coming in.
For I have had too much
Of apple-picking: I am overtired
Of the great harvest I myself desired.

30 There were ten thousand thousand fruit to touch,
Cherish in hand, lift down, and not let fall.
For all
That struck the earth,
No matter if not bruised or spiked with stubble,
Went surely to the cider-apple heap
As of no worth.
One can see what will trouble
This sleep of mine, whatever sleep it is.
Were he not gone,
40 The woodchuck could say whether it's like his
Long sleep, as I describe its coming on,
Or just some human sleep.
1914

BIRCHES

When I see birches bend to left and right
Across the lines of straighter darker trees,
I like to think some boy's been swinging them.
But swinging doesn't bend them down to stay
As ice-storms do. Often you must have seen them
Loaded with ice a sunny winter morning
After a rain. They click upon themselves
As the breeze rises, and turn many-colored
As the stir cracks and crazes their enamel.
10 Soon the sun's warmth makes them shed crystal shells
Shattering and avalanching on the snow-crust—
Such heaps of broken glass to sweep away
You'd think the inner dome of heaven had fallen.
They are dragged to the withered bracken by the load,
And they seem not to break; though once they are bowed
So low for long, they never right themselves:
You may see their trunks arching in the woods
Years afterwards, trailing their leaves on the ground
Like girls on hands and knees that throw their hair
20 Before them over their heads to dry in the sun.
But I was going to say when Truth broke in
With all her matter-of-fact about the ice-storm
I should prefer to have some boy bend them
As he went out and in to fetch the cows—
Some boy too far from town to learn baseball,
Whose only play was what he found himself,
Summer or winter, and could play alone.
One by one he subdued his father's trees
By riding them down over and over again

Until he took the stiffness out of them, 30
And not one but hung limp, not one was left
For him to conquer. He learned all there was
To learn about not launching out too soon
And so not carrying the tree away
Clear to the ground. He always kept his poise
To the top branches, climbing carefully
With the same pains you use to fill a cup
Up to the brim, and even above the brim.
Then he flung outward, feet first, with a swish,
Kicking his way down through the air to the ground. 40
So was I once myself a swinger of birches.
And so I dream of going back to be.
It's when I'm weary of considerations,
And life is too much like a pathless wood
Where your face burns and tickles with the cobwebs
Broken across it, and one eye is weeping
From a twig's having lashed across it open.
I'd like to get away from earth awhile
And then come back to it and begin over.
May no fate wilfully misunderstand me 50
And half grant what I wish and snatch me away
Not to return. Earth's the right place for love:
I don't know where it's likely to go better.
I'd like to go by climbing a birch tree,
And climb black branches up a snow-white trunk
Toward heaven, till the tree could bear no more,
But dipped its top and set me down again.
That would be good both going and coming back.
One could do worse than be a swinger of birches.
1916

THE HILL WIFE

LONELINESS

Her Word

One ought not to have to care
    So much as you and I
Care when the birds come round the house
    To seem to say good-bye;

Or care so much when they come back
    With whatever it is they sing;

The truth being we are as much
    Too glad for the one thing

As we are too sad for the other here—
10   With birds that fill their breasts
But with each other and themselves
    And their built or driven nests.

HOUSE FEAR

Always—I tell you this they learned—
Always at night when they returned
To the lonely house from far away
To lamps unlighted and fire gone gray,
They learned to rattle the lock and key
To give whatever might chance to be
Warning and time to be off in flight:
And preferring the out- to the in-door night,
They learned to leave the house-door wide
10 Until they had lit the lamp inside.

THE SMILE

Her Word

I didn't like the way he went away.
That smile! It never came of being gay.
Still he smiled—did you see him?—I was sure!
Perhaps because we gave him only bread
And the wretch knew from that that we were poor.
Perhaps because he let us give instead
Of seizing from us as he might have seized.
Perhaps he mocked at us for being wed,
Or being very young (and he was pleased
10 To have a vision of us old and dead).
I wonder how far down the road he's got.
He's watching from the woods as like as not.

THE OFT-REPEATED DREAM

She had no saying dark enough
    For the dark pine that kept
Forever trying the window-latch
    Of the room where they slept.

The tireless but ineffectual hands
    That with every futile pass
Made the great tree seem as a little bird
    Before the mystery of glass!

It never had been inside the room,
    And only one of the two   10
Was afraid in an oft-repeated dream
    Of what the tree might do.

THE IMPULSE

It was too lonely for her there,
    And too wild,
And since there were but two of them,
    And no child,

And work was little in the house,
    She was free,
And followed where he furrowed field,
    Or felled tree.

She rested on a log and tossed
    The fresh chips,   10
With a song only to herself
    On her lips.

And once she went to break a bough
    Of black alder.
She strayed so far she scarcely heard
    When he called her—

And didn't answer—didn't speak—
    Or return.
She stood, and then she ran and hid
    In the fern.   20

He never found her, though he looked
    Everywhere,
And he asked at her mother's house
    Was she there.

Sudden and swift and light as that
    The ties gave,
And he learned of finalities
    Besides the grave.
1916

THE AXE-HELVE

I've known ere now an interfering branch
Of alder catch my lifted axe behind me.
But that was in the woods, to hold my hand
From striking at another alder's roots,
And that was, as I say, an alder branch.
This was a man, Baptiste, who stole one day
Behind me on the snow in my own yard
Where I was working at the chopping-block,
And cutting nothing not cut down already.
He caught my axe expertly on the rise,
When all my strength put forth was in his favor,
Held it a moment where it was, to calm me,
Then took it from me—and I let him take it.
I didn't know him well enough to know
What it was all about. There might be something
He had in mind to say to a bad neighbor
He might prefer to say to him disarmed.
But all he had to tell me in French-English
Was what he thought of—not me, but my axe;
Me only as I took my axe to heart.
It was the bad axe-helve some one had sold me—
"Made on machine," he said, ploughing the grain
With a thick thumbnail to show how it ran
Across the handle's long drawn serpentine,
Like the two strokes across a dollar sign.
"You give her one good crack, she's snap raght off.
Den where's your hax-ead flying t'rough de hair?"
Admitted; and yet, what was that to him?

"Come on my house and I put you one in
What's las' awhile—good hick'ry what's grow
        crooked.
De second growt' I cut myself—tough, tough!"

Something to sell? That wasn't how it sounded.

"Den when you say you come? It's cost you nothing.
To-naght?"

        As well to-night as any night.

Beyond an over-warmth of kitchen stove
My welcome differed from no other welcome.
Baptiste knew best why I was where I was.

So long as he would leave enough unsaid,
I shouldn't mind his being overjoyed   40
(If overjoyed he was) at having got me
Where I must judge if what he knew about an axe
That not everybody else knew was to count
For nothing in the measure of a neighbor.
Hard if, though cast away for life with Yankees,
A Frenchman couldn't get his human rating!

Mrs. Baptiste came in and rocked a chair
That had as many motions as the world:
One back and forward, in and out of shadow,
That got her nowhere; one more gradual,   50
Sideways, that would have run her on the stove
In time, had she not realized her danger
And caught herself up bodily, chair and all,
And set herself back where she started from.
"She ain't spick too much Henglish—dat's too bad."

I was afraid, in brightening first on me,
Then on Baptiste, as if she understood
What passed between us, she was only feigning.
Baptiste was anxious for her; but no more
Than for himself, so placed he couldn't hope   60
To keep his bargain of the morning with me
In time to keep me from suspecting him
Of really never having meant to keep it.

Needlessly soon he had his axe-helves out,
A quiverful to choose from, since he wished me
To have the best he had, or had to spare—
Not for me to ask which, when what he took
Had beauties he had to point me out at length
To insure their not being wasted on me.
He liked to have it slender as a whipstock,   70
Free from the least knot, equal to the strain
Of bending like a sword across the knee.
He showed me that the lines of a good helve
Were native to the grain before the knife
Expressed them, and its curves were no false curves
Put on it from without. And there its strength lay
For the hard work. He chafed its long white body
From end to end with his rough hand shut round it.
He tried it at the eye-hole in the axe-head.
"Hahn, hahn," he mused, "don't need much taking down."   80
Baptiste knew how to make a short job long
For love of it, and yet not waste time either.

Do you know, what we talked about was knowledge?
Baptiste on his defence about the children
He kept from school, or did his best to keep—
Whatever school and children and our doubts
Of laid-on education had to do
With the curves of his axe-helves and his having
Used these unscrupulously to bring me
90   To see for once the inside of his house.
Was I desired in friendship, partly as some one
To leave it to, whether the right to hold
Such doubts of education should depend
Upon the education of those who held them?

But now he brushed the shavings from his knee
And stood the axe there on its horse's hoof,
Erect, but not without its waves, as when
The snake stood up for evil in the Garden,—
Top-heavy with a heaviness his short,
100   Thick hand made light of, steel-blue chin drawn down
And in a little—a French touch in that.
Baptiste drew back and squinted at it, pleased;
"See how she's cock her head!"
1924

STOPPING BY WOODS ON A SNOWY EVENING

Whose woods these are I think I know.
His house is in the village though;
He will not see me stopping here
To watch his woods fill up with snow.

My little horse must think it queer
To stop without a farmhouse near
Between the woods and frozen lake
The darkest evening of the year.

He gives his harness bells a shake
10   To ask if there is some mistake.
The only other sound's the sweep
Of easy wind and downy flake.

The woods are lovely, dark and deep.
But I have promises to keep,
And miles to go before I sleep,
And miles to go before I sleep.
1924

TWO TRAMPS IN MUD TIME

or, A Full-Time Interest

Out of the mud two strangers came
And caught me splitting wood in the yard.
And one of them put me off my aim
By hailing cheerily 'Hit them hard!'
I knew pretty well why he dropped behind
And let the other go on a way.
I knew pretty well what he had in mind:
He wanted to take my job for pay.

Good blocks of oak it was I split,
As large around as the chopping block;   10
And every piece I squarely hit
Fell splinterless as a cloven rock.
The blows that a life of self-control
Spares to strike for the common good
That day, giving a loose to my soul,
I spent on the unimportant wood.

The sun was warm but the wind was chill.
You know how it is with an April day
When the sun is out and the wind is still,
You're one month on in the middle of May.   20
But if you so much as dare to speak,
A cloud comes over the sunlit arch,
A wind comes off a frozen peak,
And you're two months back in the middle of March.

A bluebird comes tenderly up to alight
And turns to the wind to unruffle a plume,
His song so pitched as not to excite
A single flower as yet to bloom.
It is snowing a flake: and he half knew
Winter was only playing possum.   30
Except in color he isn't blue,
But he wouldn't advise a thing to blossom.

The water for which we may have to look
In summertime with a witching-wand,
In every wheelrut's now a brook,
In every print of a hoof a pond.
Be glad of water, but don't forget
The lurking frost in the earth beneath
That will steal forth after the sun is set
And show on the water its crystal teeth.   40

The time when most I loved my task
These two must make me love it more
By coming with what they came to ask.
You'd think I never had felt before
The weight of an axe-head poised aloft,
The grip on earth of outspread feet,
The life of muscles rocking soft
And smooth and moist in vernal heat.

50

Out of the woods two hulking tramps
(From sleeping God knows where last night,
But not long since in the lumber camps.)
They thought all chopping was theirs of right.
Men of the woods and lumberjacks,
They judged me by their appropriate tool.
Except as a fellow handled an axe,
They had no way of knowing a fool.

60

Nothing on either side was said.
They knew they had but to stay their stay
And all their logic would fill my head:
As that I had no right to play
With what was another man's work for gain.
My right might be love but theirs was need.
And where the two exist in twain
Theirs was the better right—agreed.

70

But yield who will to their separation,
My object in living is to unite
My avocation and my vocation
As my two eyes make one in sight.
Only where love and need are one,
And the work is play for mortal stakes,
Is the deed ever really done
For Heaven and the future's sakes.
1936

THE FIGURE A POEM MAKES[1]

Abstraction is an old story with the philosophers, but it has been like a new toy in the hands of the artists of our day. Why can't we have any one quality of poetry we choose by itself? We can have in thought. Then it will go hard if we can't in practice. Our lives for it.

Granted no one but a humanist much cares how sound a poem is if it is only *a* sound. The sound is the gold in the ore. Then we will have the sound out alone

---

1. This essay first appeared as a preface to the *Complete Poems of Robert Frost*, published in 1949.

and dispense with the inessential. We do till we make the discovery that the object in writing poetry is to make all poems sound as different as possible from each other, and the resources for that of vowels, consonants, punctuation, syntax, words, sentences, meter are not enough. We need the help of context—meaning —subject matter. That is the greatest help towards variety. All that can be done with words is soon told. So also with meters—particularly in our language where there are virtually but two, strict iambic and loose iambic. The ancients with many were still poor if they depended on meters for all tune. It is painful to watch our sprung-rhythmists straining at the point of omitting one short from a foot for relief from monotony. The possibilities for tune from the dramatic tones of meaning struck across the rigidity of a limited meter are endless. And we are back in poetry as merely one more art of having something to say, sound or unsound. Probably better if sound, because deeper and from wider experience.

Then there is this wildness whereof it is spoken. Granted again that it has an equal claim with sound to being a poem's better half. If it is a wild tune, it is a poem. Our problem then is, as modern abstractionists, to have the wildness pure; to be wild with nothing to be wild about. We bring up as aberrationists, giving way to undirected associations and kicking ourselves from one chance suggestion to another in all directions as of a hot afternoon in the life of a grasshopper. Theme alone can steady us down. Just as the first mystery was how a poem could have a tune in such a straightness as meter, so the second mystery is how a poem can have wildness and at the same time a subject that shall be fulfilled.

It should be of the pleasure of a poem itself to tell how it can. The figure a poem makes. It begins in delight and ends in wisdom. The figure is the same as for love. No one can really hold that the ecstasy should be static and stand still in one place. It begins in delight, it inclines to the impulse, it assumes direction with the first line laid down, it runs a course of lucky events, and ends in a clarification of life—not necessarily a great clarification, such as sects and cults are founded on, but in a momentary stay against confusion. It has denouement. It has an outcome that though unforeseen was predestined from the first image of the original mood—and indeed from the very mood. It is but a trick poem and no poem at all if the best of it was thought of first and saved for the last. It finds its own name as it goes and discovers the best waiting for it in some final phrase at once wise and sad—the happy-sad blend of the drinking song.

No tears in the writer, no tears in the reader. No surprise for the writer, no surprise for the reader. For me the initial delight is in the surprise of remembering something I didn't know I knew. I am in a place, in a situation, as if I had materialized from cloud or risen out of the ground. There is a glad recognition of the long lost and the rest follows. Step by step the wonder of unexpected supply keeps growing. The impressions most useful to my purpose seem always those I was unaware of and so made no note of at the time when taken, and the conclusion is come to that like giants we are always hurling experience ahead of us to pave the future with against the day when we may want to strike a line of purpose across it for somewhere. The line will have the more charm for not being mechanically straight. We enjoy the straight crookedness of a good walking stick. Modern instruments of precision are being used to make things crooked as if by eye and hand in the old days.

I tell how there may be a better wildness of logic than of inconsequence. But the logic is backward, in retrospect, after the act. It must be more felt than seen ahead like prophecy. It must be a revelation, or a series of revelations, as much for the poet as for the reader. For it to be that there must have been the greatest freedom of the material to move about in it and to establish relations in it regardless of time and space, previous relation, and everything but affinity. We prate of freedom. We call our schools free because we are not free to stay away from them till we are sixteen years of age. I have given up my democratic prejudices and now willingly set the lower classes free to be completely taken care of by the upper classes. Political freedom is nothing to me. I bestow it right and left. All I would keep for myself is the freedom of my material—the condition of body and mind now and then to summons aptly from the vast chaos of all I have lived through.

Scholars and artists thrown together are often annoyed at the puzzle of where they differ. Both work from knowledge; but I suspect they differ most importantly in the way their knowledge is come by. Scholars get theirs with conscientious thoroughness along projected lines of logic; poets theirs cavalierly and as it happens in and out of books. They stick to nothing deliberately, but let what will stick to them like burrs where they walk in the fields. No acquirement is on assignment, or even self-assignment. Knowledge of the second kind is much more available in the wild free ways of wit and art. A schoolboy may be defined as one who can tell you what he knows in the order in which he learned it. The artist must value himself as he snatches a thing from some previous order in time and space into a new order with not so much as a ligature clinging to it of the old place where it was organic.

More than once I should have lost my soul to radicalism if it had been the originality it was mistaken for by its young converts. Originality and initiative are what I ask for my country. For myself the originality need be no more than the freshness of a poem run in the way I have described: from delight to wisdom. The figure is the same as for love. Like a piece of ice on a hot stove the poem must ride on its own melting. A poem may be worked over once it is in being, but may not be worried into being. Its most precious quality will remain its having run itself and carried away the poet with it. Read it a hundred times: it will forever keep its freshness as a metal keeps its fragrance. It can never lose its sense of a meaning that once unfolded by surprise as it went.
1949

T. S. ELIOT ■■■■■■■■■■■■■■■■■■■■■■

In prestige and influence, T. S. Eliot is the most important critic and poet of the twentieth century. His criteria and judgments, set forth in a substantial body of critical essays, have had a dominant influence on current literary criticism. Likewise, his poetry, especially since the appearance of *The Waste Land* in 1922, has been so regnant that one might almost say Eliot is modern poetry, and modern poetry, Eliot. Most of the younger critics and poets of our time (the novelists are quite another matter) reflect in one way or another the impress of his theory and practice.

THE REVOLT AGAINST THE
NINETEENTH CENTURY

The influence of the nineteenth century persisted well into the twentieth, but by the 1920's a general revolt was in progress. Eliot was a leader in the literary revolt: he led both in the reappraisal of nineteenth-century literature (especially the poetry) and in the revision of nineteenth-century estimates of earlier literature. The resulting change in literary opinion was quite as radical as that which had occurred in the time of Wordsworth, or in the time of Dryden.

The poetry of the nineteenth-century romantics, Eliot thought, was too personal and too emotional: it was concerned too much with the poet himself and with the poet as separate and distinct from other people; it was also emotionally unrestrained and deficient in intellectual energy. "Poetry," Eliot declared, "is not a turning loose of emotion, but an escape from emotion; it is not the expression of personality, but an escape from personality." A good poet undergoes in the writing of his poetry, he thought, a "process of depersonalization": "What happens is a continual surrender of himself as he is at the moment to something which is more valuable. The progress of an artist is a continual self-sacrifice, a continual extinction of personality."

Eliot challenged also the romantic conception of the poet as oracle or seer, and of poetry as a product of inspiration. He thought rather of the poet as a craftsman, expert in his craft and laboriously devoted to it. Great art, he believed, results only through "concentrating upon a task which is a task in the same sense as the making of an efficient engine or the turning of a jug or a table-leg." Apropos of Shelley's famous lines,

> The world's great age begins anew,
> The golden years return,
> The earth doth like a snake renew
> Her winter weeds outworn. . . .

Eliot remarked, "It is not easy to see propriety in an image which divests a snake of 'winter weeds.'" The remark is characteristic of his critical approach. Shelley's image is a "blemish" because it doesn't make sense. Looked at in such a way, nineteenth-century poetry seemed to abound in blemishes that could be attributed to careless workmanship or to a relaxation of intellect or to both.

Eliot objected, moreover, to the whole spirit of the preceding century: its cheerfulness, optimism, and hopefulness; its confidence in man's innate goodness and his improvement by means of the mechanisms of science and politics. In opposition to all this, Eliot reasserted the Christian view, which he felt had been weakened and diluted by Protestant liberalism: the view that stresses man's sinfulness, his need for redemption, the necessity of suffering. The bearing of this view on the poet is seen in his belief that "poetry not only must be found only *through* suffering but can find its material only *in* suffering."

Dissatisfaction with the nineteenth century led to the conviction that nothing less was needed than a revolution in poetic method and poetic taste. The revolution was, in part, a return to older models: to Dante, to the late Elizabethan dramatists, and to the English metaphysical poets of the seventeenth century (these being, with the addition of the nineteenth-century French symbolists, the most important literary influences on Eliot's own poetry). In thirty or forty cogent essays on this older literature (see especially his *Selected Essays, 1917–1932*), he elucidated works of art with a new rigor and "corrected" the taste of the age. The radical nature of his corrections can be inferred from a few examples. Shakespeare (whose idolatry the nineteenth century carried to the farthest reach) appeared in some of Eliot's comments to suffer by comparison with Jonson. *Hamlet,* we were told, is "an artistic failure": "Shakespeare tackled a problem which proved too much for him." Jonson, on the other hand, was praised for un-Shakespearean virtues: his "bold, even shocking and terrifying directness"; his "immense dramatic constructive skill"; his "simple and single effect." Equally dissonant with the nineteenth-century attitude was a comparison drawn between Dryden and Milton in such a way as to make Dryden appear in the more favorable light: "The great advantage of Dryden over Milton," Eliot observed, "is that while Dryden is always in control of his ascent, and can rise or fall at will (and how masterfully, like his own Timotheus, he directs the transitions!), Milton has elected a perch from which he cannot afford to fall, and from which he is in danger of slipping." To Eliot, the grand style, whether of Shakespeare or of Milton, was likely to be a little suspect.

He admired especially the seventeenth-century metaphysical poets —Donne, Crashaw, Marvell (all of whom had been largely discredited in the nineteenth century)—and regretted that in later times "their virtue," which was "something permanently valuable," had been lost. At their best, Eliot said, the metaphysical poets "were engaged in the task of trying to find the verbal equivalent for states of mind and feeling. And this means both that they are more mature, and that they wear better, than later poets." He drew a sharp contrast between the "mistiness" and "vagueness" of a poem by William Morris (of the nineteenth century) and "the bright, hard precision" of a poem by Andrew Marvell. He praised Marvell's "wit," which he defined as "a tough reasonableness beneath the slight lyric grace," and added, "You cannot find it in Shelley or Keats or Wordsworth." In any event, Eliot's reappraisals (the examples cited above are taken from essays published in the 1920's) proved enormously influential, and especially his revival of the English seventeenth century. For Eliot's younger disciples, Donne became almost the pattern of the perfect poet; Marvell's "To His Coy Mistress," almost a touchstone of excellence.

If Eliot was the paraclete of modern criticism, his exegetes are now legion; they have been conspicuous in the literary journals and, more recently, in many textbooks on the "right" understanding of literature; they appear, perhaps, to have been too much warped by his powerful attraction, for not only his general approach but his very terminology has become part of the present-day academic stock-in-trade. Possibly Eliot has been more "successful" as a critical influence than he himself could wish.

POETIC METHOD

Dr. Johnson first used the expression "metaphysical poets," and objected that in their poetry "the most heterogeneous ideas are yoked by violence together." "The force of this impeachment," Eliot remarked, "lies in the failure of the conjunction, the fact that often the ideas are yoked but not united." The greatest poetry, Eliot believes, is an ordering of experience; it therefore necessarily uses heterogeneous materials; but it must unite them, not merely yoke them by violence together, into a new and meaningful pattern. The following famous passage from his essay "The Metaphysical Poets" gives an important clue to Eliot's own method in poetry:

> When a poet's mind is perfectly equipped for its work, it is constantly amalgamating disparate experience; the ordinary man's experience is chaotic, irregular, fragmentary. The latter falls in love, or reads Spinoza, and these two experiences have nothing to do with each other, or with the noise of the typewriter or the smell of cooking; in the mind of the poet these experiences are always forming new wholes.

The result may be poetry in which, as Eliot puts it, there is "a development by rapid association of thought which requires considerable agility on the part of the reader." If the bold juxtapositions and abrupt transitions of this method present an extraordinary difficulty, Eliot's defense is that modern poetry, more than any other, "must be *difficult*," because, he argues,

> Our civilization comprehends great variety and complexity, and this variety and complexity, playing upon a refined sensibility, must produce various and complex results. The poet must become more and more comprehensive, more allusive, more indirect, in order to force, to dislocate if necessary, language into his meaning. . . . Hence we get something which looks very much like the conceit—we get, in fact, a method curiously similar to that of the "metaphysical poets," similar also in its use of obscure words and of simple phrasing.

The classic example of the method thus described is *The Waste Land*.[1] Here is a reordering of experience into a new whole. The experience is comprehensive, complex, and varied; it includes the past as well as the present, reading (one's reading is a part of one's "experience") as well as observation; it is generalized in the sense that it is not intended to be personal to the poet, though Eliot confesses in his notes to the poem that some of the associations are "arbitrary," and the notes themselves are perhaps a confession that complete impersonality is not achieved. The poem is a description of the poet's consciousness of the world and the life of man, a "verbal equivalent for states of mind and feeling." Eliot has said that "the only way of expressing emotion in the form of art is by finding an 'objective correlative'; in other words, a set of objects, a situation, a chain of events which shall be the formula of that *particular* emotion; such that when the external facts, which must terminate in sensory experience, are given, the emotion is immediately evoked."

The Waste Land is, in part, a collection of characters and scenes

---

1. For a detailed examination of the poem, the reader is referred to Cleanth Brooks, "The Waste Land: Critique of the Myth," *Modern Poetry and the Tradition*, 136–172.

drawn from the modern world: Madame Sosostris, the fortuneteller, with her pack of cards; the crowd crossing London Bridge in the early morning fog; the woman sitting at her dressing table and talking or trying to talk with her husband, or lover; the woman in an English pub discussing Lil with another woman; Mr. Eugenides, the Smyrna merchant, and his invitation to the Metropole for a weekend; the affair of the typist and the clerk; the girl from Highbury and her adventure in a canoe on the Thames; and others. These characters and scenes are symbols of the degradation and despair of the modern world.

But "realistic" scenes like these are only a part of the poet's representation. His aim is to show these things (for the poetic consciousness so incorporates them) in relation to other things, to show them both in time and in eternity, and thereby achieve a rich dimensional development. The modern scene is shown, first, in relation to the historical past; and it is evident that there has been a decline, a loss. Literary allusions and borrowed phrases often serve the purpose (among other purposes) of suggesting and pointing up this contrast. The bored woman at the gaudy dressing table is compared unfavorably with Cleopatra, whom age could not wither nor custom stale, the comparison being suggested by the verbal reminiscence of Shakespeare's description of Cleopatra's barge. Eliot's woman is "synthetic"; so is his description of her—purposely so. The Thames, now littered with "cardboard boxes, cigarette ends/Or other testimony of summer nights," has deteriorated since Elizabethan times, when it was the scene of stately bridals (suggested by the line from Spenser's "Prothalamion"), and Elizabeth and Leicester were rowed on its surface in a splendid barge. Deterioration is everywhere: the pack of cards, now used for trivial purposes, was formerly a part of an ancient ritual; the typist is a degradation of Goldsmith's "lovely woman"; Sweeney and Mrs. Porter lack the dignity of Marvell's lovers (suggested by the verbal echo of a line in "To His Coy Mistress"); Mr. Eugenides ill becomes the historic dignity of Smyrna.

Further development in dimension (or depth of perspective) is achieved by showing the contemporary scene in a frame of reference that is essentially timeless and that is drawn from ancient myths. Old Tiresias, who has suffered all, knowing "both sides of love," and "foresuffered all," having the power to foresee the future, is a dispassionate spectator and chorus. If the contrasts between the present and the past seem to emphasize the deterioration of the present, the commentary of Tiresias seems to suggest the possibility, at least, that the decline may be more apparent than real. The Fisher King, from the Grail legend, and the desert country, repeatedly described, are also symbols of timelessness, as are other symbols in the poem: the evil of the world is as old as the world itself. The present evil, however, is not nullified, or even mitigated, by the larger frames of reference; it is given added weight and significance, rather, when seen in the perspective of man's long and ageless experience.

STYLE

An exalted style seemed to Eliot out of keeping with the modern temper. Still less did he like the high-flown manner of the nineteenth-century poets. He once quoted D. H. Lawrence's remarks on modern poetry, as follows,

> "The essence of poetry with us in this age of stark and unlovely actualities is a stark directness, without a shadow of a lie, or a shadow of deflection anywhere. Everything can go, but this stark, bare, rocky directness of statement; this alone makes poetry today."

He then went on to say of Lawrence's dictum,

> This speaks to me of that at which I have long aimed, in writing poetry; to write poetry which should be essentially poetry, with nothing "poetic" about it, poetry standing naked in its bare bones, or poetry so transparent that we should not see the poetry, but that which we are meant to see through the poetry, poetry so transparent that in reading it we are intent on what the poem *points at,* and not on the poetry, this seems to me the thing to try for.[2]

Critics of Eliot have often pointed out the chief characteristics of his way of writing poetry: the conversational tone, the vocabulary at once colloquial and unusual, the rapid association of ideas, the irregular verse form, the flash of wit, the omission of connecting links. These characteristics (suggesting the influence of Donne) are more emphasized in *The Waste Land* than in *Four Quartets*. In the latter work, there is more "ordonnance" (a quality mentioned by Eliot in his praise of Lancelot Andrewes); the structure is less fragmentary, the progression less interrupted; there is perhaps a loss of "wit," the contrasts being less violent, but a gain in meditative seriousness. There is still poetic variety, the parts of the poems composing the *Four Quartets* ranging variously between the intense lyric in exact meter and the conversational piece in the relaxed rhythms of prose. There is the same control of ascent and descent that Eliot so much admired in Dryden. There is, also, in the *Four Quartets*, as in the earlier work of this rigorous classicist, great verbal precision and the careful, exact placing of words together. Eliot the classicist speaks in the following passage in "Little Gidding":

> . . . where every word is at home,
> Taking its place to support the others. . . .
> The common word exact without vulgarity,
> The formal word precise but not pedantic,
> The complete consort dancing together.

2. Quoted in F. O. Matthiessen, *The Achievement of T. S. Eliot,* 89–90.

THE CHRISTIAN TRADITION AND THE
MODERN INTELLECTUAL MAN

The doctrine of man's sinfulness is basic in the Christian tradition. "All have sinned," according to Saint Paul, "and come short of the glory of God" (Romans 3:23). The Christian view emphasizes man's imperfection, his wretchedness, his need of redemption. The appropriate attitude for man in this state of affairs is not pride in his goodness but contrition for his faults: men should be bound together in a common humility. The way of salvation is not social amelioration but inner purification. David's prayer, "Create in me a clean heart, O God, and renew a right spirit within me" (Psalms 51:10), strikes at the root of the matter. The Christian life, therefore, is not self-congratulatory and easy, for Christianity at its best imposes a difficult discipline. Eliot's position on the religious question is shown quite clearly in a passage like the following from *Thoughts After Lambeth* (1931):

> Thought, study, mortification, sacrifice: it is such notions as these that should be impressed upon the young—who differ from the young of other times merely in having a different middle-aged generation behind them. You will never attract the young by making Christianity easy; but a good many can be attracted by finding it difficult: difficult both to the disorderly mind and to the unruly passions.

Salvation is by God's grace, but man's penitence and penance are a necessary condition to the operation of divine grace.

Eliot's poetry shows a steady progression toward religious belief. It is the tortuous progress of the modern intellectual man who recognizes the necessity of religion, but for whom a spontaneous, simple faith is difficult, if not impossible. The poems are an honest record; there are no easy affirmations; the poet has not put down what one would like to feel, though unable actually to feel it; there would be no point in that. What the poems give instead is something more valuable: a dramatic and symbolical description of the complex consciousness of a modern intellectual mind.

"The Love Song of J. Alfred Prufrock," a dramatic monologue, is a consummate picture of the ineffectualness of the modern intellectual. Prufrock's condition is symbolized at the very beginning of the poem by the comparison between the evening and a patient etherized upon a table. His condition is one of distress and restlessness (for the patient under ether is not really quiet, but distressed and infinitely restless) and, at the same time, of complete paralysis. He is unable to answer questions, either great or small, or to arrive at a decision. He is incapable of action. He is bored by the petty round of tea parties and social calls. He lacks motivation because he is without conviction or belief. Contrasts are suggested with heroic figures of the past: with Hamlet, who, though greatly perturbed by the task thrust upon him, was nevertheless a passionate, heroic figure; with Michelangelo, who epitomizes the creative energy of the Italian Renaissance; with John the Baptist, the first Christian martyr. The presence of allusions like these gives the poem a religious implication: Hamlet, Michelangelo, and John the Baptist were energized by a passionate belief; Prufrock is separated from them by the distance between health and neurosis.

The ironic futility of "Prufrock" is continued in *The Waste Land*, but the despair is greater and the religious implications correspondingly more emphatic. It is as if the poet meant to suggest that modern man must be reduced to utter despair before there can be a conscious striving toward religious faith. Many passages in *The Waste Land* point to a religious interpretation. The desert passages recall the Old Testament in both tone and language. Compare, for example, Eliot's "Son of man,/ You cannot say, or guess, for you know only/ A heap of broken images" with Ezekiel's "Son of man, can these bones live? And I answered, O Lord God, thou knowest." Ecclesiastes, Chapter 12, describes a waste land similar to Eliot's: ". . . and the grasshopper shall be a burden, and desire shall fail. . . ." The allusion to Christ's agony and death ("After the torchlight red on sweaty faces/ After the frosty silence in the garden/ After the agony. . . .") suggests the Christian solution. The poem, however, reaches out to include all religions. Christ is associated with other "hanged gods" and becomes one of many examples (though the example, Eliot would say, most available to the Western world) of the basic doctrine of life through death. Among the illustrations of the doctrine in the poem are the corpse buried in the garden, which the Dog (possibly representing modern science) threatens to exhume and thereby prevent the rebirth of life, and the drowned Phoenician Sailor, whose eyes undergo a supernatural transformation. The whole poem is built, Cleanth Brooks believes, on this central paradox: "Life devoid of meaning is death; sacrifice, even the sacrificial death, may be life-giving, an awakening to life."[3] The Sanskrit words at the end of the poem (meaning "give, sympathize, control," and "the peace which passeth understanding") point up the unity and antiquity of religious beliefs.

Between *The Waste Land* and the *Four Quartets* (published as a whole in 1943) Eliot developed in the direction of a less complex poetry and a more mature religious attitude. In the late 1920's he announced his conversion to Anglo-Catholicism, and his work since that time, both in prose and in poetry, has reflected this commitment, though looking back, we can now see that such a development was implicit in the earlier writings. The *Four Quartets* may be regarded as a series of religious meditations. The work consists of four poems

3. *Modern Poetry and the Tradition*, 137.

—"Burnt Norton," "East Coker," "The Dry Salvages," and "Little Gidding"—and each poem is developed through five movements, somewhat after the manner of the sonata form in music.

The series reaches its culmination in "Little Gidding," which takes its name from a famous Anglican shrine in Huntingdonshire, where Nicholas Ferrar and his family, in 1625, retired to lead a life of religious devotion, and where Charles I, "a broken king," came to pray. It is a place, the poet says, "where prayer has been valid." The protagonist of the poem visits Little Gidding to pray, or at least to assume the attitude of prayer: "You are here to kneel." But genuine prayer is almost infinitely difficult (the reported consciousness still resembles that of the protagonist of *The Waste Land* in its complexity), for "prayer is more/ Than an order of words, the conscious occupation/ Of the praying mind, or the sound of the voice praying." The position of the modern man is very different from that of the seventeenth-century worshipers at Little Gidding. To the modern visitor, even with the best of intentions, this shrine, or any other shrine, is likely to be only "a shell, a husk of meaning."

"Little Gidding," like Keats's "Cold Pastoral," teases us out of thought as doth eternity. Man is the prisoner of time; everything about him is in a state of flux; human history is a record of flux, symbolized by the transmuting of the four elements in Part 2. But man is capable of liberation from time ("This is the use of memory"). He is capable of moments of illumination when the timeless touches or intersects the temporal ("the intersection of the timeless moment," "this intersection time"); the meeting with the "dead master" during the bombing of London is such a moment. The meaning of history ("love of a country," "old factions," "old policies") is grasped only in "a symbol," a timeless abstraction wrung from the temporal flux.

Experience, the poem seems to say, is a preparation for the "intersection time," the moment of insight or revelation. The preparation is a purgation, a purification as by fire: indeed, fire seems the dominant symbol of the poem. In Part 1, the sun shines with "pentecostal fire." In Part 2, fire appears as "the flickering tongue" of a bomber (shockingly contrasted with the "cloven tongues" of Pentecost). Part 4 reiterates the fire motif, particularly in "the intolerable shirt of flame," the Nessus shirt of Hercules. But in whatever manifestation, the fire is for man's behoof; it is "refining" (this is the lesson of the dead master); it is "devised" by "Love."

"Little Gidding" attempts the reconciliation of opposites. (The symbol of the dance, where conflicting members are joined in harmony, is twice used.) Only through the largest possible synthesis, Eliot seems to say, can man achieve a true integration. Such a goal, the poem demonstrates, requires great effort of mind and spirit. If we rightly experience the poet's own effort, his conclusion that "all shall be well" (which echoes Saint Paul's "all things work together for good") may take on a new and valid meaning.

LIFE AND WORKS

T. S. Eliot was born in St. Louis, Missouri, in 1888 and educated in the St. Louis schools, Milton Academy, and Harvard (B.A. 1909; M.A. 1910); he did further graduate study at the Sorbonne and Oxford. He worked for a while in Lloyd's Bank in London; founded *The Criterion,* an important literary journal; became a director of the publishing house of Faber and Faber; became a British subject in 1927; was Charles Eliot Norton Professor of Poetry at Harvard in 1933–1934; received the Nobel prize for literature in 1948. His *The Waste Land* ushered in a new era in poetry and his *The Sacred Wood* a new era in criticism, both appearing in the early 1920's. His verse plays have not had a comparable influence in the dramatic field, though his fourth, *The Cocktail Party* (1950), was a Broadway hit. His most mature poetry is found in *Four Quartets* (1943). His most valuable literary essays were collected in a volume of *Selected Essays* (selected, that is, by the author himself) in 1935. By 1950 he had become a name throughout the land of his birth, and indeed throughout the English-speaking world.

H. R. Williamson, *The Poetry of T. S. Eliot* (1932); F. O. Matthiessen, *The Achievement of T. S. Eliot* (1935, revised edition 1947); *T. S. Eliot: A Selected Critique,* editor, Leonard Unger (1948); H. L. Gardner, *The Art of T. S. Eliot* (1949).

THE LOVE SONG OF J. ALFRED PRUFROCK

S'io credesse che mia risposta fosse
A persona che mai tornasse al mondo,
Questa fiamma staria senza piu scosse.
Ma perciocche giammai di questo fondo
Non torno vivo alcun, s'i'odo il vero,
Senza tema d'infamia ti rispondo.

Let us go then, you and I,
When the evening is spread out against the sky
Like a patient etherised upon a table;
Let us go, through certain half-deserted streets,
The muttering retreats
Of restless nights in one-night cheap hotels
And sawdust restaurants with oyster-shells:
Streets that follow like a tedious argument
Of insidious intent

S'io . . . rispondo: If I could believe that my answer might be to a person who should ever return into the world, this flame would stand without more quiverings; but inasmuch as, if I hear the truth, never from this depth did any living man return, without fear of infamy I answer thee (Dante's *Inferno,* Canto 27, lines 61–66).

To lead you to an overwhelming question . . .   10
Oh, do not ask, "What is it?"
Let us go and make our visit.

In the room the women come and go
Talking of Michelangelo.

The yellow fog that rubs its back upon the window-panes,
The yellow smoke that rubs its muzzle on the window-panes
Licked its tongue into the corners of the evening,
Lingered upon the pools that stand in drains,
Let fall upon its back the soot that falls from chimneys,
Slipped by the terrace, made a sudden leap,   20
And seeing that it was a soft October night,
Curled once about the house, and fell asleep.

And indeed there will be time
For the yellow smoke that slides along the street,
Rubbing its back upon the window-panes;
There will be time, there will be time
To prepare a face to meet the faces that you meet;
There will be time to murder and create,
And time for all the works and days of hands
That lift and drop a question on your plate;   30
Time for you and time for me,
And time yet for a hundred indecisions,
And for a hundred visions and revisions,
Before the taking of a toast and tea.

In the room the women come and go
Talking of Michelangelo.

And indeed there will be time
To wonder, "Do I dare?" and, "Do I dare?"
Time to turn back and descend the stair,
With a bald spot in the middle of my hair—
(They will say: "How his hair is growing thin!")   40
My morning coat, my collar mounting firmly to the chin,
My necktie rich and modest, but asserted by a simple pin—
(They will say: "But how his arms and legs are thin!")
Do I dare
Disturb the universe?
In a minute there is time
For decisions and revisions which a minute will reverse.

For I have known them all already, known them all:
Have known the evenings, mornings, afternoons,   50
I have measured out my life with coffee spoons;
I know the voices dying with a dying fall

10. The dots here and elsewhere in the poem are the author's and do not denote omissions.
52. dying fall: The phrase is from Shakespeare's *Twelfth Night*, I, i, 4.

Beneath the music from a farther room.
   So how should I presume?
And I have known the eyes already, known them all—
The eyes that fix you in a formulated phrase,
And when I am formulated, sprawling on a pin,
When I am pinned and wriggling on the wall,
Then how should I begin

60   To spit out all the butt-ends of my days and ways?
   And how should I presume?

And I have known the arms already, known them all—
Arms that are braceleted and white and bare
(But in the lamplight, downed with light brown hair!)
Is it perfume from a dress
That makes me so digress?
Arms that lie along a table, or wrap about a shawl.
   And should I then presume?
   And how should I begin?

    .   .   .   .   .

70   Shall I say, I have gone at dusk through narrow streets
And watched the smoke that rises from the pipes
Of lonely men in shirt-sleeves, leaning out of windows? . . .

I should have been a pair of ragged claws
Scuttling across the floors of silent seas.

    .   .   .   .   .

And the afternoon, the evening, sleeps so peacefully!
Smoothed by long fingers,
Asleep . . . tired . . . or it malingers,
Stretched on the floor, here beside you and me.
Should I, after tea and cakes and ices,

80   Have the strength to force the moment to its crisis?
But though I have wept and fasted, wept and prayed,
Though I have seen my head (grown slightly bald) brought in upon a platter,
I am no prophet—and here's no great matter;
I have seen the moment of my greatness flicker,
And I have seen the eternal Footman hold my coat, and snicker,
And in short, I was afraid.

And would it have been worth it, after all,
After the cups, the marmalade, the tea,
Among the porcelain, among some talk of you and me,

90   Would it have been worth while,
To have bitten off the matter with a smile,
To have squeezed the universe into a ball

---

83. prophet: an allusion to John the Baptist, whose head was brought to Herod "in a charger" (see Matthew 14).

92. into a ball: Compare Marvell's "To His Coy Mistress," lines 41–42: "Let us roll all our strength and all/ Our sweetness up into one ball."

To roll it toward some overwhelming question,
To say: "I am Lazarus, come from the dead,
Come back to tell you all, I shall tell you all"—
If one, settling a pillow by her head,
   Should say: "That is not what I meant at all;
   That is not it, at all."

And would it have been worth it, after all,
Would it have been worth while,   100
After the sunsets and the dooryards and the sprinkled streets,
After the novels, after the teacups, after the skirts that trail along the floor—
And this, and so much more?—
It is impossible to say just what I mean!
But as if a magic lantern threw the nerves in patterns on a screen:
Would it have been worth while
If one, settling a pillow or throwing off a shawl,
And turning toward the window, should say:
   "That is not it at all,
   That is not what I meant, at all."   110

     .   .   .   .   .

No! I am not Prince Hamlet, nor was meant to be;
Am an attendant lord, one that will do
To swell a progress, start a scene or two,
Advise the prince; no doubt, an easy tool,
Deferential, glad to be of use,
Politic, cautious, and meticulous;
Full of high sentence, but a bit obtuse;
At times, indeed, almost ridiculous—
Almost, at times, the Fool.

I grow old . . . I grow old . . .   120
I shall wear the bottoms of my trousers rolled.

Shall I part my hair behind? Do I dare to eat a peach?
I shall wear white flannel trousers, and walk upon the beach.
I have heard the mermaids singing, each to each.

I do not think that they will sing to me.

I have seen them riding seaward on the waves
Combing the white hair of the waves blown back
When the wind blows the water white and black.

We have lingered in the chambers of the sea
By sea-girls wreathed with seaweed red and brown   130
Till human voices wake us, and we drown.
1917

94. Lazarus: See John 11.
117. Full . . . sentence: full of wisdom, said of Chaucer's "clerk of Oxenford." See the Prologue to *The Canterbury Tales*, line 306.

THE WASTE LAND

"NAM Sibyllam quidem Cumis ego ipse oculis meis vidi in ampulla pendere, et cum illi pueri dicerent: Σίβυλλα τί θέλεις; respondebat illa: ἀποθανεῖν θέλω."

1. THE BURIAL OF THE DEAD

April is the cruellest month, breeding
Lilacs out of the dead land, mixing
Memory and desire, stirring
Dull roots with spring rain.
Winter kept us warm, covering
Earth in forgetful snow, feeding
A little life with dried tubers.
Summer surprised us, coming over the Starnbergersee
With a shower of rain; we stopped in the colonnade,
10   And went on in sunlight, into the Hofgarten,
And drank coffee, and talked for an hour.
Bin gar keine Russin, stamm' aus Litauen, echt deutsch.
And when we were children, staying at the archduke's,
My cousin's, he took me out on a sled,
And I was frightened. He said, Marie,
Marie, hold on tight. And down we went.
In the mountains, there you feel free.
I read, much of the night, and go south in the winter.

What are the roots that clutch, what branches grow
20   Out of this stony rubbish? Son of man,
You cannot say, or guess, for you know only
A heap of broken images, where the sun beats,
And the dead tree gives no shelter, the cricket no relief,
And the dry stone no sound of water. Only
There is shadow under this red rock,

In the following annotations on "The Waste Land," Eliot's own notes (from his *Collected Poems*, 1936) are identified by quotation marks and by (Eliot) after each note. Supplementary notes have been supplied by the editors.
"Not only the title, but the plan and a good deal of the incidental symbolism of the poem were suggested by Miss Jessie L. Weston's book on the Grail legend: *From Ritual to Romance* (Cambridge). Indeed, so deeply am I indebted, Miss Weston's book will elucidate the difficulties of the poem much better than my notes can do; and I recommend it (apart from the great interest of the book itself) to any who think such elucidation of the poem worth the trouble. To another work of anthropology I am indebted in general, one which has influenced our generation profoundly; I mean *The Golden Bough;* I have used especially the two volumes *Adonis, Attis, Osiris.* Anyone who is acquainted with these works will immediately recognise in the poem certain references to vegetation ceremonies." (Eliot)
"NAM . . . ἀποθανεῖν θέλω": "Yes, and I myself saw with my own eyes the Sibyl of Cumae hanging in a cage; and when the children cried at her, 'Sibyl, what do you want?' she used to reply, 'I want to die.'" Petronius, *Satyricon,* XLVIII.

(Come in under the shadow of this red rock),
And I will show you something different from either
Your shadow at morning striding behind you
Or your shadow at evening rising to meet you;
I will show you fear in a handful of dust.   30

> *Frisch weht der Wind*
> *Der Heimat zu*
> *Mein Irisch Kind,*
> *Wo weilest du?*

"You gave me hyacinths first a year ago;
"They called me the hyacinth girl."
—Yet when we came back, late, from the Hyacinth garden,
Your arms full, and your hair wet, I could not
Speak, and my eyes failed, I was neither
Living nor dead, and I knew nothing,   40
Looking into the heart of light, the silence.
Oed' und leer das Meer.

Madame Sosostris, famous clairvoyante,
Had a bad cold, nevertheless
Is known to be the wisest woman in Europe,
With a wicked pack of cards. Here, said she,
Is your card, the drowned Phoenician Sailor,
(Those are pearls that were his eyes. Look!)
Here is Belladonna, the Lady of the Rocks,
The lady of situations.   50
Here is the man with three staves, and here the Wheel,
And here is the one-eyed merchant, and this card,
Which is blank, is something he carries on his back,
Which I am forbidden to see. I do not find
The Hanged Man. Fear death by water.
I see crowds of people, walking round in a ring.
Thank you. If you see dear Mrs. Equitone,
Tell her I bring the horoscope myself:
One must be so careful these days.

12. Bin . . . deutsch: I am no Russian, I come from Lithuania, true German.
20. Son of man: "Cf. Ezekiel 2:1." (Eliot)
23. cricket no relief: "Cf. Ecclesiastes 12:5." (Eliot)
31. Frisch . . . du: "V. Tristan und Isolde, I, verses 5–8." (Eliot) "The wind blows fresh homeward, my Irish child, where do you tarry?" From the opera by Wagner.
42. Oed' . . . Meer: "Id. III, verse 24." (Eliot) "Desolate and empty the sea."
46. pack of cards: "I am not familiar with the exact constitution of the Tarot pack of cards, from which I have obviously departed to suit my own convenience. The Hanged Man, a member of the traditional pack, fits my purpose in two ways: because he is associated in my mind with the Hanged God of Frazer, and because I associate him with the hooded figure in the passage of the disciples to Emmaus in Part V. The Phoenician Sailor and the Merchant appear later; also the 'crowds of people,' and Death by Water is executed in Part IV. The Man with Three Staves (an authentic member of the Tarot pack) I associate, quite arbitrarily, with the Fisher King himself." (Eliot) Frazer is the author of *The Golden Bough;* the Fisher King is the impotent ruler of the waste land described in *From Ritual to Romance.*
48. Those . . . eyes: from Ariel's song in Shakespeare's *The Tempest*, Act I, scene ii, line 398.

60 Unreal City,
Under the brown fog of a winter dawn,
A crowd flowed over London Bridge, so many,
I had not thought death had undone so many.
Sighs, short and infrequent, were exhaled,
And each man fixed his eyes before his feet.
Flowed up the hill and down King William Street,
To where Saint Mary Woolnoth kept the hours
With a dead sound on the final stroke of nine.
There I saw one I knew, and stopped him, crying: "Stetson!
70 "You who were with me in the ships at Mylae!
"That corpse you planted last year in your garden,
"Has it begun to sprout? Will it bloom this year?
"Or has the sudden frost disturbed its bed?
"Oh keep the Dog far hence, that's friend to men,
"Or with his nails he'll dig it up again!
"You! hypocrite lecteur!—mon semblable,—mon frère!"

2. A GAME OF CHESS

The chair she sat in, like a burnished throne,
Glowed on the marble, where the glass
Held up by standards wrought with fruited vines
80 From which a golden Cupidon peeped out
(Another hid his eyes behind his wing)
Doubled the flames of sevenbranched candelabra
Reflecting light upon the table as
The glitter of her jewels rose to meet it,
From satin cases poured in rich profusion;
In vials of ivory and coloured glass
Unstoppered, lurked her strange synthetic perfumes,
Unguent, powdered, or liquid—troubled, confused

60. Unreal City: "Cf. Baudelaire:
'Fourmillante cité, cité pleine de rêves,
'Où le spectre en plein jour raccroche le passant.' " (Eliot)
"Swarming city, city full of dreams, where a ghost in broad daylight accosts the passerby." From "Les Sept Vieillards."
63. I had . . . so many: "Cf. *Inferno* III, 55–57:
'si lunga tratta
di gente, ch'io non avrei mai creduto
che morte tanta n'avesse disfatta.' " (Eliot)
"So long a train of people, I never should have believed death had undone so many."
64. Sighs . . . exhaled: "Cf. *Inferno* IV, 25–27:
'Quivi, secondo che per ascoltare,
'non avea pianto, ma' che di sospiri,
'che l'aura eterna facevan tremare.' " (Eliot)
"Here, as one listened, there was no complaining, but only sighs, which made the eternal air tremble."
68. With . . . nine: "A phenomenon which I have often noticed." (Eliot)
70. Mylae: Roman naval victory over Carthage in 260 B.C.
74. Dog: "Cf. the Dirge in Webster's *White Devil*." (Eliot) The lines referred to occur in Act V, scene iv of John Webster's play: "But keep the wolf far thence, that's foe to men,/ For with his nails he'll dig them up again." The "corpse" has been taken to refer to the fertility god, and the "sprouting" to the god's resurrection. An

And drowned the sense in odours; stirred by the air
That freshened from the window, these ascended   90
In fattening the prolonged candle-flames,
Flung their smoke into the laquearia,
Stirring the pattern on the coffered ceiling.
Huge sea-wood fed with copper
Burned green and orange, framed by the coloured
     stone,
In which sad light a carvèd dolphin swam.
Above the antique mantel was displayed
As though a window gave upon the sylvan scene
The change of Philomel, by the barbarous king
So rudely forced; yet there the nightingale   100
Filled all the desert with inviolable voice
And still she cried, and still the world pursues,
"Jug Jug" to dirty ears.
And other withered stumps of time
Were told upon the walls; staring forms
Leaned out, leaning, hushing the room enclosed.
Footsteps shuffled on the stair.
Under the firelight, under the brush, her hair
Spread out in fiery points
Glowed into words, then would be savagely still.   110

"My nerves are bad to-night. Yes, bad. Stay with me.
"Speak to me. Why do you never speak. Speak.
"What are you thinking of? What thinking? What?
"I never know what you are thinking. Think."

I think we are in rats' alley
Where the dead men lost their bones.

"What is that noise?"
               The wind under the door.

analogous concept occurs in Romans 6:5: "For if we have been planted together in the likeness of His death, we
shall be also in the likeness of His resurrection."
76. hypocrite . . . frere: "V. Baudelaire, Preface to *Fleurs du Mal*." (Eliot) "Hypocritical reader, my likeness, my brother."
77. The chair . . . throne: "Cf. *Antony and Cleopatra*, II, ii, l. 190." (Eliot) The famous passage in Shakespeare describing Cleopatra's barge begins "The barge she sat in, like a burnished throne. . . ."
92. laquearia: "V. *Aeneid*, I, 726:
     'dependent lychni laquearibus aureis incensi, et noctem flammis funalia vincunt.' " (Eliot)
"Lighted lamps hang from the fretted ceiling of gold, and flaming torches overcome the night."
98. sylvan scene: "V. Milton, *Paradise Lost*, IV, 140." (Eliot) Here Milton describes the Garden of Eden as
first viewed by Satan.
99. Philomel: "V. Ovid, *Metamorphoses*, VI, Philomela." (Eliot) Here Ovid tells the story of the rape of
Philomela by Tereus, the cutting out of her tongue, and her subsequent change into a nightingale. The words
"jug, jug" (l. 103) were used by English poets to represent the nightingale's song. See, for example, John Lyly's
"Alexander and Campaspe": "What bird so sings, yet does so wail? / Oh, 'tis the ravished nightingale, / Jug,
jug, jug, jug, tereu, she cries, / And still her woes at midnight rise."
100. nightingale: "Cf. Part III, l. 204." (Eliot)
115. rats' alley: "Cf. Part III, l. 195." (Eliot)
118. The wind: "Cf. Webster: 'Is the wind in that door still?' " (Eliot) The quotation is from John Webster's
The Devil's Law Case, Act III, scene ii, line 162.

"What is that noise now? What is the wind doing?"
120   Nothing again nothing.

                                "Do
"You know nothing? Do you see nothing? Do you remember
"Nothing?"

              I remember
Those are pearls that were his eyes.
"Are you alive, or not? Is there nothing in your head?"

                                  But
O O O O that Shakespeherian Rag—
It's so elegant
130 So intelligent
"What shall I do now? What shall I do?"
"I shall rush out as I am, and walk the street
"With my hair down, so. What shall we do to-morrow?
"What shall we ever do?"
                    The hot water at ten.
And if it rains, a closed car at four.
And we shall play a game of chess,
Pressing lidless eyes and waiting for a knock upon the door.

When Lil's husband got demobbed, I said—
140 I didn't mince my words, I said to her myself,
HURRY UP PLEASE ITS TIME
Now Albert's coming back, make yourself a bit smart.
He'll want to know what you done with that money he gave you
To get yourself some teeth. He did, I was there.
You have them all out, Lil, and get a nice set,
He said, I swear, I can't bear to look at you.
And no more can't I, I said, and think of poor Albert,
He's been in the army four years, he wants a good time,
And if you don't give it him, there's others will, I said.
150 Oh is there, she said. Something o' that, I said.
Then I'll know who to thank, she said, and give me a straight look.
HURRY UP PLEASE ITS TIME
If you don't like it you can get on with it, I said.
Others can pick and choose if you can't.
But if Albert makes off, it won't be for lack of telling.
You ought to be ashamed, I said, to look so antique.

125. Those . . . eyes: "Cf. Part I, l. 37, 48." (Eliot)
137. game of chess: "Cf. the game of chess in Middleton's *Women Beware Women*." (Eliot) In Act II, scene ii, of Thomas Middleton's play, a chess game is used to distract the attention of a mother-in-law while her daughter-in-law is being seduced by a highborn lover, the husband being absent.
141. HURRY . . . TIME: the call denoting closing time in an English pub.
172. Good . . . night: The line is taken from Ophelia's mad speech in *Hamlet*, Act IV, scene v, line 74.
176. Sweet . . . song: "V. Spenser, *Prothalamion*." (Eliot) The line is the refrain of Edmund Spenser's poem.

(And her only thirty-one.)
I can't help it, she said, pulling a long face,
It's them pills I took, to bring it off, she said.
(She's had five already and nearly died of young George.)   160
The chemist said it would be all right, but I've never been the same.
You *are* a proper fool, I said.
Well, if Albert won't leave you alone, there it is, I said,
What you get married for if you don't want children?
HURRY UP PLEASE ITS TIME
Well, that Sunday Albert was home, they had a hot gammon,
And they asked me in to dinner, to get the beauty of it hot—
HURRY UP PLEASE ITS TIME
HURRY UP PLEASE ITS TIME
Goonight Bill. Goonight Lou. Goonight May. Goonight.   170
Ta ta. Goonight. Goonight.
Good night ladies, good night, sweet ladies, good night, good night.

3. THE FIRE SERMON

The river's tent is broken: the last fingers of leaf
Clutch and sink into the wet bank. The wind
Crosses the brown land, unheard. The nymphs are departed.
Sweet Thames, run softly, till I end my song.
The river bears no empty bottles, sandwich papers,
Silk handkerchiefs, cardboard boxes, cigarette ends
Or other testimony of summer nights. The nymphs are departed.
And their friends, the loitering heirs of city directors;   180
Departed, have left no addresses.
By the waters of Leman I sat down and wept . . .
Sweet Thames, run softly till I end my song,
Sweet Thames, run softly, for I speak not loud or long.
But at my back in a cold blast I hear
The rattle of the bones, and chuckle spread from ear to ear.
A rat crept softly through the vegetation
Dragging its slimy belly on the bank
While I was fishing in the dull canal
On a winter evening round behind the gashouse   190
Musing upon the king my brother's wreck
And on the king my father's death before him.
White bodies naked on the low damp ground

182. By . . . wept: See Psalms, Chapter 137: "By the rivers of Babylon, there we sat down, yea, we wept,
when we remembered Zion." "Leman" is the Swiss name for Lake Geneva. The three dots, here and elsewhere in
the poem, are the author's, and do not denote omissions.
192. king . . . death: "Cf. *The Tempest,* I, ii." (Eliot) Compare especially lines 389–391: "Sitting on a bank,/
Weeping again the King my father's wrack,/ This music crept by me upon the waters. . . ." Eliot's passage
alludes obliquely to the Fisher King of the Grail legend.

And bones cast in a little low dry garret,
Rattled by the rat's foot only, year to year.
But at my back from time to time I hear
The sound of horns and motors, which shall bring
Sweeney to Mrs. Porter in the spring.
O the moon shone bright on Mrs. Porter
200 And on her daughter
They wash their feet in soda water
Et O ces voix d'enfants, chantant dans la coupole!

Twit twit twit
Jug jug jug jug jug jug
So rudely forc'd.
Tereu

Unreal City
Under the brown fog of a winter noon
Mr. Eugenides, the Smyrna merchant
210 Unshaven, with a pocket full of currants
C.i.f. London: documents at sight,
Asked me in demotic French
To luncheon at the Cannon Street Hotel
Followed by a weekend at the Metropole.
At the violet hour, when the eyes and back
Turn upward from the desk, when the human engine waits
Like a taxi throbbing waiting,
I Tiresias, though blind, throbbing between two lives,
Old man with wrinkled female breasts, can see

196. But . . . hear: "Cf. Marvell, *To His Coy Mistress.*" (Eliot) The especially relevant lines are: "But ever at my back I hear/ Time's winged chariot, hurrying near. . . ."
197. The sound . . . bring: "Cf. Day, *Parliament of Bees:*
        'When of the sudden, listening, you shall hear,
        'A noise of horns and hunting, which shall bring
        'Actaeon to Diana in the spring,
        'Where all shall see her naked skin. . . .' " (Eliot)
199. O the moon: "I do not know the origin of the ballad from which these lines are taken: it was reported to me from Sydney, Australia." (Eliot) Eliot may possibly have known also the popular American song whose chorus begins with the line, "O the moon shines tonight on pretty Redwing."
202. Et . . . coupole: "V. Verlaine, *Parsifal.*" (Eliot) "And O the voices of the children chanting in the choir."
210. currants: "The currants were quoted at a price 'carriage and insurance free to London'; and the Bill of Lading etc. were to be handed to the buyer upon payment of the sight draft." (Eliot)
218. Tiresias: "Tiresias, although a mere spectator and not indeed a 'character,' is yet the most important personage in the poem, uniting all the rest. Just as the one-eyed merchant, seller of currants, melts into the Phoenician Sailor, and the latter is not wholly distinct from Ferdinand Prince of Naples, so all the women are one woman, and the two sexes meet in Tiresias. What Tiresias *sees*, in fact, is the substance of the poem. The whole passage from Ovid is of great anthropological interest:
        '. . . . Cum Iunone iocos et maior vestra profecto est
        Quam, quae contingit maribus,' dixisse, 'voluptas.'
        Illa negat; placuit quae sit sententia docti
        Quaerere Tiresiae: venus huic erat utraque nota.
        Nam duo magnorum viridi coeuntia silva
        Corpora serpentum baculi violaverat ictu
        Deque viro factus, mirabile, femina septem
        Egerat autumnos; octavo rursus eosdem
        Vidit et 'est vestrae si tanta potentia plagae,'
        Dixit 'ut auctoris sortem in contraria mutet,

At the violet hour, the evening hour that strives   220
Homeward, and brings the sailor home from sea,
The typist home at teatime, clears her breakfast, lights
Her stove, and lays out food in tins.
Out of the window perilously spread
Her drying combinations touched by the sun's last rays,
On the divan are piled (at night her bed)
Stockings, slippers, camisoles, and stays.
I Tiresias, old man with wrinkled dugs
Perceived the scene, and foretold the rest—
I too awaited the expected guest.   230
He, the young man carbuncular, arrives,
A small house agent's clerk, with one bold stare,
One of the low on whom assurance sits
As a silk hat on a Bradford millionaire.
The time is now propitious, as he guesses,
The meal is ended, she is bored and tired,
Endeavours to engage her in caresses
Which still are unreproved, if undesired.
Flushed and decided, he assaults at once;
Exploring hands encounter no defence;   240
His vanity requires no response,
And makes a welcome of indifference.
(And I Tiresias have foresuffered all
Enacted on this same divan or bed;
I who have sat by Thebes below the wall
And walked among the lowest of the dead.)

Nunc quoque vos feriam!' percussis anguibus isdem
Forma prior rediit genetivaque venit imago.
Arbiter hic igitur sumptus de lite iocosa
Dicta Iovis firmat; gravius Saturnia iusto
Nec pro materia fertur doluisse suique
Iudicis aeterna damnavit lumina nocte,
At pater omnipotens (neque enim licet inrita cuiquam
Facta dei fecisse deo) pro lumine adempto
Scire futura dedit poenamque levavit honore.'' (Eliot)

"Jupiter, by chance, well drenched with nectar, laid aside all weighty cares, and engaged in some free jokes with Juno, in her idle moments, and said: 'Decidedly the pleasure of you females, is greater than that which falls to the lot of us males.' She denied it. It was agreed between them, to ask what was the opinion of the experienced Tiresias. To him both pleasures were well known. For he had separated with a blow of his staff two bodies of large serpents as they were coupling in a green wood; and (passing strange) become a woman from a man, he had spent seven autumns. In the eighth, he again saw the same serpents, and said, 'If the power of a stroke given you is so great as to change the condition of the giver into the opposite one, I will now strike you again.' Having struck the same snakes, his former sex returned, and his original shape came again. He, therefore, being chosen as umpire in this sportive contest, confirmed the words of Jove. The daughter of Saturn is said to have grieved more than was fit, and not in proportion to the subject; and she condemned the eyes of the umpire to eternal darkness. But the omnipotent father (for it is not allowed any God to cancel the acts of another Deity) gave him the knowledge of things to come, in recompense for his loss of sight, and alleviated his punishment by this honour." Ovid's *Metamorphoses*, III, 320–338. Translation of Henry T. Riley.

221. brings . . . sea: "This may not appear as exact as Sappho's lines, but I had in mind the 'longshore' or 'dory' fisherman, who returns at nightfall." (Eliot) Eliot refers to Sappho's apostrophe to the Evening Star: 'Hesperus, you bring home all things the bright morning dispersed—the sheep, the goat, the child to its mother." Byron paraphrased Sappho in the famous stanza in *Don Juan* (III: 107) beginning: "Oh, Hesperus! thou bringest all good things—/ Home to the weary, to the hungry cheer. . . ." See also the well-known line from Robert Louis Stevenson's "Requiem": "Home is the sailor, home from sea."

Bestows one final patronising kiss,
And gropes his way, finding the stairs unlit . . .

250 She turns and looks a moment in the glass,
Hardly aware of her departed lover;
Her brain allows one half-formed thought to pass:
"Well now that's done; and I'm glad it's over."
When lovely woman stoops to folly and
Paces about her room again, alone,
She smoothes her hair with automatic hand,
And puts a record on the gramaphone.

"This music crept by me upon the waters"
And along the Strand, up Queen Victoria Street.
O City city, I can sometimes hear
260 Beside a public bar in Lower Thames Street,
The pleasant whining of a mandoline
And a clatter and a chatter from within
Where fishmen lounge at noon: where the walls
Of Magnus Martyr hold
Inexplicable splendour of Ionian white and gold.

    The river sweats
    Oil and tar
    The barges drift
    With the turning tide
270   Red sails
    Wide
    To leeward, swing on the heavy spar.
    The barges wash
    Drifting logs
    Down Greenwich reach
    Past the Isle of Dogs.
        Weialala leia
        Wallala leialala

    Elizabeth and Leicester
280   Beating oars

253. When . . . folly: "V. Goldsmith, the song in *The Vicar of Wakefield*." (Eliot) The lines, in Chapter 24,
are as follows: "When lovely woman stoops to folly,/ And finds too late that men betray,/ What charm can
soothe her melancholy?/ What art can wash her guilt away?/ The only art her guilt to cover,/ To hide her
shame from every eye,/ To give repentance to her lover,/ And wring his bosom—is to die."
257. This . . . waters: "V. *The Tempest*, as above." (Eliot) See the note on line 192.
264. Magnus Martyr: "The interior of St. Magnus Martyr is to my mind one of the finest among Wren's
interiors. See *The Proposed Demolition of Nineteen City Churches* (P. S. King & Son, Ltd.)." (Eliot)
266. The river sweats: "The Song of the (three) Thames-daughters begins here. From line 292 to 306 inclusive they speak in turn. V. *Götterdämmerung*, III, i: the Rhine-daughters." (Eliot) In the passage referred to
in Wagner's work, the three Rhine-daughters lament the loss of the gold entrusted to their custody.
279. Elizabeth and Leicester: "V. Froude, *Elizabeth*, Vol. I, ch. iv, letter of De Quadra to Philip of Spain:
'In the afternoon we were in a barge, watching the games on the river. (The queen) was alone with Lord Robert
and myself on the poop, when they began to talk nonsense, and went so far that Lord Robert at last said, as I
was on the spot there was no reason why they should not be married if the queen pleased.' " (Eliot) De Quadra, a
Catholic bishop, was Spanish Ambassador at Elizabeth's court.

The stern was formed
A gilded shell
Red and gold
The brisk swell
Rippled both shores
Southwest wind
Carried down stream
The peal of bells
White towers
    Weialala leia   290
    Wallala leialala

"Trams and dusty trees.
Highbury bore me. Richmond and Kew
Undid me. By Richmond I raised my knees
Supine on the floor of a narrow canoe."

"My feet are at Moorgate, and my heart
Under my feet. After the event
He wept. He promised 'a new start.'
I made no comment. What should I resent?"

"On Margate Sands.   300
I can connect
Nothing with nothing.
The broken fingernails of dirty hands.
My people humble people who expect
Nothing."
          la la

To Carthage then I came

Burning burning burning burning
O Lord Thou pluckest me out
O Lord Thou pluckest   310

burning

293. Highbury . . . Undid me: "Cf. *Purgatorio*, V. 133:
                            'Ricorditi di me, che son la Pia;
                            'Siena mi fe', disfecemi Maremma,' " (Eliot)
"Remember me, who am La Pia; Siena made me, Maremma unmade me."
307. To Carthage . . . came: "V. St. Augustine's *Confessions*: 'to Carthage then I came, where a cauldron
of unholy loves sang all about mine ears.' " (Eliot)
308. Burning . . . burning: "The complete text of Buddha's Fire Sermon (which corresponds in importance
to the Sermon on the Mount) from which these words are taken, will be found translated in the late Henry
Clarke Warren's *Buddhism in Translation* (Harvard Oriental Series). Mr. Warren was one of the great pioneers
of Buddhist studies in the Occident." (Eliot)
309. O Lord . . . out: "From St. Augustine's *Confessions* again. The collocation of these two representatives
of eastern and western asceticism, as the culmination of this part of the poem, is not an accident." (Eliot)

4. DEATH BY WATER

Phlebas the Phoenician, a fortnight dead,
Forgot the cry of gulls, and the deep sea swell
And the profit and loss.
                    A current under sea
Picked his bones in whispers. As he rose and fell
He passed the stages of his age and youth
Entering the whirlpool.
                    Gentile or Jew
320   O you who turn the wheel and look to windward,
Consider Phlebas, who was once handsome and tall as you.

5. WHAT THE THUNDER SAID

After the torchlight red on sweaty faces
After the frosty silence in the gardens
After the agony in stony places
The shouting and the crying
Prison and palace and reverberation
Of thunder of spring over distant mountains
He who was living is now dead
We who were living are now dying
330   With a little patience

Here is no water but only rock
Rock and no water and the sandy road
The road winding above among the mountains
Which are mountains of rock without water
If there were water we should stop and drink
Amongst the rock one cannot stop or think
Sweat is dry and feet are in the sand
If there were only water amongst the rock
Dead mountain mouth of carious teeth that cannot
          spit
340   Here one can neither stand nor lie nor sit

What the Thunder Said: "In the first part of Part V three themes are employed: the journey to Emmaus,
the approach to the Chapel Perilous (see Miss Weston's book) and the present decay of eastern Europe."
(Eliot) For the journey to Emmaus, see Luke, Chapter 24.
322. torchlight: The opening lines refer to events preceding the crucifixion of Christ. See particularly Luke
22:23.
357. hermit-thrush: "This is *Turdus aonalaschkae pallasii*, the hermit-thrush which I have heard in Quebec
County. Chapman says (*Handbook of Birds of Eastern North America*) 'it is most at home in secluded woodland
and thickety retreats. . . . Its notes are not remarkable for variety or volume, but in purity and sweetness of
tone and exquisite modulation they are unequalled.' Its 'water-dripping song' is justly celebrated." (Eliot)
360. The third: "The following lines were stimulated by the account of one of the Antarctic expeditions (I
forget which, but I think one of Shackleton's): it was related that the party of explorers, at the extremity of

There is not even silence in the mountains
But dry sterile thunder without rain
There is not even solitude in the mountains
But red sullen faces sneer and snarl
From doors of mudcracked houses
    If there were water
  And no rock
  If there were rock
  And also water
  And water   350
  A spring
  A pool among the rock
  If there were the sound of water only
  Not the cicada
  And dry grass singing
  But sound of water over a rock
  Where the hermit-thrush sings in the pine trees
  Drip drop drip drop drop drop drop
  But there is no water

Who is the third who walks always beside you?   360
When I count, there are only you and I together
But when I look ahead up the white road
There is always another one walking beside you
Gliding wrapt in a brown mantle, hooded
I do not know whether a man or a woman
—But who is that on the other side of you?

What is that sound high in the air
Murmur of maternal lamentation
Who are those hooded hordes swarming
Over endless plains, stumbling in cracked earth   370
Ringed by the flat horizon only
What is the city over the mountains
Cracks and reforms and bursts in the violet air
Falling towers
Jerusalem Athens Alexandria
Vienna London
Unreal

their strength, had the constant delusion that there was *one more member* than could actually be counted."
(Eliot) See also the journey to Emmaus, Luke, Chapter 24. Eliot's account is symbolical of the resurrection of
the fertility god, and the lack of faith and consequent blindness in the waste land.
367–377. What . . . Unreal: "Cf. Hermann Hesse, *Blick ins Chaos*: 'Schon ist halb Europa, schon ist zumin-
dest der halbe Osten Europas auf dem Wege zum Chaos, fährt betrunken im heiligem Wahn am Abgrund
entlang und singt dazu, singt betrunken und hymnisch wie Dmitri Karamasoff sang. Ueber diese Lieder lacht
der Bürger beleidigt, der Heilige und Seher hört sie mit Tränen.' " (Eliot) "Already half of Europe, already at
least half of Eastern Europe, is on the way to chaos, going drunk in holy folly along the edge of the abyss and
singing drunken hymns as Dmitri Karamasoff did. The burgher laughs scornfully at these songs while the saint
and seer hear them with tears." The allusion is to Dostoievski's *The Brothers Karamazov.*

A woman drew her long black hair out tight
And fiddled whisper music on those strings
380 And bats with baby faces in the violet light
Whistled, and beat their wings
And crawled head downward down a blackened wall
And upside down in air were towers
Tolling reminiscent bells, that kept the hours
And voices singing out of empty cisterns and exhausted
    wells.

In this decayed hole among the mountains
In the faint moonlight, the grass is singing
Over the tumbled graves, about the chapel
There is the empty chapel, only the wind's home.
390 It has no windows, and the door swings,
Dry bones can harm no one.
Only a cock stood on the rooftree
Co co rico co co rico
In a flash of lightning. Then a damp gust
Bringing rain

Ganga was sunken, and the limp leaves
Waited for rain, while the black clouds
Gathered far distant, over Himavant.
The jungle crouched, humped in silence.
400 Then spoke the thunder
DA
Datta: what have we given?
My friend, blood shaking my heart
The awful daring of a moment's surrender
Which an age of prudence can never retract

388. **chapel:** the Chapel Perilous (see Jessie L. Weston's *From Ritual to Romance*, already referred to) where, according to the legends of the Holy Grail, the knight must endure supernatural terrors as a preparation for his quest.

393. **Co . . . rico:** The crowing of the cock has at least a double association: the dispersal of ghosts and evil spirits (see *Hamlet*, Act I, scene ii, line 160) and Peter's denial of Christ (see Matthew 26:74).

402. **Datta:** " 'Datta, dayadhvam, damyata' (Give, sympathise, control). The fable of the meaning of Thunder is found in the *Brihadaranyaka-Upanishad*, 5, 1. A translation is found in Deussen's *Sechzig Upanishads des Veda*, p. 489." (Eliot)

408. **draped . . . spider:** "Cf. Webster, *The White Devil*, V, vi:
        '. . . they'll remarry
    Ere the worm pierce your winding-sheet, ere the spider
    Make a thin curtain for your epitaphs.' " (Eliot)

412. **the key:** "Cf. *Inferno*, XXXIII, 46:
        'ed io sentii chiavar l'uscio di sotto
        all'orribile torre.'
[". . . and below I heard the door of the horrible tower being closed up," said by Ugolino to Dante] Also F. H. Bradley, *Appearance and Reality*, p. 346: 'My external sensations are no less private to myself than are my thoughts or my feelings. In either case my experience falls within my own circle, a circle closed on the outside; and, with all its elements alike, every sphere is opaque to the others which surround it. . . . In brief, regarded as an existence which appears in a soul, the whole world for each is peculiar and private to that soul.' " (Eliot)

417. **broken Coriolanus:** the hero of Shakespeare's play of that name, a Roman general and aristocrat, who fell the victim of his own pride and the people's ingratitude.

425. **Fishing:** "V. Weston: *From Ritual to Romance*: chapter on the Fisher King." (Eliot) "The title of Fisher,"

By this, and this only, we have existed
Which is not to be found in our obituaries
Or in memories draped by the beneficent spider
Or under seals broken by the lean solicitor
In our empty rooms   410
DA
Dayadhvam: I have heard the key
Turn in the door once and turn once only
We think of the key, each in his prison
Thinking of the key, each confirms a prison
Only at nightfall, aethereal rumours
Revive for a moment a broken Coriolanus
DA
Damyata: The boat responded
Gaily, to the hand expert with sail and oar   420
The sea was calm, your heart would have responded
Gaily, when invited, beating obedient
To controlling hands

              I sat upon the shore
Fishing, with the arid plain behind me
Shall I at least set my lands in order?
London Bridge is falling down falling down falling down
Poi s'ascose nel foco che gli affina
Quando fiam uti chelidon—O swallow swallow
Le Prince d'Aquitaine à la tour abolie   430
These fragments I have shored against my ruins
Why then Ile fit you. Hieronymo's mad againe.
Datta. Dayadhvam. Damyata.
    Shantih shantih shantih
1922

says Miss Weston, "has, from the earliest ages, been associated with Deities who were held to be specially connected with the origin and preservation of life." In Eliot's treatment, the Fisher King, like Christ and the
Fertility gods, is symbolical of life through death.
428. Poi . . . affina: "V. *Purgatorio,* XXVI, 148:
          ' "Ara vos prec per aquella valor
          que vos guida al som de l'escalina,
          sovegna vos a temps de ma dolor."
          Poi s'ascose nel foco che gli affina.' " (Eliot)
" 'Now I pray you by that power which guides you to the top of this stairway, be mindful of my pain in proper
season.' He hid himself then in the fire which refines them." In this passage, the purgatorial fires consume the
lusts of the flesh.
429. Quando . . . swallow: "V. *Pervigilium Veneris.* Cf. Philomela in Parts II and III." (Eliot) "When shall
I be like the swallow," from *Pervigilium Veneris,* a medieval poem describing the joy of nature on the night of
Venus.
430. Le Prince . . . abolie: "V. Gerard de Nerval, Sonnet *El Desdichado.*" (Eliot) "The Prince of Aquitaine
in the ruined tower."
432. Why . . . againe: "V. Kyd's *Spanish Tragedy,*" (Eliot) The first sentence occurs in Act IV, scene i, of
Thomas Kyd's *Spanish Tragedy,* where Hieronymo agrees to present at court a play by which he secretly plans
to take revenge on the murderers of his son; the second sentence is the subtitle of the play.
434. Shantih: "Shantih. Repeated as here, a formal ending to an Upanishad. 'The Peace which passeth understanding' is our equivalent to this word." (Eliot) See Philippians 4:7: "And the peace of God, which passeth all
understanding. . . ."

LITTLE GIDDING

1

Midwinter spring is its own season
Sempiternal though sodden towards sundown,
Suspended in time, between pole and tropic.
When the short day is brightest, with frost and fire,
The brief sun flames the ice, on pond and ditches,
In windless cold that is the heart's heat,
Reflecting in a watery mirror
A glare that is blindness in the early afternoon.
And glow more intense than blaze of branch, or brazier,
10   Stirs the dumb spirit: no wind, but pentecostal fire
In the dark time of the year. Between melting and freezing
The soul's sap quivers. There is no earth smell
Or smell of living thing. This is the spring time
But not in time's covenant. Now the hedgerow
Is blanched for an hour with transitory blossom
Of snow, a bloom more sudden
Than that of summer, neither budding nor fading,
Not in the scheme of generation.
Where is the summer, the unimaginable
20   Zero summer?

        If you came this way,
Taking the route you would be likely to take
From the place you would be likely to come from,
If you came this way in may time, you would find the hedges
White again, in May, with voluptuary sweetness.
It would be the same at the end of the journey,
If you came at night like a broken king,
If you came by day not knowing what you came for,
It would be the same, when you leave the rough road
30   And turn behind the pig-sty to the dull façade
And the tombstone. And what you thought you came for
Is only a shell, a husk of meaning
From which the purpose breaks only when it is fulfilled
If at all. Either you had no purpose
Or the purpose is beyond the end you figured
And is altered in fulfilment. There are other places
Which also are the world's end, some at the sea jaws,

Little Gidding: a village in Huntingdonshire, England, to which Nicholas Ferrar and his family retired in 1625 in order to lead a life of religious devotion. Ferrar's ideal, which he attempted to realize at Little Gidding, was a religious community based upon the Christian family. Owing to civil war, the community was scattered in 1647 and the chapel reduced to a ruin. The chapel was restored in the nineteenth century, but the community was never revived. Little Gidding has remained, nevertheless, a famous shrine of the Anglican Church.
10. pentecostal fire: The reference is to the outpouring of the Spirit on the day of Pentecost. Compare Acts

Or over a dark lake, in a desert or a city—
But this is the nearest, in place and time,
Now and in England.   40

        If you came this way,
Taking any route, starting from anywhere,
At any time or at any season,
It would always be the same: you would have to put off
Sense and notion. You are not here to verify,
Instruct yourself, or inform curiosity
Or carry report. You are here to kneel
Where prayer has been valid. And prayer is more
Than an order of words, the conscious occupation
Of the praying mind, or the sound of the voice praying.   50
And what the dead had no speech for, when living,
They can tell you, being dead: the communication
Of the dead is tongued with fire beyond the language of the living.
Here, the intersection of the timeless moment
Is England and nowhere. Never and always.

2
Ash on an old man's sleeve
Is all the ash the burnt roses leave.
Dust in the air suspended
Marks the place where a story ended.
Dust inbreathed was a house—   60
The wall, the wainscot and the mouse.
The death of hope and despair,
    This is the death of air.

There are flood and drouth
Over the eyes and in the mouth,
Dead water and dead sand
Contending for the upper hand.
The parched eviscerate soil
Gapes at the vanity of toil,
Laughs without mirth.   70
    This is the death of earth.

Water and fire succeed
The town, the pasture and the weed.

2:3–4: "And there appeared unto them cloven tongues like as of fire, and it sat upon each of them. And they
were all filled with the Holy Ghost, and began to speak with other tongues, as the Spirit gave them utterance."
27. broken king: King Charles I visited Little Gidding in 1633 and in 1642, and legend has it that he sought
shelter there after his final defeat at the battle of Naseby in 1645.
63. death of air: F. O. Matthiessen points out the relation of the opening of the second part to the following
sentence from Heraclitus, which expresses both "the ceaseless flux" and "the reconciliation of opposites"
("Eliot's Quartets," Kenyon Review, Spring 1943, p. 173): "Fire lives in the death of air, and air in the death of
fire; water lives in the death of earth, and earth in the death of water."

Water and fire deride
The sacrifice that we denied.
Water and fire shall rot
The marred foundations we forgot,
Of sanctuary and choir.
    This is the death of water and fire.

80 In the uncertain hour before the morning
    Near the ending of interminable night
    At the recurrent end of the unending
After the dark dove with the flickering tongue
    Had passed below the horizon of his homing
    While the dead leaves still rattled on like tin
Over the asphalt where no other sound was
    Between three districts whence the smoke arose
    I met one walking, loitering and hurried
As if blown towards me like the metal leaves
90   Before the urban dawn wind unresisting.
    And as I fixed upon the down-turned face
That pointed scrutiny with which we challenge
    The first-met stranger in the waning dusk
    I caught the sudden look of some dead master
Whom I had known, forgotten, half recalled
    Both one and many; in the brown baked features
    The eyes of a familiar compound ghost
Both intimate and unidentifiable.
    So I assumed a double part, and cried
100   And heard another's voice cry: 'What! are *you* here?'
Although we were not. I was still the same,
    Knowing myself yet being someone other—
    And he a face still forming; yet the words sufficed
To compel the recognition they preceded.
    And so, compliant to the common wind,
    Too strange to each other for misunderstanding,
In concord at this intersection time
    Of meeting nowhere, no before and after,
    We trod the pavement in a dead patrol.
110 I said: 'The wonder that I feel is easy,
    Yet ease is cause of wonder. Therefore speak:
    I may not comprehend, may not remember.'
And he: 'I am not eager to rehearse
    My thought and theory which you have forgotten.

80. uncertain hour: The background of the following passage is the bombing of London in World War II.
83–84. dark dove . . . homing: The German bombers had returned to Germany after making a raid on London.
94. dead master: called three lines later a "compound ghost," and apparently not to be identified with any single poet.
107. intersection time: See "the intersection of the timeless moment," part 1, line 54: the intersection of the temporal and the timeless in a moment of revelation. Eliot's "intersection time" is essentially the concept of the divine incarnation.

These things have served their purpose: let them be.
So with your own, and pray they be forgiven
   By others, as I pray you to forgive
   Both bad and good. Last season's fruit is eaten
And the fullfed beast shall kick the empty pail.
   For last year's words belong to last year's language   120
   And next year's words await another voice.
But, as the passage now presents no hindrance
   To the spirit unappeased and peregrine
   Between two worlds become much like each other,
So I find words I never thought to speak
   In streets I never thought I should revisit
   When I left my body on a distant shore.
Since our concern was speech, and speech impelled us
   To purify the dialect of the tribe
   And urge the mind to aftersight and foresight,   130
Let me disclose the gifts reserved for age
   To set a crown upon your lifetime's effort.
   First, the cold friction of expiring sense
Without enchantment, offering no promise
   But bitter tastelessness of shadow fruit
   As body and soul begin to fall asunder.
Second, the conscious impotence of rage
   At human folly, and the laceration
   Of laughter at what ceases to amuse.
And last, the rending pain of re-enactment   140
   Of all that you have done, and been; the shame
   Of motives late revealed, and the awareness
Of things ill done and done to others' harm
   Which once you took for exercise of virtue.
   Then fools' approval stings, and honour stains.
From wrong to wrong the exasperated spirit
   Proceeds, unless restored by that refining fire
   Where you must move in measure, like a dancer.'
The day was breaking. In the disfigured street
   He left me, with a kind of valediction,   150
   And faded on the blowing of the horn.

3

There are three conditions which often look alike
Yet differ completely, flourish in the same hedgerow:
Attachment to self and to things and to persons, detachment

---

129. **To purify . . . tribe:** Helen L. Gardner ("Four Quartets: a Commentary," in *T. S. Eliot: A Study of His Writings by Several Hands*, ed. B. Rajan) gives the annotation that this line is a reminiscence of Mallarmé's "Donner un sens plus pur aux mots de la tribu" in "Le Tombeau d'Edgar Allan Poe." Miss Gardner goes on to make the following comment, the wisdom of which Eliot's annotators might do well to remember: "The contexts are so different that the reference does not illuminate the passage in 'Little Gidding.' It appears to be a lovely line accidentally remembered for the precision of its definition of the poet's function."

From self and from things and from persons; and, growing between
    them, indifference
Which resembles the others as death resembles life,
Being between two lives—unflowering, between
The live and the dead nettle. This is the use of memory:
For liberation—not less of love but expanding

160 Of love beyond desire, and so liberation
From the future as well as the past. Thus, love of a country
Begins as attachment to our own field of action
And comes to find that action of little importance
Though never indifferent. History may be servitude,
History may be freedom. See, now they vanish,
The faces and places, with the self which, as it could, loved them,
To become renewed, transfigured, in another pattern.

Sin is Behovely, but
All shall be well, and

170 All manner of thing shall be well.
If I think, again, of this place,
And of people, not wholly commendable,
Of no immediate kin or kindness,
But some of peculiar genius,
All touched by a common genius,
United in the strife which divided them;
If I think of a king at nightfall,
Of three men, and more, on the scaffold
And a few who died forgotten

180 In other places, here and abroad,
And of one who died blind and quiet,
Why should we celebrate
These dead men more than the dying?
It is not to ring the bell backward
Nor is it an incantation
To summon the spectre of a Rose.
We cannot revive old factions
We cannot restore old policies
Or follow an antique drum.

190 These men, and those who opposed them
And those whom they opposed
Accept the constitution of silence
And are folded in a single party.
Whatever we inherit from the fortunate
We have taken from the defeated
What they had to leave us—a symbol:

168. Behovely: useful, profitable, needful. The entire sentence, Miss Gardner points out, is taken from the fourteenth-century English mystic, Dame Julian of Norwich.
178. three men: a reference to the executions of King Charles I (in 1649) and his arch supporters Strafford and Laud.

A symbol perfected in death.
And all shall be well and
All manner of thing shall be well
By the purification of the motive   200
In the ground of our beseeching.

4
The dove descending breaks the air
With flame of incandescent terror
Of which the tongues declare
The one discharge from sin and error.
The only hope, or else despair
    Lies in the choice of pyre or pyre—
    To be redeemed from fire by fire.
Who then devised the torment? Love.
Love is the unfamiliar Name   210
Behind the hands that wove
The intolerable shirt of flame
Which human power cannot remove.
    We only live, only suspire
    Consumed by either fire or fire.

5
What we call the beginning is often the end
And to make an end is to make a beginning.
The end is where we start from. And every phrase
And sentence that is right (where every word is at home,
Taking its place to support the others,   220
The word neither diffident nor ostentatious,
An easy commerce of the old and the new,
The common word exact without vulgarity,
The formal word precise but not pedantic,
The complete consort dancing together)
Every phrase and every sentence is an end and a beginning,
Every poem an epitaph. And any action
Is a step to the block, to the fire, down the sea's throat
Or to an illegible stone: and that is where we start.
We die with the dying: 230
See, they depart, and we go with them.
We are born with the dead:
See, they return, and bring us with them.
The moment of the rose and the moment of the yew-tree
Are of equal duration. A people without history
Is not redeemed from time, for history is a pattern

181. one . . . quiet: John Milton. Miss Gardner observes that "Milton, whom Mr. Eliot once found so anti-
pathetic as a poet and a man, is very much in mind throughout the poem."
201. ground . . . beseeching: from Dame Julian also (see Gardner).

Of timeless moments. So, while the light fails
On a winter's afternoon, in a secluded chapel
History is now and England.
240   With the drawing of this Love and the voice of this Calling

We shall not cease from exploration
And the end of all our exploring
Will be to arrive where we started
And know the place for the first time.
Through the unknown, remembered gate
When the last of earth left to discover
Is that which was the beginning;
At the source of the longest river
The voice of the hidden waterfall
250   And the children in the apple-tree
Not known, because not looked for
But heard, half-heard, in the stillness
Between two waves of the sea.
Quick now, here, now, always—
A condition of complete simplicity
(Costing not less than everything)
And all shall be well and
All manner of thing shall be well
When the tongues of flame are in-folded
260   Into the crowned knot of fire
And the fire and the rose are one.
1943

240. With . . . Calling: from "The Cloud of Unknowing," by an anonymous English mystic of the fourteenth century (see Gardner).
261. fire . . . rose: "The rose, the symbol of natural beauty and natural love, is one with the fire, the love by which all things are made" (Gardner).

TRADITION AND THE INDIVIDUAL TALENT

1

In English writing we seldom speak of tradition, though we occasionally apply its name in deploring its absence. We cannot refer to "the tradition" or to "a tradition"; at most, we employ the adjective in saying that the poetry of So-and-so is "traditional" or even "too traditional." Seldom, perhaps, does the word appear except in a phrase of censure. If otherwise, it is vaguely approbative, with the implication, as to the work approved, of some pleasing archæological reconstruction. You can hardly make the word agreeable to English ears without this comfortable reference to the reassuring science of archæology.

Certainly the word is not likely to appear in our appreciations of living or

From *Selected Essays 1917–1932* by T. S. Eliot, copyright, 1932, by Harcourt, Brace and Company, Inc. Reprinted by permission of Harcourt, Brace and Company, Inc., and Faber and Faber, Ltd.

dead writers. Every nation, every race, has not only its own creative, but its own critical turn of mind; and is even more oblivious of the shortcomings and limitations of its critical habits than of those of its creative genius. We know, or think we know, from the enormous mass of critical writing that has appeared in the French language the critical method or habit of the French; we only conclude (we are such unconscious people) that the French are "more critical" than we, and sometimes even plume ourselves a little with the fact, as if the French were the less spontaneous. Perhaps they are; but we might remind ourselves that criticism is as inevitable as breathing, and that we should be none the worse for articulating what passes in our minds when we read a book and feel an emotion about it, for criticizing our own minds in their work of criticism. One of the facts that might come to light in this process is our tendency to insist, when we praise a poet, upon those aspects of his work in which he least resembles any one else. In these aspects or parts of his work we pretend to find what is individual, what is the peculiar essence of the man. We dwell with satisfaction upon the poet's difference from his predecessors, especially his immediate predecessors; we endeavour to find something that can be isolated in order to be enjoyed. Whereas if we approach a poet without this prejudice we shall often find that not only the best, but the most individual parts of his work may be those in which the dead poets, his ancestors, assert their immortality most vigorously. And I do not mean the impressionable period of adolescence, but the period of full maturity.

Yet if the only form of tradition, of handing down, consisted in following the ways of the immediate generation before us in a blind or timid adherence to its successes, "tradition" should positively be discouraged. We have seen many such simple currents soon lost in the sand; and novelty is better than repetition. Tradition is a matter of much wider significance. It cannot be inherited, and if you want it you must obtain it by great labour. It involves, in the first place, the historical sense, which we may call nearly indispensable to any one who would continue to be a poet beyond his twenty-fifth year; and the historical sense involves a perception, not only of the pastness of the past, but of its presence; the historical sense compels a man to write not merely with his own generation in his bones, but with a feeling that the whole of the literature of Europe from Homer and within it the whole of the literature of his own country has a simultaneous existence and composes a simultaneous order. This historical sense, which is a sense of the timeless as well as of the temporal and of the timeless and of the temporal together, is what makes a writer traditional. And it is at the same time what makes a writer most acutely conscious of his place in time, of his own contemporaneity.

No poet, no artist of any art, has his complete meaning alone. His significance, his appreciation is the appreciation of his relation to the dead poets and artists. You cannot value him alone; you must set him, for contrast and comparison, among the dead. I mean this as a principle of æsthetic, not merely historical, criticism. The necessity that he shall conform, that he shall cohere, is not one-sided; what happens when a new work of art is created is something that happens simultaneously to all the works of art which preceded it. The existing monuments form an ideal order among themselves, which is modified by the introduction of the new (the really new) work of art among them. The existing order is complete before the new work arrives; for order to persist after the supervention of novelty, the *whole* existing order must be, if ever so slightly, altered; and so the relations, proportions, values of each work of art toward the whole are re-adjusted; and this is conformity between the old and the new. Whoever has approved this idea of order, of the form of European, of English literature will not find it preposterous that the past should be altered by the present as much as the present is directed by the past. And the poet who is aware of this will be aware of great difficulties and responsibilities.

In a peculiar sense he will be aware also that he must inevitably be judged by the standards of the past. I say judged, not amputated, by them; not judged to be as good as, or worse or better than, the dead; and certainly not judged by the canons of dead critics. It is a judgment, a comparison, in which two things are measured by each other. To conform merely would be for the new work not really to conform at all; it would not be new, and would therefore not be a work of art. And we do not quite say that the new is more valuable because it fits in; but its fitting in is a test of its value—a test, it is true, which can only be slowly and cautiously applied, for we are none of us infallible judges of conformity. We say: it appears to conform, and is perhaps individual, or it appears individual, and may conform; but we are hardly likely to find that it is one and not the other.

To proceed to a more intelligible exposition of the relation of the poet to the past: he can neither take the past as a lump, an indiscriminate bolus, nor can he form himself wholly on one or two private admirations, nor can he form himself wholly upon one preferred period. The first course is inadmissible, the second is an important experience of youth, and the third is a pleasant and highly desirable supplement. The poet must be very conscious of the main current, which does not at all flow invariably through the most distinguished reputations. He must be quite aware of the obvious fact that art never improves, but that the material of art is never quite the same. He must be aware that the mind of Europe—the mind of his own country—a mind which he learns in time to be much more important than his own private mind—is a mind which changes, and that this change is a development which abandons nothing *en route*, which does not superannuate either Shakespeare, or Homer, or the rock drawing of the Magdalenian draughtsmen. That this development, refinement perhaps, complication certainly, is not, from the point of view of the artist, any improvement. Perhaps not even an improvement from the point of view of the psychologist or not to the extent which we imagine; perhaps only in the end based upon a complication in economics and machinery. But the difference between the present and the past is that the conscious present is an awareness of the past in a way and to an extent which the past's awareness of itself cannot show.

Some one said: "The dead writers are remote from us because we *know* so much more than they did." Precisely, and they are that which we know.

I am alive to a usual objection to what is clearly part of my programme for the *métier* of poetry. The objection is that the doctrine requires a ridiculous amount of erudition (pedantry), a claim which can be rejected by appeal to the lives of poets in any pantheon. It will even be affirmed that much learning deadens or perverts poetic sensibility. While, however, we persist in believing that a poet ought to know as much as will not encroach upon his necessary receptivity and necessary laziness, it is not desirable to confine knowledge to whatever can be put into a useful shape for examinations, drawing-rooms, or the still more pretentious modes of publicity. Some can absorb knowledge, the more tardy must sweat for it. Shakespeare acquired more essential history from Plutarch than most men could from the whole British Museum. What is to be insisted upon is that the poet must develop or procure the consciousness of the past and that he should continue to develop this consciousness throughout his career.

What happens is a continual surrender of himself as he is at the moment to something which is more valuable. The progress of an artist is a continual self-sacrifice, a continual extinction of personality.

There remains to define this process of depersonalization and its relation to the sense of tradition. It is in this depersonalization that art may be said to approach the condition of science. I, therefore, invite you to consider, as a suggestive analogy, the action which takes place when a bit of finely filiated platinum is introduced into a chamber containing oxygen and sulphur dioxide.

2

Honest criticism and sensitive appreciation are directed not upon the poet but upon the poetry. If we attend to the confused cries of the newspaper critics and the *susurrus* of popular repetition that follows, we shall hear the names of poets in great numbers; if we seek not Blue-book knowledge but the enjoyment of poetry, and ask for a poem, we shall seldom find it. I have tried to point out the importance of the relation of the poem to other poems by other authors, and suggested the conception of poetry as a living whole of all the poetry that has ever been written. The other aspect of this Impersonal theory of poetry is the relation of the poem to its author. And I hinted, by an analogy, that the mind of the mature poet differs from that of the immature one not precisely in any valuation of "personality," not being necessarily more interesting, or having "more to say," but rather by being a more finely perfected medium in which special, or very varied, feelings are at liberty to enter into new combinations.

The analogy was that of the catalyst. When the two gases previously mentioned are mixed in the presence of a filament of platinum, they form sulphurous acid. This combination takes place only if the platinum is present; nevertheless the newly formed acid contains no trace of platinum, and the platinum itself is apparently unaffected; has remained inert, neutral, and unchanged. The mind of the poet is the shred of platinum. It may partly or exclusively operate upon the experience of the man himself; but, the more perfect the artist, the more completely separate in him will be the man who suffers and the mind which creates; the more perfectly will the mind digest and transmute the passions which are its material.

The experience, you will notice, the elements which enter the presence of the transforming catalyst, are of two kinds: emotions and feelings. The effect of a work of art upon the person who enjoys it is an experience different in kind from any experience not of art. It may be formed out of one emotion, or may be a combination of several; and various feelings, inhering for the writer in particular words or phrases or images, may be added to compose the final result. Or great poetry may be made without the direct use of any emotion whatever: composed out of feelings solely. Canto XV of the *Inferno* (Brunetto Latini) is a working up of the emotion evident in the situation; but the effect, though single as that of any work of art, is obtained by considerable complexity of detail. The last quatrain gives an image, a feeling attaching to an image, which "came," which did not develop simply out of what precedes, but which was probably in suspension in the poet's mind until the proper combination arrived for it to add itself to. The poet's mind is in fact a receptacle for seizing and storing up numberless feelings, phrases, images, which remain there until all the particles which can unite to form a new compound are present together.

If you compare several representative passages of the greatest poetry you see how great is the variety of types of combination, and also how completely any semi-ethical criterion of "sublimity" misses the mark. For it is not the "greatness," the intensity, of the emotions, the components, but the intensity of the artistic process, the pressure, so to speak, under which the fusion takes place, that counts. The episode of Paolo and Francesca employs a definite emotion, but the intensity of the poetry is something quite different from whatever intensity in the supposed experience it may give the impression of. It is no more intense, furthermore, than Canto XXVI, the voyage of Ulysses, which has not the direct dependence upon an emotion. Great variety is possible in the process of transmutation of emotion: the murder of Agamemnon, or the agony of Othello, gives an artistic effect apparently closer to a possible original than the scenes from Dante. In the *Agamemnon*, the artistic emotion approximates to the emotion of an actual spectator; in *Othello* to the emotion of the protagonist himself. But the difference between art and the event is always absolute; the combination which is the murder of Agamemnon is probably as complex as that which is the voyage of Ulysses. In either case there has been a fusion of elements. The ode of Keats contains a number of feelings which have nothing particular to do with the nightingale, but which the nightingale, partly, perhaps, because of its attractive name, and partly because of its reputation, served to bring together.

The point of view which I am struggling to attack is perhaps related to the metaphysical theory of the substantial unity of the soul: for my meaning is, that the poet has, not a "personality" to express, but a particular medium, which is only a medium and not a personality, in which impressions and experiences combine in peculiar and unexpected ways. Impressions and experiences which are important for the man may take no place in the poetry, and those which become important in the poetry may play quite a negligible part in the man, the personality.

I will quote a passage which is unfamiliar enough to be regarded with fresh attention in the light—or darkness—of these observations:

> And now methinks I could e'en chide myself
> For doating on her beauty, though her death
> Shall be revenged after no common action.
> Does the silkworm expend her yellow labours
> For thee? For thee does she undo herself?
> Are lordships sold to maintain ladyships
> For the poor benefit of a bewildering minute?

Why does yon fellow falsify highways,
And put his life between the judge's lips,
To refine such a thing—keep horse and men
To beat their valours for her? . . .[1]

In this passage (as is evident if it is taken in its context) there is a combination of positive and negative emotions: an intensely strong attraction toward beauty and an equally intense fascination by the ugliness which is contrasted with it and which destroys it. This balance of contrasted emotion is in the dramatic situation to which the speech is pertinent, but that situation alone is inadequate to it. This is, so to speak, the structural emotion, provided by the drama. But the whole effect, the dominant tone, is due to the fact that a number of floating feelings, having an affinity to this emotion by no means superficially evident, have combined to give us a new art emotion.

It is not in his personal emotions, the emotions provoked by particular events in his life, that the poet is in any way remarkable or interesting. His particular emotions may be simple, or crude, or flat. The emotion in his poetry will be a very complex thing, but not with the complexity of the emotions of people who have very complex or unusual emotions in life. One error, in fact, of eccentricity in poetry is to seek for new human emotions to express; and in this search for novelty in the wrong place it discovers the perverse. The business of the poet is not to find new emotions, but to use the ordinary ones and, in working them up into poetry, to express feelings which are not in actual emotions at all. And emotions which he has never experienced will serve his turn as well as those familiar to him. Consequently, we must believe that "emotion recollected in tranquillity" is an inexact formula. For it is neither emotion, nor recollection, nor, without distortion of meaning, tranquillity. It is a concentration, and a new thing resulting from the concentration, of a very great number of experiences which to the practical and active person would not seem to be experiences at all; it is a concentration which does not happen consciously or of deliberation. These experiences are not "recollected," and they finally unite in an atmosphere which is "tranquil" only in that it is a passive attending upon the event. Of course that is not quite the whole story. There is a great deal, in the writing of poetry, which must be conscious and deliberate. In fact, the bad poet is usually unconscious where he ought to be conscious, and conscious where he ought to be unconscious. Both errors tend to make him "personal." Poetry is not a turning loose of emotion, but an escape from emotion; it is not the expression of personality, but an escape from personality. But, of course, only those who have personality and emotions know what it means to want to escape from these things.

3

This essay proposes to halt at the frontier of metaphysics or mysticism, and confine itself to such practical conclusions as can be applied by the reasonable person interested in poetry. To divert interest from the poet to the poetry is a laudable aim: for it would conduce to a juster estimation of actual poetry, good

1. From Cyril Tourneur's *The Revenger's Tragedy*, III, v.

and bad. There are many people who appreciate the expression of sincere emotion in verse, and there is a smaller number of people who can appreciate technical excellence. But very few know when there is an expression of *significant* emotion, emotion which has its life in the poem and not in the history of the poet. The emotion of art is impersonal. And the poet cannot reach this impersonality without surrendering himself wholly to the work to be done. And he is not likely to know what is to be done unless he lives in what is not merely the present, but the present moment of the past, unless he is conscious, not of what is dead, but of what is already living.

1917